D1592984

BROTHERS ON THE
SANTA FE AND CHIHUAHUA TRAILS

BROTHERS ON THE
SANTA FE AND CHIHUAHUA TRAILS

Edward James Glasgow and William Henry Glasgow
1846–1848

Edited and Annotated by Mark L. Gardner
Foreword by Marc Simmons

UNIVERSITY PRESS OF COLORADO

Published by the University Press of Colorado
P.O. Box 849
Niwot, Colorado 80544

The University Press of Colorado is a cooperative publishing enterprise supported, in part, by
Adams State College, Colorado State University, Fort Lewis College, Mesa State College, Metropolitan
State College of Denver, University of Colorado, University of Northern Colorado, University of
Southern Colorado, and Western State College of Colorado.

The paper used in this publication meets the minimum requirements of the American National Stand-
ard for Information Sciences—Permanence of Paper for Printed Library Materials. ANSI Z39.48–1984

∞

Library of Congress Cataloging-in-Publication Data

Glasgow, Edward James, 1820–1908.
    Brothers on the Santa Fe and Chihuahua Trails / Edward James Glasgow and William
Henry Glasgow, 1846–1848; edited and annotated by Mark L. Gardner; foreword by
Marc Simmons. — 1st ed.
        p.   cm.
    Includes bibliographical references and index.
    ISBN 0-87081-291-2
    1. Southwest, New — Description and travel.   2. Southwest, New — History — To
1848.   3. Glasgow, Edward James, 1820–1908 — Journeys — Southwest, New.   4.
Glasgow, William Henry, 1822–1897 — Journeys — Southwest, New.   5. Mexican
War, 1846–1848 —Personal narratives.   6. Santa Fe Trail.   7. Doniphan's Expedition,
1846–1847.   I. Glasgow, William Henry, 1822–1897.   II. Gardner, Mark L.   III. Title.
F786.G57   1993
979 — dc20   93-19433
                                                                                    CIP

10   9   8   7   6   5   4   3   2   1

To Mom and Dad,
Claude and Venita Gardner
Breckenridge, Missouri

CONTENTS

FOREWORD

The Santa Fe Trail, after a period of scholarly and popular neglect, has come into its own again. Since May 1987, when President Ronald Reagan signed a congressional bill elevating it to the status of national historic trail and giving the National Park Service responsibility for its historical interpretation, the Santa Fe Trail has become something of a media darling. If the spate of recent trail books, magazine articles, and newspaper features, together with videos and films, does not quite constitute an avalanche, it would at least qualify as a small landslide — one created by the public's new push for information and stories about the old Santa Fe Trail.

In the wake of a resurgent popular interest in the subject, scholars, too, are beginning to take another look at trail history and to examine aspects that earlier researchers passed over or missed. An example can be seen in the recent studies of Susan Calafate Boyle (under contract to the National Park Service) and David Sandoval, who have explored and illuminated the significant role of native New Mexican and Chihuahuan merchants in the overland trade.

Another major topic that has received insufficient attention has to do with the biographies and business practices of the chief figures involved in the Missouri mercantile firms that engaged in active trade with the northern Mexican provinces. The lives of these men, who were wedded to the so-called commerce of the prairies, proved to be anything but humdrum. Although they devoted much time to their account books, juggling the profit and loss columns, they were also men of action, periodically abandoning their writing desks to follow the hazardous trail leading to Santa Fe and distant markets beyond.

Among the leading exemplars of this class of western American businessmen were the Glasgow brothers of St. Louis — Edward James and William Henry. Often mentioned in passing by early-day writers concerned with the Santa Fe trade, the Glasgows have never been the subject of a detailed study devoted exclusively to them. That has been a glaring omission, for not only were they prominent in international commerce but they also played a role in events surrounding the conduct of the Mexican War in New Mexico and Chihuahua.

Neglect of the Glasgows is remedied by publication of this book. Mark L. Gardner, one of the ablest of the new generation of Santa Fe Trail scholars, spent seven years assembling and editing writings of the Glasgow brothers that deal with the Mexican War period. To that he has added a substantial Introduction representing a skillfully drawn portrait of the lives of the two Glasgows, and he includes much new data on their father, William Glasgow, Sr., who launched them in their business careers.

Studies of individual merchants — their practices, successes, and failures — remain one of the largest untapped areas for Santa Fe Trail research. Such work requires the locating of elusive business records, personal correspondence, and contemporary newspaper accounts. It also necessitates a thorough understanding of commercial transactions, including bookkeeping, as they were handled in the nineteenth century. Gardner's careful and authoritative treatment of the Glasgows can well serve as a model for future works in this category. Not only has he given us a book highly useful for understanding the business history of the Santa Fe Trail, but he has also produced one that most readers who enjoy historical accounts will find challenging and entertaining to read. This book, then, should be regarded as an important contribution to the literature of the trail and to the ever-engaging saga of westward expansion.

MARC SIMMONS

PREFACE

I first learned of the Mexican War–era letters of Edward James Glasgow and William Henry Glasgow in 1984 from an article by James Neal Primm describing the Clark Family Collection,[1] then on loan to the Missouri Historical Society in St. Louis, and of which the letters were a part. I contacted the curator of manuscripts at the society, Peter Michel, about getting copies and the possibility of publishing them. Peter kindly supplied me with photocopies of all the letters and also the name of the owner, Mrs. Valerie J. Anderson of Vero Beach, Florida. I was by that time considering the letters as the possible subject for my master's thesis and asked Mrs. Anderson for her permission to use the letters and also for permission to publish them in the future. She agreed. I chose another topic for the thesis, however, and the Glasgows were put on hold — but not forgotten. In 1987 I renewed my work on the Glasgows. I contacted Mrs. Anderson again, but she had by that time sold the letters. She gave me the name of Richard C. Frajola, of Danbury, Connecticut, the individual who had handled the transaction, and I wrote him seeking the name and address of the purchaser. Mr. Frajola was very helpful, forwarding my inquiry to Mr. Wade Shipley of Lovington, New Mexico, the current owner of the Glasgow letters. Mr. Shipley was extremely cooperative and enthusiastic, granting me permission to continue with my project. During my research in 1987, Peter Michel brought to my attention William H. Glasgow's "Memorandums," of which the Missouri Historical Society had a typescript. He provided me with a copy, and I was pleasantly surprised to see that it contained a section on William's experiences from 1846 to 1848, the same time period as the letters. I decided that this section would be included with the letters in my projected book. I was working with this typescript when I was contacted by W. Merrill Glasgow of Houston, Texas, a great grandson of William Henry. He had obtained my name through Mary Seematter at the Missouri Historical Society, who had also worked with the Glasgow materials. Mr. Glasgow informed me that he had the original "Memorandums" in his possession as well as several images of his great grandfather. Mr. Glasgow approved of my project and provided me with copies of numerous family documents, including the "Memorandums" and an original diary book kept by William.

Also while conducting my research on the letters, I noted that historian William Connelley, in his book *Doniphan's Expedition*, quoted frequently from letters written to him by Edward Glasgow iin 1906 and 1907. I contacted the Kansas State Historical Society in Topeka hoping that this correspondence might survive in their collections. Although Connelley's collection had been split up upon his death, the society had a good portion of it, and the letters Edward had written to him were there. I was furnished copies and permission to use them. These letters form Part III.

Thoughout the editing of the Glasgow materials, every effort has been made to reproduce them exactly as they were written, including original punctuation and spelling. One exception is that sentences that ended in a dash have been changed to end in a period. All items within brackets are the editor's.

NOTE

1.   James Neal Primm, "Seal of the Territory of Louisiana: A Discovery amid a Clark Family Collection," *Gateway Heritage* 4 (Spring 1984): 17–21.

ACKNOWLEDGMENTS

My interest in the Glasgow family, particularly the brothers Edward James and William Henry, began with their letters written on the Santa Fe and Chihuahua trails during the Mexican War. As I delved deeper into the brothers' lives, however, I found a much larger story. What I discovered was an amazing family of mercantile capitalists whose business endeavors stretched from Europe to Mexico's Pacific coast and spanned a century.

Following the Glasgows' sometimes complicated trail brought me into contact with archives and institutions across the country. The staffs of the following were extremely helpful: Missouri Historical Society; State Historical Society of Missouri; Joint Collection: University of Missouri, Western Historical Manuscript Collection/State Historical Society of Missouri Manuscripts (WHMC/SHSM); National Archives; Kansas State Historical Society; Baker Library, Harvard University Graduate School of Business Administration; University of New Mexico Library, Special Collections; Denver Public Library, Western History Department; New Mexico State Records Center and Archives; Colorado Historical Society; Jefferson National Expansion Memorial, National Park Service; Missouri Botanical Garden; Museum of New Mexico; Colorado College Library; and Bent's Old Fort National Historic Site.

From the above list there are certain individual staff members who deserve special notice for their efforts on my behalf. They are Peter Michel and Mary Seematter of the Missouri Historical Society; Fae Sotham and Marie Concannon of the State Historical Society of Missouri; Patricia A. Michaelis of the Kansas State Historical Society; Florence Lathrop of Baker Library; Cindy Stewart of the Joint Collection: WHMC/SHSM; Michael T. Meier of the National Archives; Kathleen Moenster of the Jefferson National Expansion Memorial; and Willow Powers of the Laboratory of Anthropology, Museum of New Mexico.

Numerous friends and fellow scholars have been very generous in providing me with assistance. They are Dr. David Sandoval, Janet Lecompte, Dr. Adrian Bustamante, William Gwaltney, Barton Barbour, Mary and Leo Gamble, Bruce Dale, Dr. Leo E. Oliva, Richard C. Frajola, Pauline Fowler, Dan and Carol Sharp, Denise Sanders, William Y. Chalfant, Dr. Richard Forry, Dr. Susan Calafate Boyle, Paul Bentrup, Daniel Muldoon, Frances Hurd Stadler, and Dr. Betty Burnett. In this category I must make special mention of Dr. Marc Simmons. During my research trips to New Mexico, Marc put me up several times at his home in Cerrillos and made available to me his outstanding library. Marc also lent a hand when I needed items from New Mexico institutions he frequently visits for his own research. Above all, Marc was always willing to share his findings and offer guidance and enthusiasm for my efforts. He is a fine friend and a scholar I admire greatly.

My Glasgow research naturally brought me into contact with descendants of the Glasgow brothers, all extremely supportive and a pleasure to know. They are Mr. and Mrs. William G. Bowling of St. Louis; Edward J. Glasgow of Nashville, Tennessee; Isabel Glasgow of El Paso, Texas; and W. Merrill Glasgow of Houston, Texas. I am particularly indebted to William Bowling and Merrill Glasgow for permission to publish W. H. Glasgow's "Memorandums." At my request, Merrill had copies made of many family portraits, some of which appear in this book. Edward J. Glasgow, a grandson of the first Edward J., now owns the miniature of Edward painted in 1840, and he generously allowed it to be photographed for this publication. A very important individual in my work on the Glasgows has been Mr. Wade Shipley of Lovington, New Mexico, the owner of the letters written by the Glasgow brothers during the Mexican War. For the support, enthusiasm, and friendship he and his wife, Betty, showed me, I am both extremely grateful and fortunate. I would also like to acknowledge the previous owner of the Glasgow letters, Mrs. Valerie J. Anderson of Vero Beach, Florida, for her gracious cooperation and permission to begin my work on the letters.

Last, I cannot bring this list of illustrious individuals to a close without adding my wife's name to it. Katie and I wed four years before this work was completed. I am sure that when we married she did not know what a hold the Glasgows had on me; she does now, and we are still together. Katie conducted research for me, sacrificed some of our vacation time for my research, and, if that wasn't enough, had our first child (Christiana) in the midst of all this. Her support and love have contributed immensely to this publication. Thank you Katie Davis Gardner.

M.L.G.

Give my love to Ma and to all the folks at home and say I will return as soon as I possibly can, consistent with the proper attention my business demands, and my duty requires.

Edward James Glasgow
May 27, 1846

The traders, mostly young men from the eastern cities, were fine hearty fellows, who employ their capital in this trade because it combines pleasure with profit, and the excitement and danger of the journey through the Indian country are more agreeable than the monotonous life of a city merchant.

George A.F. Ruxton
Adventures in Mexico and the Rocky Mountains, 1847

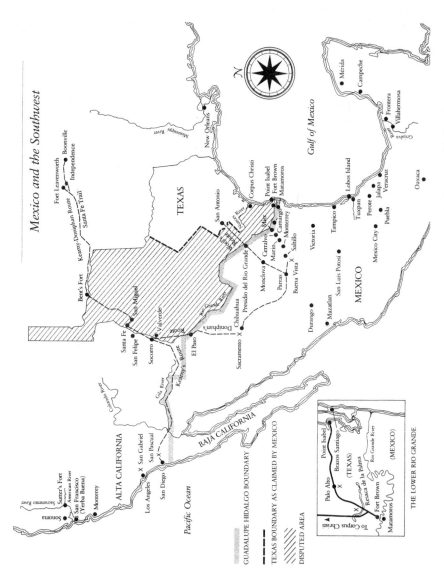

Mexico and the Southwest

Map reproduced courtesy of the Amon Carter Museum.

BROTHERS ON THE
SANTA FE AND CHIHUAHUA TRAILS

EDITOR'S INTRODUCTION

In 1906 and 1907 historian William E. Connelley was preparing a massive book entitled *War with Mexico, 1846–1847: Doniphan's Expedition and the Conquest of New Mexico and California.* It consisted largely of a reprint of veteran John T. Hughes's 1847 account of the expedition but was also filled with numerous notes by Connelley that elaborated at length on the various incidents and personalities involved. Much of this information Connelley gathered directly from the participants and their descendants. Several old soldiers and at least one trader were still alive to recount the exciting experiences of over half a century before. Fortunately, much of Connelley's correspondence survives, including eleven letters written to him by former Southwest trader Edward James Glasgow.[1]

Glasgow was more than eighty-six years old at the time but was still willing to provide Connelley with whatever information he could: a description of the trade of New Mexico and Chihuahua, an account of the Battle of Sacramento, memories of some of the traders and military men he knew, and a short biographical sketch of his life. But Edward James was unaware, or had forgotten, that the letters he and his brother, William Henry Glasgow, had written on that trip sixty years before had been carefully preserved. Addressed to family members in St. Louis, the letters described in detail their journey and hardships from Independence to Chihuahua. Also unknown to him was a manuscript by William Henry Glasgow that related those same adventures. Together, the letters and manuscript were a treasure trove of information that historians like Connelley dream about, but the documents were destined to remain unknown far beyond Connelley's lifetime.

The letters, written from May 1846 to March 1848, and an excerpt from William H. Glasgow's journal, or "Memorandums," covering that same period, form the central portion of this book. Through the intimate and candid writings of the Glasgow brothers, one witnesses firsthand the U.S.

occupation of northern Mexico, a tumultuous period that changed forever the face of the Southwest. Even more intriguing, one sees this conquest from the perspective of the civilian trader, who was forced to follow in the rear of the Army of the West while it slowly wended its way from one victory to another.

It is not simply the historical record contained in the Glasgow writings that makes them important, however. Just as priceless is their reflection of nineteenth-century values and attitudes, the cultural baggage they and others carried to the farthest reaches of Mexico. The documents also convey an excellent feeling for St. Louis society as well as insight into the relationships of a close and loving family, a family whose roots are easily traced to eighteenth-century Delaware.

The Glasgow brothers' father, William Glasgow, Sr., was born at Christiana, Delaware, on October 4, 1787, the son of James and Eleanor Glasgow.[2] One source states that as a young man he worked at the Brandywine Flour Mills before traveling to Cádiz, Spain, for his health.[3] Another account, which does not mention William's health, says that he traveled to Europe in 1812 "on commercial business."[4] According to family history, he was secretary to the U.S. consul while at Cádiz.[5]

The year 1815 saw William on his way back to the United States, and late 1816 found him on the banks of the Mississippi River in the frontier community of St. Louis.[6] "Being kindly received by the French inhabitants and the few American families of the village," stated an 1868 newspaper biography of Glasgow, "he concluded to take up his abode here and engage in mercantile pursuits."[7] In 1817 William was a member of the firm of Porter, Glasgow & Niven (or Nivin), which had just opened their "new Store, with all New Goods, in the place recently occupied by Theo. Hunt, Papin's house, two doors below 'Washington Hall.' "[8]

John Mason Peck, an early Baptist missionary to St. Louis, reminisced that in 1818 the town was "crowded with inhabitants. . . . Every house and room that could shelter persons was occupied. . . . The storekeepers, most of whom were without families, in many instances, kept 'bachelor's hall' in their counting-rooms, and cooked their own meals."[9] This is probably an accurate description of William Glasgow's situation — but only for a short while, for

William Glasgow, Sr. (1787–1876), merchant and father of the Glasgow brothers, from a daguerreotype made probably in the 1850s. (Courtesy of the Missouri Historical Society, St. Louis.)

on November 19, 1818, he married sixteen-year-old Sarah Mitchell at Belleville, Illinois.[10] Glasgow had moved to Belleville, a few miles southeast of St. Louis, that year, perhaps to open a branch store of the Porter, Glasgow & Niven firm.[11]

Two sons were born to the Glasgows at Belleville: Edward James Glasgow on June 7, 1820, and William Henry Glasgow on February 19, 1822.[12] Edward was named for his grandfather Edward Mitchell, a minister and revolutionary war veteran who had migrated west from Virginia in 1818.[13] Roughly a year after the birth of William Henry, the Glasgows moved to Herculaneum, Missouri, a lead-mining town on the Mississippi, south of St. Louis.[14] "The little settlement," as it was described by Paul Wilhelm in May 1823, "consisting of scarcely 20 houses is most romantic, being near a really impressive group of cliffs, of varying shapes, some entirely devoid of all vegetation, while others are attractively overgrown."[15] Here William Glasgow

Sarah Mitchell Glasgow (1801–1883), mother of the Glasgow brothers, from a daguerreotype probably taken in the 1850s. (GPN Por-G-8, courtesy of the Missouri Historical Society, St. Louis.)

"had a general store for sale of merchandise" and operated the nearby Sandy lead mines.[16]

In 1827 William Glasgow and his family, now larger by one with the birth of Eleanor Ann Glasgow on May 1, 1824, moved back to St. Louis.[17] William was at this time a partner of James Ross in the firm of Ross & Glasgow.[18] Ross, the father-in-law of William's older brother, James, was a Wilmington, Delaware, merchant who had come to Missouri about 1819 along with his son-in-law and John Aull. The trio settled at Chariton, a new community up the Missouri River, where they "engaged in mercantile pursuits."[19] From all appearances, Ross and Glasgow met with success, for by 1832, when Ross died, their firm had interests in stores at Chariton, Fayette, Herculaneum, and St. Louis.[20]

St. Louis in the 1830s was no doubt an exciting setting for the Glasgow children to grow up in (Mary Susan was the last addition in 1829[21]),

Eleanor Ann Glasgow Clark (1824–1894), the older of the Glasgow brothers two sisters, in an 1853 portrait by de Franca. Eleanor married George Rogers Hancock Clark. (Por-C-93c, courtesy of the Missouri Historical Society, St. Louis.)

especially so for the brothers. It had become "the great depot of all the Fur Trading Companies to the Upper Missouri and Rocky Mountains," wrote artist George Catlin, "and their starting place; and also for the Santa Fe, and other Trading Companies, who reach the Mexican borders overland, to trade for silver bullion."[22] The Mississippi riverfront, with its steamboats, trappers, Indians, and boatmen, was an exotic place, as was William Clark's home, which was filled with Indian "curiosities" from his famous expedition with Meriwether Lewis and service as superintendent of Indian Affairs. Edward recalled in later years his youthful visits to the "museum" in Clark's council chamber. It was filled with "bows and arrows, battle clubs, stone axes, birch bark canoes which were suspended from the ceiling, Indian dresses, decorated with feathers, [and] bones of mastodones."[23]

Although the Far West surely seemed very close to those who called St. Louis their home, the city was no longer the frontier outpost that William Glasgow had known. St. Louis had a population of nearly 6,000 in 1830,

Mary Susan Glasgow Clark (1829–1921), the youngest of the Glasgow siblings, probably painted in the early 1850s. The majority of the Glasgow brothers' letters are written to Mary Susan. (Por-C, courtesy of the Missouri Historical Society, St. Louis.)

and five years later it numbered over 8,000 and was growing.[24] The Glasgow brothers did not have to go east for their schooling but attended St. Charles College and St. Louis University.[25] Supplemental to their formal education must have been the practical one they received by observing their father's many business ventures, from investments in steamboats to the manufacture and exportation of tobacco.[26]

The formative years ended quickly for both brothers. In 1840, at the age of twenty, Edward James embarked on an adventure that marked the beginning of his long career as a merchant. In August of that year he left New York on a ship bound for Mexico. His destination was that country's Pacific coast, where he was to conduct business for Glasgow, Harrison, Valois & Co. The firm was sending two merchandise-laden sailing ships, a brig and a bark, to Mazatlan.[27] The cargoes, "principally dry goods," were selected for the

Edward James Glasgow (1820–1908). This striking miniature was painted in
Philadelphia in 1840 as Edward was preparing to depart for Mazatlan, Mexico.
(Courtesy of Edward J. Glasgow, Nashville, Tennessee.)

Mexican trade at either Mazatlan or Guaymas, both active seaports.[28] Before
departing, Edward was appointed U.S. consul at Guaymas by President Martin
Van Buren.[29]

    Glasgow, Harrison, Valois & Co. was composed of James Glasgow (Ed-
ward's uncle), James Harrison, Mariano de Valois, Daniel Boyd, Edward J.
Glasgow, and William Glasgow (Edward's father).[30] With years of experience
as merchants at St. Louis, Chariton, and Fayette, the elder Glasgows and
Harrison were familiar with this foreign commerce. Since William Becknell's
successful trading expedition from Missouri to Santa Fe in 1821, caravans
of traders had departed annually from central and western Missouri to peddle
U.S. and European textiles and other dry goods in the markets of Mexico.
The Glasgows and Harrison catered to many of these traders, offering "Santa
Fe goods" direct from New York and Philadelphia houses.[31] In 1831 Harrison

James Glasgow (1784–1856). An uncle of the Glasgow brothers, James was a
Missouri merchant and senior member of the firm of Glasgow, Harrison, Valois &
Co. This portrait, the only one known, appeared in the *Glasgow Missourian* of January
4, 1917. (Courtesy of the State Historical Society of Missouri, Columbia.)

actually took goods himself, evidently in partnership with the Glasgows,
traveling all the way to Chihuahua on one of these caravans.[32]

Valois, a native of Mexico, was also a veteran of the Mexican trade and
"had been for several years engaged in working the gold and silver mines of
Chihuahua."[33] During spring and summer 1839, he and some fellow
Chihuahua merchants had blazed a trail from Chihuahua to the state of
Arkansas.[34] Harrison, then located in western Arkansas, had become acquainted with Valois while trading in Chihuahua a few years before and now
apparently encountered the Mexican merchant once again. Harrison's favorable impression of him led to Valois's joining in the Glasgows' venture.[35]
Someone like Valois, who thoroughly knew the country, the language, and
the business, would be a definite asset. Boyd's qualifications, in contrast, are
not so clear. In addition to his own interests in the undertaking, Boyd seems
to have been representing those of his brother James, as a letter from William

Glasgow written in 1843 speaks of a large settlement with the Boston firm of James Boyd & Son in connection with the closing up of their Mexico business.[36] James Boyd & Son is listed in the Boston directories of the period as "saddlers." There are no entries for Daniel Boyd.[37]

Despite the experience of most of the partners, sending their wares by sea to a distant Mexican port was far more ambitious, and perhaps riskier, than transporting them in wagons over the Santa Fe Trail. There was, however, a distinct advantage to this mode of operation that all Santa Fe traders were well aware of. Merchants who re-exported foreign goods from Atlantic ports by sea were eligible for drawbacks on those goods, rebates of the duties collected by U.S. customs officers. These drawbacks were not available to the overland traders, who paid U.S. duties on their imported European goods and, once they reached Santa Fe, Mexican duties as well. This situation gave a decided edge in the Mexican trade to merchants operating through the seaports, who were essentially paying only one tariff.[38]

After forty-two days of sailing, with a three-day stopover in Havana to replenish water supplies, Edward landed at Vera Cruz, on the Gulf of Mexico. While the firm's ships sailed south and around Cape Horn, Edward and partners Valois and Boyd traveled overland across Mexico by stagecoach.[39] At Durango the trio left their coach and purchased mules for the final leg of their journey, which took them over the Sierra Madres to Mazatlan. Upon arrival, the partners temporarily split up. Edward and Valois left on a twenty-six-day trip for Hermosillo and Guaymas while Boyd remained in Mazatlan. It would be close to two months before their ships arrived, and the partners wanted to determine Guaymas's suitability for business.[40]

At Guaymas Edward received some shocking information. An American there told him that his trusted partner, Valois, was in debt to a Guaymas merchant to the amount of $40,000! Edward carried the bad news back to Boyd in Mazatlan. Fearing that their goods would be confiscated by the Mexican authorities to satisfy Valois's debt, the two decided to buy their partner out. They offered him $13,000. Valois, however, did not want to be bought out, even though he had invested no capital in their venture. Only when the two threatened to take charge of the ships when they arrived and return immediately to New York with the cargoes did he relent. Glasgow, Harrison, Valois & Co. was no more.[41]

"This was one of the greatest trials of my life," Edward wrote many years later. "I was inexperienced, only 20 years old, in a strange country and feared

James Harrison (1803–1870). A one-time Chihuahua trader and partner with the Glasgows in the Mexican trade at Mazatlan. He was later a member of the St. Louis firm of Chouteau, Harrison & Valle, iron entrepreneurs. (Courtesy of the Missouri Historical Society, St. Louis.)

I would incur Mr. Harrison's displeasure."[42] That the young merchant had acted correctly, though, is confirmed by a letter from Edward's father early in 1841. William wrote his son that "Mr. Harrison is astonished with the conduct of Valois and is much pleased with the arrangement you have made with him; thinks you have got clear of him on good terms."[43] In the same letter, he cautioned Edward, "You must not be discouraged; you have had a rough time of it but it is the life of a young man to be compelled to act his part and exert his energies."

Mazatlan was decided upon as the "preferable point for business."[44] One of the firm's vessels, appropriately named the *California*, arrived at that port on January 28. According to the consular returns for Mazatlan, the *California* was burthen 189 tons and had a crew of thirteen Americans and a cargo recorded simply as "Sundries."[45] This merchandise and that brought by the other vessel, whose name is not revealed in the surviving Glasgow correspondence, was consigned to the commission house of Parrott & Co.[46] As Edward was to remain at Mazatlan, he resigned his appointment as U.S. consul at Guaymas.[47] The young Glasgow had thus survived the initial hardships of establishing his family's business interests in Mexico, but letters from his father at St. Louis reveal additional problems that threatened the success of their enterprise, now operating under the name of Glasgow, Harrison, Boyd & Co.

Slow communications between Mazatlan and the States and the delays in shipping home returns proved to be the firm's greatest hardships. It was critical to the concern that the returns reach the United States before the bills came due on their goods. Edward's father wrote him on March 8, 1841, that "if you can only manage to send in money in a short time after the ship leaves we will feel easy here but the expectation of money by return of the ship has been all frustrated by your letter [of] the 11th and we must make arrangements to meet the bills due in July, say, $89,000. in other ways." Edward had informed his partners that the *California* would be returning with a cargo of brazilwood.[48]

The *California* departed Mazatlan for the United States on February 21, less than a month after its arrival in Mexico.[49] Sometime during March or April, Daniel Boyd also left for the States, possibly with a return.[50] Through the following summer and fall, Edward remained alone at Mazatlan, occasionally serving as vice-consul for the port.[51] October 1841 saw Boyd and the *California* on their way back to Mazatlan, Boyd via St. Louis and New Orleans. It also saw the elder partners troubled by the political climate in Mexico. News had reached the United States of a revolution, led by Antonio López de Santa Anna and others, that had broken out in August. There was a possibility that the returning *California* might not be allowed to enter its new cargo at Mazatlan and Edward would have to send the ship south, perhaps to the port of Valparaiso, Chile, or Callao, Peru. William wrote his son on October 28 discussing these matters and also the closing of the Mazatlan concern. Yet he added that "if there should be a change of the Govt. and the ports of Mexico be opened for the reception of our goods and the export of bullion, I have no doubt you will make further trial of the business." His uncle James and Harrison, however, felt "considerable anxiety in the present unsettled state of the country about the difficulty and the danger of delay in getting home funds of former shipments."[52]

The revolution was short-lived, and on October 14 Santa Anna became president of the Republic of Mexico.[53] But this was not the end of the partners' worries. In early 1842 they received word from Edward that it was probable that most of the goods Boyd had shipped to Mazatlan with the return of the *California* were prohibited and could not be entered there without risk of confiscation.[54] William wrote to his son on February 12 that because the ship "will have been dispatched before this reaches you it is useless to suggest any new plan to adopt. You will, being on the spot, be better able to judge of the best course to pursue in [the] future but let your every aim be directed to the most speedy remittance." Before closing his letter, he added, "Our situation now becomes every day more alarming, money is very scarce and we have bills due four months from this time which we expect will be paid by your remittances."[55]

The *California* and its cargo were sent to Valparaiso.[56] These complications must have been frustrating for Edward, who was far from home and trying to conduct a profitable business for his family in Mexico and now South America. But he was not the only member of the firm to meet obstacles. The elder partners were not experiencing a great deal of luck themselves.

On July 3, 1841, a petition from Glasgow, Harrison, Boyd & Co. was presented to the U.S. Senate by Senator Lewis F. Linn of Missouri "praying that the charges made at the US Mints for refining imported bullion may be discontinued."[57] The partners had discovered that the cost of separating the small portion of gold usually found in Mexican silver bullion was cheaper at European mints than it was at the U.S. mint, and they had apparently been sending some of their returns overseas in consequence. If the U.S. mint provided this service "gratis," they wrote in their petition, "it would make it an Object for merchants to make their shipments of Bullion to this country instead of sending it to Europe and would largely increase the importation . . . of Bullion into the United States." The merchants also pointed out that approximately two British warships annually visited the Pacific ports from Guaymas south, providing merchants with "a regular and safe conveyance of the precious metals to England." The partners hoped that if the charges for separating metals were dropped, an arrangement would be made with the U.S. Navy "by which our merchants trading to the Coast of the Pacific may enjoy equal facilities with those afforded by European powers & without incurring the commissions & expenses to which they are at present subjected by having to ship to England or France."[58]

But the partners' petition met strong opposition from the director of the mint at Philadelphia, who did not like the idea of separating their bullion for free. In a letter to the Senate Committee on Finance, he defended the higher U.S. mint charge and argued that at the most economical refineries in Europe the partners would only be saving 1 percent of the value of the bullion. "Our country may be said to be on the road from Spanish America to Europe," he wrote. "Does not our proximity to the mines give us an advantage greater than is sufficient to countervail the increased cost of parting the mixed metals? or, in other words, would not the cost of freight, insurance, and other charges of transportation, reach to one per cent. of the value of the metals?"[59] The Committee on Finance answered the director's question when it resolved that it is "not expedient to enact a law in accordance with the prayer of the petition."[60]

The committee's decision, reported nearly a year later, on April 27, 1842, probably came too late to have any effect on the Glasgows' enterprise. Plans were already under way for the closing of their Mazatlan business. After the California delivered its "prohibited" cargo at Valparaiso, it returned to Mazatlan, where it was loaded with a cargo of brazilwood and $40,000 worth of bullion.[61] William Glasgow had strongly advised Edward that if a large return was to be sent by sea, it would be important that someone accompany it to the States, and this Edward did, leaving Mazatlan on June 23, 1842.[62]

The five-and-a-half-month journey around Cape Horn was broken up somewhat by a stopover in Valparaiso so that Edward could close up the business at that port.[63] He arrived there on August 17 and three days later wrote a playful letter to Sarah Lane Glasgow, wife of his cousin, William Glasgow, Jr., in St. Louis. In this letter, Edward described the Chilean port as a "fine, lively bustling place," but he was much more enamored of the women he found there, taking up most of three pages writing about them. One in particular, "a very handsome darkeyed beauty with cheeks as red as a turkey's nose," was the cause of a little humiliation. Noticing her while "walking up town," Edward

> looked at her with all the eyes in my head and she sort'a [?] looked back again at me, [and] when I brushed past her I gave her another peep, and saw she was peeping too, and at last, after she had gone on, I looked around,

and may I be flogged with a bag of feathers if she was'nt cutting her left
eye around at me still.

I was on the point of going up and asking her if she "believed in "love
at first sight", when I walked jam up against a post in the side-walk, that
knocked the breath out of me. I was mad at every pretty girl I saw for nearly
ten minutes after.[64]

When Edward wrote the above letter he expected that it would be a week
before he could continue his long voyage to the States. His partner Boyd,
however, was far ahead of him, reaching the United States sometime before
September 12. The date of Boyd's departure from Mazatlan, his route, and
conveyance are not known. What is known is that he arrived none too soon
with a much-needed return. Before Boyd's arrival, the financial situation of
the firm had become increasingly critical, for a letter written by William Carr
Lane, Sarah Lane Glasgow's father, on the above date reveals that one of the
Glasgows at St. Louis had planned a trip to Mexico, probably to speed up the
returns. According to Lane, Boyd's arrival in the United States and the
knowledge that Edward James was on his way home with another return
caused the trip to be "abandoned." Lane remarked that "these returns appear
to make the Glasgows easy."[65]

Easy or not, the Glasgows were evidently unwilling to risk further delays
with any remaining returns. When Boyd left again for Mexico approximately
three months later, he had a young William Henry Glasgow at his side. During
the years previous, William had been busy working as a clerk for another of
the family's enterprises in St. Louis: Gay, Glasgow & Co., "large importers of
sugar and tobacco from Havana."[66] Now twenty years old, William would
travel with Boyd to Mazatlan, eventually returning by way of Chihuahua and
Santa Fe to Independence, Missouri. He would bring back a valuable return
in silver specie and an additional item that was priceless — a written record
of his experiences.

William Henry Glasgow faithfully wrote down each day's activities on
his Mexican journey of 1842–1843 in what must have ended up being
several small diaries. Only one, however, is known to exist today. It is fortunate
that William at some point transferred all his entries (making some minor

William Henry Glasgow (1822–1897). This portrait of William, painted by artist Manuel Joachim de Franca, dates to the early 1850s. (Courtesy of W. Merrill Glasgow, Houston, Texas.)

revisions and additions in the process) to one journal book and entitled it "Memorandums of a Trip Through Mexico in 1842 & 1843." Filled with detailed descriptions of Mexican villages, people, and customs, William's "Memorandums" are an entertaining and fascinating record of his travels.[67] Yet for the most part, they give little indication that he was on family business. A few key journal passages, however, confirm that he had an important mission beyond pleasure and adventure.[68]

Boyd and William Henry set sail from New Orleans on the schooner *Virginia Antoinette* on December 1, 1842. Landing at Tampico, they traveled overland via San Luis Potosí and Guadalajara to the Pacific port of San Blas. From there they boarded a Mexican sloop and on January 14, 1843, arrived in Mazatlan. William had much to say about his brother's base of operations:

> Mazatlan is quite a handsome Mexican town, containing about 10,000 Inhabitants. There are no public buildings of any importance in the place, the houses are generally built of adobe (or unburt brik) and one story in height. There are however several very substantial buildings, composed of burnt brick, occupied as residences by the wealthier portion of the inhabitants. The Society here as well as in all the cities of the Republic is divided into 2 general classes. That of the Aristocracy, is composed of the descendants of the old Spaniards who pride themselves greatly upon their blood and seldom if ever intermarry with the other class. Which is composed of the descendants of the original mexicans. There are also in this place many, wealthy Foreigners, who do a large and profitable business.

William and Boyd's first stop on the morning of their arrival was "the breakfast table" of John Parrott, U.S. consul for that port and no doubt a member of the class of "wealthy foreigners" William notes in his "Memorandums." What was spoken at that table William did not record, but because Parrott was also the head of the commission firm of Parrott & Co., a house the Glasgows had dealings with, business must have been a primary topic. That evening William and Boyd attended one of the theaters in Mazatlan.

Disappointingly, William skips the following ten days in his "Memorandums." Perhaps business and preparations for his long journey toward the United States did not seem worth recording. At any rate, he begins his account again on January 24, leaving Mazatlan that morning with "2 mexican servants mounted upon mules a young American who will accompany me to the U.S. and two mules, laden with my trunk, bed, cooking utensils &

Lithograph of Mazatlan, Mexico, as it appeared in 1852. From John Russell Barrtlett's *Personal Narrative of Explorations and Incidents in Texas, New Mexico, California, Sonora, and Chihuahua* ... (1854). (Editor's collection.)

provision box. Myself & the young Am^n Mr Hodge were armed each with a double barreled rifle & pair of holster pistols for our protection from the Indians & robbers upon the road." William makes no mention of Boyd, who must have remained behind at Mazatlan.

On February 18, having traveled for more than three weeks, William arrived at Jesús Maria, a silver-mining town high in the mountains of the state of Chihuahua.[69] After checking in at the local custom house, where he also obtained a small room, William looked up his "friend" Mariano de Valois. Valois, the proprietor of a mine at Jesús Maria, greeted William with "a real Mexican hug and insisted upon my removing immediately both bag & baggage to his house." Instead, William sent his mules to Valois's yard and set up quarters in a vacant house owned by Valois. Here the two spent "the remainder of the evening until 10 oclk in conversation about business matters."

William again leaves us to speculation when he does not elaborate on the business matters that were discussed. One possible subject might have been an $1,800 note that the firm of Glasgow & Harrison held against Valois two years before and that may still have been outstanding. This note had

"Chihuahua, Mexico, Looking East," a photograph by William H. Jackson, circa 1883. (Courtesy of the Denver Public Library, Western History Department.)

apparently been left out of the settlement that Edward and Boyd had made with Valois at Mazatlan.[70] If this was the reason for William's visit, it had no obvious effect on his host, who along with his "handsome lady" went to extremes to see that William was well fed and taken care of.

On the nineteenth William noted that "upon getting up this morning [I] found myself arrived at my 21st birth day, little did I think a year ago that I should pass the day of my majority in such a rat hole as this. Who can tell where I shall pass the next one, or what Changes may Occur in the meanwhile." He remained at Jesús Maria until the following day, visiting the local mines, ore mills, and merchants. Late that morning, after breakfasting with Valois and wife, William left for the city of Chihuahua.

William was quite impressed with the Mexican state's capital, which he reached on February 27. "In the Centre of the town," he wrote, "is the Plaza upon one side of which is built a fine large Church a magnificent building in any Country, the other sides of the square are built up in good style & [are] occupied by government officers, stores, the hall of the state Congress and the American hotel." He estimated the population at 8,000 and commented that "the Commerce of this place is generally in the hands of the Americans and a few German & French merchants."

There were no rooms available at the hotel, but William found an eight-room house nearby that he rented for thirty-five dollars a month. He remained in Chihuahua until the beginning of March yet did not bother to record his activities. His next entry, on March 5, opens with the simple statement, "My business having detained me several days on this morning found myself ready to start."

William was starting for Santa Fe and would be traveling with six others, three Mexicans and three Americans. "The Company for Santa Fe," presumably merchants, had already left Chihuahua but had agreed to travel slowly to allow William's group to catch up to them. Transportation for William's party included "1 wagon loaded with our provisions & baggage & 24 mules to draw it." The provisions, which were to last their "mess" through the 580-mile trip north to Santa Fe, a part of which was over the famous Jornada del Muerto, consisted of "50^{lbs} Coffee 200 lbs dried beef 75 lbs sugar 2 bushels flour 2 bags Crackers 1 bushel beans 2 lbs Tea 50 lbs Lard 2 almos [almud, a Spanish measure] salt & a quarter of fresh Beef." Besides the provisions, their wagon also carried "a large box containing money."

On the evening of March 13 they reached El Paso del Norte on the Rio Grande, approximately 240 miles from Chihuahua. The next morning, William's party stopped at the custom house, where their guias (a "mercantile passport," according to trader and author Josiah Gregg) and wagon were checked by the collector. In El Paso William came across the owners of three wagons preparing to leave for Santa Fe and convinced them to wait for his group. He also encountered two members of the company that had preceded him out of Chihuahua. Their wagons would not arrive until the next day, as they had taken a more circular route in order to avoid the sandhills just south of El Paso. William's party had crossed these sandhills, but only after lightening their wagon by placing most of its cargo on the backs of their mules.[71]

William's party, now including the Chihuahua train, was finally ready to start north again on March 16. The only real excitement of their trip occurred the next day when a grass fire broke out in their camp and partially destroyed one of the Mexicans' wagons. The passage over the Jornada, in contrast, was cold but uneventful. The party reached Albuquerque on March 27 and was "soon (as usual) surrounded by crowds of women & children, who appeared so dextrous in the art of appropriating plates, cups knives &c

that we were compelled to put all such articles under lock & key as soon as possible." Five days later they were in Santa Fe.

William, who had never seen this well-known New Mexican city, was disappointed. "Having heard for many years of Santa Fe & the great trade of that place," he wrote, "I expected to see a place of some importance and was astonished at the wretched collection of mud hovels which compose the town." But William had more pressing affairs than sightseeing. Along with the other "owners of the wagons" in his party, he headed straight for the Governor's Palace in the center of town. Stepping into the long, whitewashed adobe building, the men asked to see Manuel Armijo, governor of New Mexico. At this point, William's "Memorandums" clearly reveal the main objective of his long journey through Mexico. Here is his description of what took place:

> We found him [Armijo] seated before a small table in a room about 16 feet square, the walls of which were ornamented by the plates of several manufactures in the U.S. and a steam Boat Bill The floor was Covered with a cheap Carpeting manufact^d in the country and around the walls were placed settees, covered with Cushions made of Calicoe and stuffed with wool
>
> The Govr is a large fine looking man of about 50 years of age, very portly, has a high & wide forehead & a penetrating eye.
>
> He arose upon our entrance and shook each of us by the hand & requested us to be seated. After a few moments Conversation we broached our business, which was to make arrangements for the payment of as little duty as possible upon the money we were to take out of the country. He told us he had nothing to do, with the administrations of the Custom House, and referred us to the Collector whom he supposed would charge us about 1 ½ %
>
> As we knew this was all gammon we left him and did not return again until 3 oclk when we called in company with the collector. and the affair was arranged by our paying 1 ½ Pr ct export duty. The legal charge for exporting coined money from the Mexican Republic is 6 pr ct. It is Contrary to law to export bullion and can only be done by smuggling or the connivance with the Custom House officers. I pulled out my purse to pay my duties, & tendered the money to the Govr but he declined receiving it & told me that it must be paid to the Collector at the Custom House. That Gent being present said it was useless trouble to go to the Custom House and would receive it then. The money was counted down upon the Gov^{r,}s

table and considering *he had nothing to do with it*, I thought he appeared to take considerable interest in the matter as he picked up and examined seperately each doubloon as I laid it down — remarking that there was a great many Counterfeits in circulation.

Where exactly William picked up the specie he was bringing to the United States is not clear. It seems logical to assume that he acquired some or all of it in Mazatlan, the base of operations for his family's firm. He also could have been collecting it from individuals along his route, such as Valois at Jesús Maria or perhaps various merchants in Chihuahua who owed the firm on previously purchased goods. Whatever the money's origins, he had just passed the last great hurdle in getting it out of Mexico and on its way to the States. All that was left now were roughly 800 miles over the Santa Fe Trail.

William and the other traders left Santa Fe on their way to Missouri that same day, April 1. Just outside of Las Vegas, on April 6, they found a caravan of Mexican merchants waiting for them. According to William's estimates, the Mexican train consisted of thirty-five wagons, 175 men, and 1,000 mules. William's party numbered eighteen Americans, twenty-two Mexican herders and servants, and an unknown quantity of wagons. The two groups kept roughly together for the next few days. But because of previous warnings that an expedition of Texans lurking in the vicinity of the trail was bent on "capturing any Mexican property that might be found upon the plains in Mexican territory," the Americans decided it best to distance themselves from their newfound companions.[72] Yet after trying various strategies, they were unable to shake the Mexicans, who eventually put in a formal request asking permission to travel with the Americans. This request was reluctantly granted, despite the American party's fears of a "skirmish"" with the Texans. The Mexicans threatened to return to Santa Fe otherwise. Such a result, William wrote, would make "a hazardous business for any of our Countrymen to visit that place afterwards."

Thoughts of Texans disappeared temporarily on April 14, when "Indian sign" was discovered along the trail in the present-day Oklahoma Panhandle. It was more than sign the next day: after crossing the Cimarron River, the caravan came upon two large camps of Kiowas and Arapahoes. As it was then too late to reach the next campsite with water, the traders had no choice but to stop for the night between the two villages, situated approximately

2 miles apart. It was not long before William and his fellow travelers found
themselves

> surrounded by about 1200 men, women & Children. The men were
> generally dressed in Moccasins & leggins made of dressed Buffaloe skins,
> no shirts, but with a loose Robe wrapped around their bodies. The women,
> were dressed in the same manner and rode astride their horses like the men
> & without a saddle. We seated them upon the ground and made them
> presents of Corn, Tobacco, flour and dried bread.

The traders' caravan left the villages early the next morning, accompanied for a short distance by a contingent of approximately 100 Indians who
traded buffalo robes to the men of the train for blankets. The merchants had
another bit of excitement the following day when they ran into a war party
of thirty Arapahoes. William and the other traders, fully armed, met the
charging band at the front of their wagons. But the Arapahoes stopped 400
yards short of the train. After some exchanges it was learned that the
Arapahoes were out hunting Pawnees — no doubt welcome news to the
traders. The Indians consequently joined the caravan, were given a "good
dinner" during the noonday stop, and camped with the traders overnight.
This was the last encounter with Indians for the rest of the trip.

It was upon approaching the Arkansas River, probably near present-day
Ingalls, Kansas, that the traders became most concerned about the Texans,
whom they expected to be in that area of the trail. Yet on April 21 the train
reached and crossed the river, the border between the United States and
Mexico, in safety. A small party in advance of them, however, had not been
so fortunate. Five Mexicans on foot entered their camp the next day. Servants
of merchant Antonio José Chavez, who had left Santa Fe for the United States
in February, they gave the shocking information that their master had been
murdered on April 8 by "a party of Texians."[73]

The traders could do nothing but continue their journey toward Missouri. Chavez's servants were put under guard, on the chance that they might
themselves have committed the murder, and a runner was sent ahead to carry
the news to Independence. On April 29 the caravan reached the area of
Chavez's murder and a small detachment from the train decided to investi-
gate. Here, near present-day Lyons, Kansas, on what was then called Owl
Creek but is today known as Jarvis,[74] the scouting party came upon fresh

campfires and spotted two men running toward some distant sandhills. In an effort to overtake these men, they were suddenly confronted by a group of twenty "ranged in order of battle." This was too much for the scouting party, which withdrew to the protection of the train. Tensions mounted again near dusk as the traders' caravan was approaching the crossing of the Little Arkansas. Two of their Mexican scouts came charging up, screaming, "Texians." The caravan now readied itself for a fight, as the scouts said that they had seen the Texans at the crossing, apparently preparing to attack the train.

But the expected battle was not to be. As William describes it,

> On coming down a long slope from the ridge, we saw a number of horses feeding about a mile below the ford and soon after a party of men making for the crossing at full speed. but before we reached it they crossed over to our side and advancing to meet us we recognised old friends from Independence who were out looking for the murderers and who fancying our men at noon to be Indians had made the best of their way out of their neighbourhood.

William, "being heartily sick of the road," joined the returning Independence posse on May 2, leaving his wagon with the caravan. But William did not like the pace at which this group was covering the 220 miles to Independence, and two days later he and three others left them behind. William, who had been away from St. Louis for over five months, was no doubt anxious to get home to family and friends. He finished the journey in under two weeks' time. The *Niles' National Register* of June 3, 1843, reported his and the other merchants' arrivals in St. Louis:

> The principal men attached to the large caravan of Santa Fe traders which lately arrived at Independence (Mo.) reached the city of St. Louis on the 17th instant [May], having with them sixteen bales and twelve boxes of silver, and a quantity of furs, belonging to Jose Gutierrer, John Pravis, James Floris, P. Arando, J. Olaro, M. Sandrue, J. C. Armigo, R. Armigo, W. Glasgow, and N. W. Greene. It is said the specie amounts to three hundred thousand dollars.

෴

Edward James Glasgow was not at St. Louis to welcome his brother home. In fact, the two had switched places: Edward had arrived at St. Louis, "via Valparaiso — Cape Horn — Boston," on January 17, 1843.[75] By June 25, however, he was in Mexico City on his way to Mazatlan, having traveled from New York and Vera Cruz.[76] Edward was making one final trip to Mazatlan to settle the affairs of Glasgow, Harrison, Boyd & Co. Edward's father wrote to him from St. Louis on July 31 with some details concerning the closing of the firm at home. He reported that James Harrison had just obtained a settlement, conducted by a referee, with James Boyd & Son of Boston. Of the monies Daniel Boyd had sent in, Harrison received $51,455.33. "He has paid off all the debt of G.H.B. & Co.," William wrote, "and got sufficient to make him quite easy here."[77]

As for Edward's interest in the firm, his father advised him that he had "asked release from G. & H. [Glasgow & Harrison] to you for all claim for loss on the business also for all acc'ts. against you on the books of G. & H. here or on the books of G. H. B. & Co., G. H. Valois & Co., here or in Mazatlan. This gives you a chance to begin free of debt and I hope your experience will be compensation for your time." In other words, instead of earning profits, Edward had learned an important lesson: mercantile pursuits are frequently a gamble. Their Mazatlan business obviously had not done well, for Daniel Boyd also appears to have been allowed nothing beyond the capital he invested in the firm and his expenses, which William estimated at $5,900. That the settlement between Harrison and James Boyd & Son required a referee suggests that there were other problems as well.[78]

But after Mazatlan thoughts of his old business would quickly pass away, for Edward was already involved in a new enterprise. Earlier in the year, apparently while in the United States, Edward had come into contact with Dr. Henry Connelly, a respected Southwest trader. The two formed a partnership to participate in the overland trade to Chihuahua. Thus, while Edward was traveling across Mexico on his way to Mazatlan, a train of wagons belonging to the firm of Connelly & Glasgow was making its way down the Santa Fe Trail. After finishing up in Mazatlan, he was to meet up with his new partner in Chihuahua.[79]

Edward could not have picked a better business associate. Twenty years Edward's senior, Connelly was a former Kentuckian who had been involved in the Chihuahua trade since 1828.[80] A description of Connelly written by Edward years later reveals the qualities that made him a desirable partner.

Dr. Henry Connelly (1800–1866). A Chihuahua trader from 1828, Connelly was a partner of Edward James Glasgow under the firm name of Connelly & Glasgow (and Glasgow & Connelly) from 1843 to 1849. (Courtesy of the Kansas State Historical Society.)

Connelly "was moderately well off," Edward wrote, "and in good standing and credit as a merchant of ability, integrity and fair dealing, besides enjoying the personal friendship of many of the influential Mexicans and all of his own countrymen in that city."[81] Connelly was also a naturalized Mexican citizen.[82] Edward would be associated with Connelly under the firm name of Connelly & Glasgow, and later Glasgow & Connelly, for the next six years.

Edward's father wrote him from St. Louis on July 31 and informed him that the last letter he had received from Connelly was written at Elm Grove on July 11, "15 miles beyond the last house on the [Santa Fe] road." Connelly had approximately twenty-two wagons, he informed his son, and a certain Gentry had twelve.[83] Gentry was merchant Reuben Gentry, who had contracted that year with an English firm at Zacatecas, Mexico, to transport their goods over the trail from Missouri.[84] From July 13 to 17, Captain Philip St. George Cooke, on his way to Fort Leavenworth in command of a detachment of U.S. dragoons, encountered the Connelly and Gentry caravan strung out along the trail both west and east of Council Grove. He reported meeting forty-two wagons and two carriages in all, which suggests that there were probably other merchants traveling with the train.[85]

The caravan reached Santa Fe by the end of September.[86] Norris Colburn, a trader who had left that city on November 15, reported to the *Missouri Republican* in St. Louis in early January that "the company of Messrs. Connelly and Glasgow. . . would reach Chihuahua about the 8th of November, but would proceed further with a large portion of their goods."[87] He also stated that the Connelly & Glasgow train consisted of forty-two wagons, which was the same amount reported by Captain Cooke. William, in his letter of July 31, advised his son to meet Connelly in Chihuahua, "as part of the goods go down in the interior to the fair and it will be important that you are both there to adopt measures for future business."[88] The fair he spoke of was the famous trade fair at San Juan de los Lagos, which was traditionally begun on December 10. Edward's brother explains the popularity of this event in his "Memorandums": "During the continuance of these fairs immense amounts of goods of all descriptions are disposed of, all merchandise sold here being exempt from all other duties except those attendant upon their first intro-duction into the country, while all sold elsewhere are burthened with an international duty of 20 per cent attending their transmition from one state in[to] any other."

But Edward was to miss the fair. On December 12, 1843, he was in Culiacán, Mexico, on his way to Chihuahua.[89] It had perhaps taken longer to settle affairs at Mazatlan than he had expected. At some point the two merchants did get together, although they were not to remain in Mexico for long. On March 10, 1844, Edward left Chihuahua for the United States, Connelly apparently following sometime later. Traveling via Santa Fe and Bent's Fort, in company with other traders and a Cheyenne Indian named Slim Face, Edward arrived in St. Louis on June 5. His party was reported to have brought in $28,000 in specie.[90]

It was three months before Connelly and Glasgow set out again for Chihuahua. In August 1843, in part because of problems with the Texans, Mexican president Santa Anna had ordered the frontier custom houses of New Mexico and Chihuahua closed to "all commerce." On March 31, 1844, however, he reopened these custom houses, the news reaching Missouri in May.[91] Probably not expecting this turn of events, Connelly and Glasgow were not able to depart Independence with a return train until shortly after the middle of September.[92] This late start brought their caravan disaster near Willow Bar in the present-day Oklahoma Panhandle.[93] A snowstorm killed approximately fifty of their mules in one night. Albert Speyer's train, which was a short distance ahead of them, lost eighty. Both Speyer and Connelly were forced to start in advance of their stranded trains for Santa Fe to acquire additional draft animals.[94] Although this was a setback, both trains did eventually reach the New Mexico capital.[95] Surprisingly, Edward took time at Cold Spring, a camping place a short distance down the trail from Willow Bar, to carve his name alongside the hundreds of others that cover the sandstone outcroppings there. His efforts are plainly visible to this day.[96]

Edward did not travel the Santa Fe Trail again until summer 1845. On August 9, he arrived in Independence with $25,000 in specie. He and another trader named Roussi, in charge of a caravan of ten wagons and forty men, had made the trip from Chihuahua in seventy-two days.[97] Reports of Connelly's whereabouts during this period are somewhat confusing. He may have accompanied Edward to Missouri. An entry of July 4, 1845, in the Mexican records at Santa Fe notes Connelly's payment of 620 pesos in taxes (6%) for specie he was exporting to the United States.[98] This specie undoubtedly made up a portion of the $25,000 that Edward was reported to have arrived with. In a journal entry for August 27, however, Lieutenant James W. Abert mentions coming across a Santa Fe–bound caravan near Point of Rocks in New Mexico, and according to a messenger they sent to the train, one of the proprietors was Dr. Connelly. The train had departed Missouri shortly after Abert's party (under John C. Frémont), which had gone around June 23.[99] It may be that Connelly left Santa Fe some time before Edward and that Edward had paid the taxes for the firm of Connelly & Glasgow, with the Mexican official only recording Connelly's name. Whatever the explanation, all that is known for certain is that Connelly was back in Mexico before Edward returned there the following year.[100]

Edward Glasgow remained in the States until spring 1846. In May of that year he was in Independence preparing for his fourth journey over the road to Santa Fe. This time he would be accompanied by brother William, who was taking his own stock of goods for what would be his first venture into the overland trade. After returning from Mexico in 1843, William had taken the position of clerk on the steamboat Lexington, a new sidewheeler with St. Louis as its home port.[101] How long he worked on the Lexington is unclear,

Edward James Glasgow's name is surrounded by several others on the sandstone outcroppings known as Inscription Rock or Signature Rock at Cold Spring, a well-known Santa Fe Trail camping spot in the present-day Oklahoma Panhandle. The inscription reads "E. J. Glasgow 1844." (Photo by Leo Gamble.)

although it is known that the Lexington was snagged and lost on the Missouri on September 16, 1845.[102]

This trip over the plains was planned as a grand affair. Tagging along with the Glasgows would be several pleasure-seekers and the Glasgows' brother-in-law George Rogers Hancock Clark, who was taking to the trail that year for his health. They would also have company from several other caravans. Josiah Gregg estimated that over $1 million in merchandise was being hauled to Mexico that season, more than three times the value of that taken in any previous year.[103] The increased amount of goods on the trail was due to the passage of the much-sought-after Drawback Act in March 1845. For the first time, overland traders who re-exported foreign goods in their original packages to Santa Fe and Chihuahua would receive drawbacks (rebates), on their U.S. duties.[104] Many of the traders that year, including the Glasgows, took advantage of the act. But Edward had an additional reason for traveling to Chihuahua: he had received the appointment of U.S. commercial agent for that city in March.[105] Shortly before their caravan left Missouri, however, the United States declared war on Mexico.[106]

On July 4, 1846, the Glasgows' train met a detachment of 180 U.S. dragoons under Captain Benjamin Moore at Pawnee Fork, near present-day Larned, Kansas. Moore had orders to halt all the traders on the trail. The Glasgows and the other merchants who had gathered at that point were later allowed to proceed to Bent's Fort but were detained there until Colonel (later General) Stephen Watts Kearny could arrive with the rest of the U.S. invading force. Starting from Bent's Fort on August 2, the various traders and their wagons, over 150 in number, followed the Army of the West over Raton Pass and into New Mexico.[107] Kearny's subsequent "bloodless" conquest of Santa Fe and claiming of New Mexico for the United States on August 18 meant little to most of the merchants, except for the important fact that no Mexican duties were collected on their cargoes. The majority of the goods were selected for the markets of Chihuahua and points farther south and were of little use in northern New Mexico.[108]

Edward met up with partner Henry Connelly either at Santa Fe or with the Army of the West as it approached the New Mexico capital. Connelly had played a minor role in the events leading up to the U.S. occupation. He was in Santa Fe when trader James Magoffin and Captain Cooke with twelve dragoons arrived ahead of the U.S. forces to "sound" Governor Armijo on the subject of a peaceful takeover. Connelly was well acquainted with both Armijo and Colonel Diego Archuleta, Armijo's second-in-command, especially so with the latter. He gave Magoffin his views on whether or not Armijo and Archuleta would offer any resistance to the U.S. forces.[109] When Captain Cooke returned to the Army of the West, Connelly accompanied him as Armijo's "commissioner."[110] What instructions he had from Armijo are unknown. According to one historian, Connelly brought back to the Mexicans a report on the strength of the American army that "created a panic among the officials, and was the principal cause of the abandonment of New Mexico by Armijo."[111] This is not substantiated by any of the primary accounts I have examined, however, including those by Connelly and the Glasgows.[112]

While the merchants were waiting for permission to leave Santa Fe with their wagons, Edward was privileged to accompany General Kearny at the head of a force of 700 troops on an enjoyable tour of the villages and pueblos along the Rio Grande below the capital city.[113] Kearny arrived back in Santa Fe from this expedition on September 11, and the trains of Connelly & Glasgow and those of many of the other traders were allowed to leave the city about nine days later.[114] But the distance they could travel in relative safety was limited. General John E. Wool was reported to be marching on Chihuahua, and until they received news of the city's capture, it was considered unwise to advance too far south.[115] In early October they reached Valverde, 157 miles from Santa Fe, and halted.[116] Connelly and a small party of traders pushed ahead of their trains to El Paso del Norte to make "an arrangemt with the authorities of Chihuahua by which we might introduce our goods without danger of confiscation." They were taken as prisoners to Chihuahua.[117] Magoffin and José Gonzales, who had preceded Connelly's party south, received the same treatment.[118]

The Glasgows and the other merchants quickly learned the fate of Connelly's party and Magoffin. "We are in no enviable situation," trader Samuel Owens wrote from Valverde on October 20, "and do not know whether to go forwards, backwards, or remain."[119] They were able to eliminate one of those options approximately three days later when they received information that a large body of Mexicans was on its way from El Paso to attack and rob them. The traders posted their own guards along the roads, hastily constructed a "fort" from their wagons, and sent an express north requesting military protection.[120] Two hundred U.S. dragoons under Captain John Henry K. Burgwin soon arrived on the scene from Albuquerque, but the attack never came, and the dragoons departed after a few days.[121] The merchants later learned that the Mexican force, numbering about 700 men, had turned back after marching about 60 miles on their way from El Paso.[122] This would be only the first of many such alarms.

The merchants and their caravan, now numbering at least 200 wagons (some accounts place the total as high as 300), remained stalled at Valverde for the next several weeks. By the end of November, provisions were both extremely scarce and expensive.[123] Despite the group's expectations, confirmed news of General Wool's much-anticipated capture of Chihuahua was not forthcoming. A stir was created in the traders' camp, however, by the arrival of a "circular" from the Chihuahua governor about November 28. It promised the traders safe entry for their goods if they dismissed their American teamsters and paid the duties that would have been charged at Santa Fe. Almost all the American traders refused to comply with the governor's conditions, but the merchants of other countries, including Britain, Mexico, and Spain, saw this as the opportunity they had been waiting for.[124]

That opportunity was dashed by Captain William Walton and a detachment of the First Regiment Missouri Mounted Volunteers that had been sent to the traders' assistance after the alarm of October 23. Walton decided to force the merchants to await the arrival of his commander, Colonel Alexander W. Doniphan. Some of the more anxious traders had already advanced to Fray Cristóbal, approximately 15 miles south, but Walton detailed troops there on December 4 to make sure the wagons went no farther.[125] Unfortunately, no one knew exactly when to expect Doniphan. He had been ordered by General Kearny to join Wool at Chihuahua but was forced to postpone that undertaking by new orders received on October 11 instructing Doniphan first to conduct a campaign against the Navajo Indians.[126]

Edward Glasgow and Samuel Owens, and possibly others, had started back for Santa Fe on December 1 in an effort to meet with Doniphan and, according to Abert, "get some positive information with reference to the place where they should be constrained to winter."[127] During their absence, the traders at Valverde, including William Glasgow, protested to Captain Walton about the detention. Although most of the American traders preferred to wait on Doniphan and the protection of his army, or until they received news of Chihuahua's capture, the traders apparently saw nothing wrong with letting those merchants proceed who wanted to. A primary concern of all of the traders was that the detention would force them to enter Chihuahua en masse with their goods. The resulting competition would be heavy. According to Abert, the protests of the merchants were aimed specifically at obtaining permission for the large train of Kerford & Jenkins to proceed, as it carried $90,000 in merchandise, all eligible for drawback. If Kerford was allowed to go on, it was understood that he would pass through Chihuahua and continue on to Zacatecas, thus leaving Chihuahua open to the other merchants. But neither a letter nor a lengthy petition prepared by the traders had "the desired effect" on the captain.[128]

Lieutenant Abert's diary indicates that William may have moved his and his brother's wagons from Valverde to the Fray Cristóbal camp on December

Doniphan's army of Missouri Volunteers marching across the Jornada del Muerto in December 1846. Connelley uses this illustration in his *Doniphan's Expedition* and credits the *Journal of William H. Richardson* ..., first published in 1847 (apparently only later additions included plates). This facsimile is from the *Centennial History of Missouri*, p. 274. (Courtesy of the State Historical Society of Missouri, Columbia.)

9, the same date as the traders' petition to Captain Walton. That evening, word reached Valverde that Doniphan was approaching.[129] On December 14 those merchants who were still camped at Valverde left to join their fellow traders waiting at Fray Cristóbal.[130] Four days later, after a majority of Doniphan's troops had passed them by, the traders were finally able to renew their journey south.[131] The merchants were required to follow with their trains in the rear of the army, a situation with which most of them were well acquainted.[132] Still, it was undoubtedly a great relief. Nearly all of them felt the same way as Edward and Owens, whom young Susan Shelby Magoffin described upon their return from Santa Fe on December 16 as "crazy to get on notwithstanding the danger they may be rushing into."[133]

On Christmas Day 1846 Doniphan and his Missourians met and defeated a superior Mexican army at Brazito, approximately 30 miles above El Paso.[134] The Glasgows and their wagons entered El Paso a few days behind the U.S. troops on January 3, 1847.[135] Doniphan would remain in El Paso until artillery he had requested from Santa Fe could join him.[136] The merchants would thus wait on Doniphan and his volunteers until the next month, some of the traders, William among them, taking the opportunity to break out their goods and make a few sales.[137] In early February two merchant trains tried to escape Doniphan's control and slip south in front of the army. One succeeded. The rest remained until February 8, when Doniphan started his troops for Chihuahua.[138] As it was now known that General Wool was not advancing on that city, Doniphan took the extra precaution of ordering the American traders and teamsters to form a battalion. They mustered two companies. The esteem in which their companions held Edward and William is evidenced by Edward's election as captain of Company A and William's being made First lieutenant.[139]

The traders received a "small sample of battle," as Edward described it later, on February 28, 1847, near the hacienda of Sacramento, 18 miles from the city of Chihuahua. Here a Mexican army under José Heredia eagerly waited behind a series of fortifications. Doniphan formed the merchants' wagons and those of his army into four parallel columns and used these to help conceal the strength of his force as he advanced upon the enemy positions. During the ensuing fight, the wagons remained close in the rear of the army to serve as defenses in case the Missourians were pushed back. But Doniphan's volunteers were again victorious, the three-and-a-half-hour battle ending with the entire Mexican army's fleeing from the field.[140] The "Traders Battalion" had remained with the wagons and technically did not see any action, although plenty of shot and shell was sent their way. A number of oxen and mules were killed, and at least one wagon was damaged.[141] Owens, the commander of the Traders Battalion and Edward's best friend, had left the wagons in charge of Edward and taken part in the attack on the enemy redoubts. He was the only American to die during the battle.[142]

The army and its merchant caravan formally entered the city of Chihuahua to the patriotic strains of "Yankee Doodle" and "Hail Columbia" on March 2.[143] Edward was again reunited with partner Connelly, who, along with the other Americans held as prisoners (except Magoffin), had acquired his freedom once the news of the American victory reached the city.[144] The rejoicing of the traders was cut short, though, by Doniphan's announcement a few days later that he would be leaving Chihuahua, giving the traders one week to prepare to depart. It was painfully obvious to the merchants that very little of their estimated $1 million in merchandise could be sold in the time Doniphan gave them, and the fate of those merchants who remained

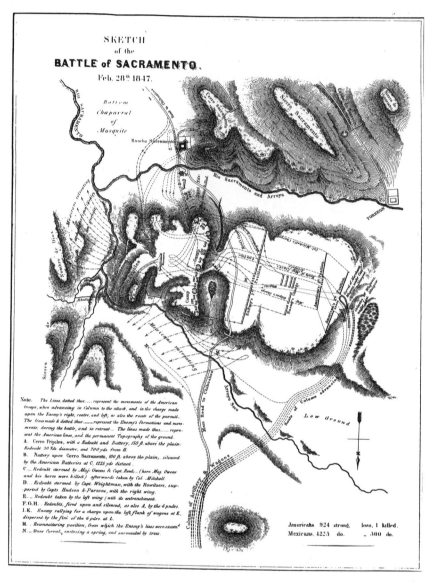

Official sketch of the Battle of Sacramento that appeared in Sen. Ex. Doc. No. 1, 30th Cong., 1st sess. (Serial 503). Note the "Corral of Merchant Wagons, under Capt. Glasgow" and "Column of Wagons, under Liet. Glasgow" at the middle right of the sketch. (Courtesy of the Denver Public Library, Western History Department.)

behind would be uncertain. With the "prospect for losing every thing" looming, the traders persuaded Doniphan to enter into treaty negotiations with the Chihuahua government, temporarily headquartered at Parral. Connelly was sent to Parral to meet with Governor Angel Trias and later returned with three Mexican commissioners charged with negotiating the terms.[145]

According to the journal of one of Doniphan's men, Connelly took a proposition from Doniphan that was to reinstate Governor Trias "in his office and evacuate the city with American forces, and the traders should pay the rates of duty as heretofore, if he [Trias] would insure them protection."[146] The journal makes no mention of the commissioners but states that Connelly returned with a counterproposal from Trias, that "he would pledge protection for the traders upon condition that the American forces would immediately evacuate the city, leaving the artillery and everything captured at Sacramento and pay liberally for all damages done Chihuahua since our possession of it. These propositions were of course rejected." Another version of the negotiations states that Doniphan proposed to the commissioners who had returned with Connelly "that if the people of Chihuahua will guaranty the safety of the American residents and traders in Chihuahua, and will hold themselves aloof from any participation in the war, he will evacuate the town and proceed on his course."[147] According to this account, "the Mexicans were favorably inclined to the terms proposed." This is contradicted by William, however, who wrote home that the negotiations failed because the commissioners were unwilling to obligate Chihuahua to remain neutral.[148]

The commissioners returned to Parral about March 24 without a treaty.[149] In a subsequent letter, William blamed the failure on Doniphan, who "fearing to compromise himself, would not accept of their propositions nor would he make any himself."[150] This letter was written after Doniphan and the volunteers had left Chihuahua, however, and the merchants who remained behind accused the colonel of "abandoning" them. Doniphan had made propositions, as the above accounts, including William's, prove. In an interesting twist, though, Doniphan claimed that the merchants were at fault. In a letter to David Waldo (a Santa Fe trader and a captain in Doniphan's regiment) written ten months later, he stated that the traders "had objected to my making a treaty for them." According to Doniphan, "the merchants by that time had come to the conclusion that a tremendous meeting & sundry resolutions would force me to stay there as long [as] there was a shirt-tail full of goods in the City."[151] Doniphan's statement also appears to be unfounded. The merchants knew that Doniphan wanted to leave Chihuahua and that there was a very good chance that he would. To scuttle any kind of a treaty would certainly not have been in their best interest. I could find no other mention of any objections by the traders in the available accounts.

The merchants did hold a meeting with Doniphan while the commissioners were in Chihuahua, perhaps because they knew that the negotiations were not going well. They pleaded with Doniphan to remain in the city. He chose to settle the matter by placing the decision in the hands of General Wool, and an express was sent to Saltillo requesting orders.[152] In his dispatch to Wool, Doniphan stated that he preferred to leave Chihuahua and join Wool's command. His troops were "wholly unfit to garrison a town or city," and their term of enlistment would expire soon. They had not received any pay since their enlistment, and many were without horses and clothing. In regard to the American merchants he was protecting, he reported that they had "several hundred thousand dollars at stake" and "violently" opposed his leaving. Yet he countered that "the merchants admit that their goods could not be sold here in five years; if they go south they will be as near the markets of Durango and Zacatecas as they now are. I am anxious and willing to protect the merchants as far as practicable; but I protest against remaining here as a mere wagon-guard."[153]

The express left Chihuahua on March 20 and returned April 23 with orders from General Zachary Taylor for the Missourians to join his command at Saltillo.[154] "As for the traders," read Taylor's orders, "they may, at their option, remain in Chihuahua, or come under the protection of your column to Saltillo."[155] The merchants, however, had reopened negotiations with the Mexican officials for a treaty, having sent Chihuahua prefecto Felix Maceyra to Parral as their "ambassador."[156] An official decree issued by the vice-governor of Chihuahua at Parral on April 2 had made their situation more ominous. The decree prohibited the sale and circulation of all goods that had come into Chihuahua with the U.S. army and forbade the issuing of guias on those goods. Any goods that were sold would be subject to confiscation.[157]

According to William, the traders instructed Maceyra to "state our willingness to pay duties &c to the gov^t and get from the vice gov^r an obligation to protect our persons & property after the army left in case we would guarantee the forces to leave the State within one month."[158] William makes no mention in his letters of Doniphan's role in this renewed effort, nor does Edward. In Doniphan's letter to Waldo, he wrote that he had refused to attempt another treaty for the traders but did tell them that "they might stipulate for their safety by making my immediate withdrawal with our forces from the State of Chihuahua & the payment of New Mexican duties the basis of a treaty on the American side." Doniphan further stated that he gave

> Dr. Conelly a written statement & directed him to send it by Mesceira to the state authorities in which I stated that if the treaty was made that I would leave with our forces in a few days — that I would use my influence to prevent Genl. Wool or any detachment of his army from marching on Chihuahua — and the Mexicans having heard that some reinforcements were coming from New Mexico I was to leave written order with Dr. Conelly directing such force not to occupy Chihuahua but to pass through as speedily as convenient.[159]

Two days before the return of Doniphan's express, the merchants received good news from Maceyra: the Chihuahua government was eager to enter into the treaty the merchants had proposed. Maceyra was due back in Chihuahua from Parral on April 28. But Doniphan, with Taylor's orders now in hand, was unwilling to wait for Maceyra. Despite the strong protests of the traders, the army began its withdrawal from Chihuahua on April 25.[160] "By dent of hard begging," as William described it, Doniphan did agree to leave a detachment of approximately 400 men until the morning of April 28, although the traders pointed out that Maceyra was not expected back until that afternoon.[161]

Without a treaty, many of the traders felt they had no choice but to follow the army, believing that their wares would be confiscated, having entered the state illegally, and that their lives would be in jeopardy if they remained.[162] Despite the Mexican decree of April 2, the merchants had been frantically disposing of their goods.[163] As the day of the army's departure quickly neared, some of the traders sold out their remaining stock to Chihuahua merchant José Cordero at low prices.[164] Others loaded up what they could and followed the army south.[165] One party of traders headed north for New Mexico, taking their returns mostly in bullion.[166] Several of the merchants, including Edward and William, had sold their livestock to the army quartermaster soon after entering Chihuahua and thus were unable to move their goods even if they wanted to. Partly because of this, Edward,

Connelly, and a few others, chose to stay with their goods and "trust to the good faith and generosity of the Mexicans." William was able to put together a team of eight mules and get away with one wagonload of merchandise, Connelly planning to claim the remainder as his own.[167]

Two days after the last of the volunteers evacuated Chihuahua, Maceyra arrived with the authority to enter into a treaty with Doniphan. Fortunately for the merchants, Maceyra was undaunted by the army's departure and decided to make the treaty with the traders, as they had "remained upon his pledge."[168] Edward sent a courier after William, which reached him at En Ramada, 145 miles to the south.[169] William returned to Chihuahua and, although business was at first slow, the brothers were optimistic and believed the worst to be over. They were as safe in Chihuahua as they would be in St. Louis, they wrote home, the Mexicans treating them in the "most polite and friendly manner."[170] Edward was even able to leave Chihuahua on a short trading trip to Parral, where he disposed of $6,000 worth of goods for cash.[171] The Glasgows and the other Americans were shaken, however, by the robbery and barbarous murder of fellow trader James Aull in his store on June 23. William wrote home about the "gloom it cast over us all We being here so few in number and one of us to be so horribly mangled for the mere purpose of plunder."[172] He did caution his family not to be alarmed, though, as Aull was killed for his money, not because he was a foreigner. The Glasgows noted the speed in which the Mexican authorities went about apprehending the suspects and the interest they demonstrated in seeing that justice was served.[173]

An unfortunate circumstance of the murder was that William, who had recently sold out his remaining goods to his brother and Connelly, had just purchased approximately $6,000 worth of merchandise from Aull. He was preparing to take these goods to Jesús Maria when the incident occurred and was consequently delayed until the authorities could complete an inventory of Aull's property.[174]

No letters survive for the period beginning July 2, 1847, and ending March 28, 1848, at which time Brigadier General Sterling Price and an American army had recently reoccupied Chihuahua and defeated General Trias at Santa Cruz de Rosales, 60 miles below the capital city. Although there is evidence that at least one letter was written in August 1847, it is probable that very few others were attempted, for during a part of this period the traders were forbidden from sending or receiving correspondence from the

United States.[175] An idea of their situation during that nine-month period is revealed in Edward's letter to his sister of March 31, 1848, in which he writes that "now that every thing is over I will confess that we have occasionally been in a little danger from our good friends the Mexicans and we were overjoyed when Gen[l] Price made his appearance in our city." William's "Memorandums" contain only a brief mention in regard to their stay in Chihuahua, but it corroborates Edward's statement. He wrote that during the twelve months after Doniphan's departure they were "subjected to all kinds of insults and indignities from the Mexicans until the second invasion of Chihuahua by Gen Price."[176] Both these statements are a marked contrast to the brothers' comments about their treatment immediately after Doniphan's withdrawal, and one wonders what events led up to or caused such a dramatic change.

The Battle of Santa Cruz de Rosales on March 16 would be the last major event of importance that the brothers would report home to their family. William departed Chihuahua on April 6 and quickly made his way to the gulf, most of the time in company with military escorts, via Parras, Monterey, and Matamoros. Edward left the following month, traveling north to Santa Fe. William arrived in St. Louis on May 14, and his elder brother got home from the plains on July 15.[177] Edward had traveled from Chihuahua with Ebenezer Pomeroy and Joseph P. Hamelin, Jr. Trail traveler Orville C. Pratt met their trains at the Great Bend of the Arkansas River and recorded in his diary that "their teams looked bad."[178] The teams were good enough to get them and their returns to the Missouri border, however, as the Liberty *Weekly Tribune* reported on July 28 that "Mr. Pomeroy, whose arrival from Chihuahua, we noticed last week, brought in $81,000. . . . Mr. GlasGow. also brought in a large amount in silver and drafts."[179]

Edward and William had survived the delays, privations, and dangers of wartime Mexico and, somewhat amazingly, had apparently come home with a good profit on their venture (Edward estimated in July 1847 that Connelly & Glasgow would make from $18,000 to $20,000 in net profits). They would never forget their experiences of the previous two years, which were at times filled with excitement and adventure but more often were frustrating and anxiety-ridden. Edward wrote to his sister Mary Susan shortly after the Battle of Sacramento that "I am sick of war and its melancholy consequences and tired of Mexico in every way. The next time I return home will be to remain there permanently."[180] As far as can be determined, for the rest of their lives, he and brother William never visited Mexico again.[181]

☙

Back in St. Louis, Edward did not remain long from commercial endeavors. In September 1849 he was operating a business on Commercial Street under the style of Glasgow & Connelly, "Wholesale Grocers, Forwarding and Commission Merchants."[182] A little over a year later, in October 1850, William H. Glasgow replaced Edward's Chihuahua trading partner, Henry Connelly, in the firm. The new name of their young business was Glasgow & Brother.[183] An advertisement for their firm in the 1859 St. Louis city directory listed the brothers as "Wholesale Grocers, And Commission Merchants, Dealers In Sugar, Coffee, Molasses and Rice."[184]

St. Louis in the 1850s was strikingly different, both in size and prominence, from the city the brothers had known as boys. In 1850 the population of St. Louis was 74,439, an increase of 352 percent over the population of ten years before.[185] More than 3,000 steamboats arrived at St. Louis each year in 1852 and 1853.[186] "St. Louis was the 'hub' of an immense system of river navigation," wrote Thomas L. Rodgers, who worked for a St. Louis mercantile firm during the period 1857–1860, and a "distributor for merchandise designed for the territory of the great West." Rodgers remembered the levee as the

> most inspiring sight on this continent. For more than a mile it was thickly lined with steamers loading the products of the West and East, and for all that distance one could walk over the piles of produce and not set foot on the ground. There were bales of hemp, hogsheads of tobacco, piles of bacon, huge piles of grain in bags, and boxes, bales, &c. of merchandise from eastern points for consumption in the city, and to be forwarded to the far West.[187]

Because of merchants such as the Glasgows, commercial ties between St. Louis and the Southwest remained very strong.[188] The brothers had made important contacts during their years on the Santa Fe and Chihuahua trails and were literate in Spanish. They consequently did a heavy business with New Mexico. But there were no long months on the trail for Edward and

Advertisement for Glasgow & Brother from the St. Louis Directory, 1859.

The St. Louis levee in 1857. (Courtesy of the State Historical Society of Missouri, Columbia.)

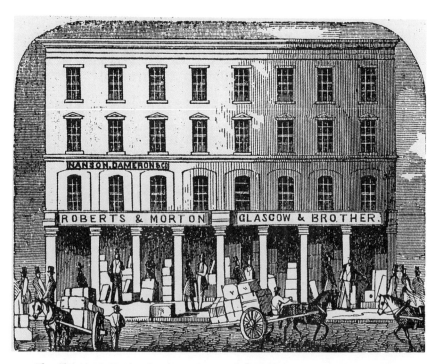

The Glasgow & Brother business, 100 North Second, as it appeared circa 1860. From Richard Edwards and M. Hopewell, Edwards's Great West (1860). (Editor's collection.)

The same location and apparently the same building pictured in the 1860 engraving of the Glasgow & Brother establishment, from a photograph taken in 1936. This structure, and many others that were a part of the nineteenth-century St. Louis business district, was razed in the late 1930s to make way for the Jefferson National Expansion Memorial (Gateway Arch). (Courtesy of the Jefferson National Expansion Memorial, National Park Service.)

William. As forwarding and commission merchants, they simply filled orders for their New Mexico customers at local and East Coast houses and oversaw the shipment of the merchandise through St. Louis. For purchasing goods, the Glasgows received a 2.5 percent commission on the total value of the merchandise. For receiving and forwarding goods they charged five cents per 100 pounds. Orders for groceries were filled at their own house, where they stocked everything from butter crackers and peppersauce to palm soap and starch.[189] In addition, Edward also oversaw the accounts of the sons of some of his New Mexico customers who were attending school in St. Louis. Edward's son, William, remembered these boys' spending their vacations in his home.[190]

Among the Glasgows' New Mexico customers were merchants Messervy & Webb (later Webb & Kingsbury), Felipe Chaves (also spelled Chavez), José

Felipe Chaves (1835–1905), merchant of Belen, New Mexico, and a long-standing customer of the Glasgows. (Courtesy of the Center for Southwest Research, University of New Mexico.)

L. Perea, Mariano Yrisarri, and François X. Aubry.[191] Mariano Yrisarri of Albuquerque was reported to keep "50 or 60^m\$ [\$60 thousand] cash on deposit with Glasgow Bros of St Louis Mo, all the time."[192] Chaves, located first in Albuquerque and later Belen, was also an important customer. Numerous letters, invoices, and statements from Glasgow & Brother, almost all of them written in Spanish, survive in the business records of Chaves at the University of New Mexico and the New Mexico State Records Center and Archives. Despite the Glasgows' grasp of the Spanish language, however, there was an occasional problem in translation, as the following episode involving Chaves illustrates:

> At one time Don Felipe Chaves, who was a very rich man and had a large store, sent to Mr. Glasgow a long list of goods that he wished to order.

Felipe Chaves's store (the two-story building at right) at Belen, New Mexico, in 1875. The one-story structure to the left is said to have been used for storage. This was one destination of goods ordered from Glasgow, Brother & Co. of St. Louis. (Courtesy of the Center for Southwest Research, University of New Mexico.)

Among other things he wanted *un caso grande*. That was a large kettle in which to cook for the working men at lambing or shearing time. Mr. Glasgow knew Spanish very well, but took that item to read *una casa grande*, a big house.

When the bill came at the end of the year, there was an item of a big house for $15,000. And the kettle never did come. Don Felipe had to go to St. Louis and upon arriving he told Mr. Glasgow that there was a mistake in his bill since he had never ordered a big house. They hunted up the bill and had a good laugh. Don Felipe paid for the house and years afterwards it was sold for him by Mr. Glasgow for eighty thousand dollars. So what was a bad mistake worked out in the end.[193]

Surviving credit reports on their firm provide a revealing look at the Glasgows and their business. "Wealthy, — bus[iness]. heavy, — & in the best of cred[it].," reads the June 1852 report of the Mercantile Agency, New York, on Glasgow & Brother. Another, for July 1853, states that "this house in good

William Henry Glasgow and son Edward James Glasgow, Jr. (1853–1902), circa
1857. (Courtesy of W. Merrill Glasgow, Houston, Texas.)

reputation here, do a fair bus.[,] good char[acter]. & standing & v[er]y. good
for th[ei]r. contracts." An entry for December 1857 estimates that their "bus.
with New Mexico am[oun]ts to 100ᵐ [$100,000] per annum" and a report
of May 22, 1858, notes that "their New Mexican customers have arrived,
and will have a lar[ge] amt of money with them." In December 1858 the
credit agency added that "their Mexican trade is consid^d very profitable, but
requires great care & vigilance."[194]

The Glasgows were doing very well. The 1860 census for St. Louis valued
Edward's real estate at $6,000 and his personal estate at $65,000.[195]
William's real estate was listed as worth $175,000 and his personal estate
$75,000.[196] The brothers were also family men by this time. William had
married Mary Frances Wright on October 22, 1850.[197] She died in 1857,
leaving him with one son, Edward James Glasgow, Jr.[198] In December 1860
William took another wife, Carlota Nestora Fales of Cuba.[199] Edward had

This 1862 photo shows several members of the Glasgow family at Ingleside, the home of William Henry Glasgow. Mary Susan Glasgow Clark can be seen third from the left. Next to her, reading a paper, is her father William Glasgow, Sr., and on his left is Mary's husband, Jefferson Kearny Clark. William H. Glasgow is third from the right holding his daughter Anita Damon, and on his left is his second wife, Carlota. (Courtesy of the Missouri Historical Society, St. Louis.)

married Harriet Clark Kennerly, fondly called "Tea" (or "Tee"), on October 29, 1856.[200] Edward's residence was at 234 Locust in 1860, and William's was an impressive brick home that he called Ingleside, located on Natural Bridge Road.[201]

The decade of the 1860s brought with it the Civil War. Its impact on the Glasgows' business, by then based at 100 North Second, was minimal, at least as it is presented in the credit reports of the Mercantile Agency.[202] The war dramatically affected the brothers' personal lives, however, as it did those of most St. Louisans. According to James Thomas, a free black who was living in St. Louis during the war, "The old and wealthy families of St Louis were all southern in sentiment with few exceptions."[203] This appears to have been the case with the Glasgows.[204] The exception, surprisingly, was their cousin,

William Glasgow, Jr., who stood firmly by the Union.[205] As St. Louis was controlled by the North throughout the conflict, pronounced Southern sympathies placed one at a definite disadvantage. Many sympathizers were singled out early on and subjected to assessments of money and property.[206] Undoubtedly because of this and other distasteful consequences of martial law, William H. Glasgow and brother-in-law Jefferson Kearny Clark temporarily abandoned the United States for Canada in 1862.[207]

Neither Edward nor William Henry took up arms during the war, although several of their friends and relatives did. Meriwether Lewis Clark, a half brother of Jefferson who had served under Kearny and Doniphan during the Mexican War, became a colonel in the Confederate States Army.[208] Edward's brother-in-law, William Clark Kennerly, another veteran of Doniphan's expedition, also enlisted in the Southern forces. When Kennerly was to be married in Alabama in 1864, sister Tea had some "good gray cloth" smuggled through the lines as a woman's cape so that he might have a new uniform for the ceremony.[209] It is not difficult to imagine the part merchant Edward James Glasgow must have played in acquiring this cloth for his wife.

The end of the hostilities found the Glasgows luckier than most. Their families were still intact and their business was thriving. In 1862 the brothers had taken in their salesman, Benjamin H. Batte, as a partner, and the style of the firm was changed to Glasgow, Brother & Co. The Mercantile Agency's report for October 1867 stated that they were "a safe reliable firm doing a profitable bus[iness] & worth 150^m$ [$150,000]." In 1871 the Glasgows took in another partner, John O'Fallon Clark, their bookkeeper and, incidentally, their nephew as well, a son of sister Eleanor. The last changes in their business occurred in 1875 when Batte sold out his interests to the other partners and Edward J. Glasgow, Jr., son of William Henry, became a new member of the firm. "It is a family concern," reported the Mercantile Agency in May 1876, "& the members do most of their own work & doubtless m[a]ke money in the bus besides adding to their wealth from the income of their sev[era]l estates. Are est[imated] wor[th] in the neighborhood of 1 million $ & good for contracts."[210]

As indicated by their directory advertisement of 1859 quoted above, the New Mexican trade was just one aspect of the Glasgows' business. Edward wrote in his reminiscences that they were "dealing principally in Brazil coffee which we imported largely from Rio Janiro and in Louisiana sugar and rice."[211] The credit report of March 15, 1879, elaborates on their coffee

The St. Louis riverfront, from a stereoview circa late 1860s. (Courtesy of the Library of Congress.)

trade, stating that Glasgow, Brother & Co. "buy Coffee at the seaboard from importers giving their paper at 90 days regular terms [and] sell to who[le-sale] dealers in St. Louis on 30 & 60 days. this is their princ^p bus & it takes but little actual cap[i]t[al] to carry it."[212]

That same report, an exceptionally detailed one, also provides information on their Southwest trade, which had changed by this late date. "They still do some trade with old and new Mexico," it informs us, "receive shipments of wool from there & fill orders for Grocs. but this portion of their bus[iness] is much smaller than formerly & is still decreasing." After discussing the firm's liabilities and worth of the partners in real estate, the report ends with the statement that "the firm is one of the oldest & best here, the char[acter] of its members is beyond reproach. Their credit in this market is practically unlimited & tho[ugh] our former ests are too high the firm is regar^d safe for contracts & worth net at a low est[imate] 200^m to 300^m."[213] It is ironic that just a few months later the business ended "disastrously."[214]

The exact cause, or causes, of the failure of Glasgow, Brother & Co. is not disclosed in the writings of either Edward or William that I have examined. Neither is it explained in the reports of the Mercantile Agency. Edward's son William, however, remembered the basics of what happened. He wrote in 1949 that

> The large quantities of coffee and sugar handled, had to be bought many months in advance and the gradual but persistent decline in the selling price caused the failure of the partnership.
>
> Being only thirteen years of age I heard little of the family talk except Uncle Jeff's [Jefferson Kearny Clark] snort of displeasure when bankruptsy proceedings were contemplated.[215]

Although the circumstances of the failure were not reported by the Mercantile Agency, the firm's increasing financial problems were, despite the Glasgows' extreme discretion about their troubled situation, which often led them to decline to give the credit agency the information it sought. What is revealed in the Mercantile Agency's reports is that in May 1879 Glasgow, Brother & Co. was financially "embarrassed" and was seeking an extension from its creditors. The firm, according to the Mercantile Agency, was offering to pay 25 percent of its debt in cash and the balance in one year. The agency's investigator noted in his report that this development, combined with William Henry's borrowing of several thousand dollars against some of his property in March, "puts a dubious aspect on their affairs."[216]

The next report of the Mercantile Agency, dated June 30, was much worse. William Henry had given a deed of trust, it stated, "on all his R[eal]E[state] to secure $156,242 for cr[editor]s." The liabilities of the essentially bankrupt firm, the agency learned, totaled over $200,000.[217] The Glasgows informed the Mercantile Agency that most of their creditors had agreed to a settlement proposal. According to "other sources," this was 25 percent in cash and William's trust deed mentioned above as the balance. Negotiations would continue, however, through the summer,[218] as creditors

William Henry Glasgow, circa 1865. (Courtesy of W. Merrill Glasgow, Houston, Texas.)

were located all across the country, from New York to New Mexico, and getting them all to agree to the same settlement proved difficult. Some insight on the problem is provided in a letter to Felipe Chaves of August 26, 1879:

> we can tell you that several of the creditors wish to make private settlements, taking houses, lands, or a discount in money, but to protect those in New Mexico, we have always refused any settlement that was not general and equitable to all; and we will continue under all circumstances to protect the interests of all equally, in case someone wants to gain some advantage.
>
> For a long while the only obstacle for completing the settlement of our business has been the unwillingness of Senor Don Jose Perea and his brother and his son whose signatures in writing are needed to complete matters, according to our understanding. Everyone else has signed some time ago with the exception of one man in Baltimore who wrote that although he would prefer to make a private settlement (as mentioned above) nevertheless, he would sign the agreement if all the others signed.[219]

It appears that by the end of September all the creditors had signed off on the agreement. The final settlement, according to the Mercantile Agency, was a payment of 25 percent in cash on the creditors' claims and a transfer of Glasgow-owned real estate to a separate party as trustee for the creditors' benefit. The Mercantile Agency reported on October 21 that Glasgow, Brother & Co. had announced their dissolution to date from October 1.[220]

⁂

When his firm failed in 1879, Edward was fifty-nine years old. He and his wife had two sons, Julian Kennerly and William Jefferson, ages seventeen and thirteen, respectively. William Henry was fifty-seven. His family consisted of Carlota, his second wife, and two sons and two daughters. They were Edward James, Jr., age twenty-six and a partner in his father's business; Jefferson Clark, eleven; Anita Damon, eighteen; and Mary Susan, ten.[221] Retirement at this time was probably not an option for the Glasgow brothers, and they would pursue future endeavors separately.

It is likely that after the demise of Glasgow, Brother & Co. William Henry stood better financially than did Edward. William's real estate holdings were much larger than his brother's at the time of the crisis, and he appears to

William Henry Glasgow in a photo taken probably in the 1890s. (Courtesy of the Missouri Historical Society, St. Louis.)

have done some shrewd maneuvering of his assets once he realized their firm was in trouble.[222] Beginning in 1882 William H. Glasgow is listed in the St. Louis city directories as the president of the St. Louis Wine Co. The company manufactured Home Bitters and Sanative Cordial and offered at wholesale champagnes, brandies, and gin.[223] Five years later William was listed as a car manufacturer.[224] He had become the president of the St. Charles Car Company, manufacturers of "all kinds of railway equipments," in 1886.[225] At the time of his death he was receiving a monthly salary of $500 and owned over 500 shares in the company.[226]

William Henry Glasgow died on August 29, 1897, while in Manitou, Colorado. He was seventy-six years old. According to one obituary, he had "gone with his daughters to spend the hot months in Colorado and was stricken down with typhoid fever."[227] His body was brought back to St. Louis, and he was buried in Bellefontaine Cemetery. His grave is today surmounted by an impressive obelisk near the family plot of the famous explorer William Clark.[228] William Henry left a will bequeathing all his

Edward James Glasgow and grandchildren Joseph Magoffin Glasgow and Octavia
Magoffin Glasgow. (Courtesy of Isabel Glasgow, El Paso, Texas.)

property and belongings to his children — his wife had died six years before. William's estate inventory, prepared by his son Edward James, Jr., and dated October 1, put his worth at over $100,000.[229]

Edward James Glasgow survived his brother by several years. Although he had lost almost everything in the failure of Glasgow, Brother & Co., including his house at 1510 Washington, he had continued in the commission business under his own name.[230] How successful he was, however, is questionable. The Mercantile Agency could not recommend him for credit in October 1879. About a year and a half later, the credit agency commented that he was "a v[er]y worthy gentleman whom everyone would like to see succeed but whose chances for anything more than a living at best are consid[ered] v[er]y small."[231] By 1900 Edward was retired and living together with his son Julian.[232] Tea had died in 1898, and his second son, William Jefferson, a graduate of West Point, was serving with the U.S. Army in Matanzas, Cuba.[233]

In his later years, Edward James was sought by writers and historians for his knowledge of the Mexican trade and the U.S. conquest of New Mexico and Chihuahua.[234] In his interviews and correspondence, he seldom failed to mention that he and other members of the Traders Battalion formed by Colonel Doniphan in 1847 were denied pensions by the government.[235] Missouri congressman Harry M. Coudrey introduced a bill in the House of Representatives to grant the old trader a pension, but Edward's death shortly thereafter apparently ended the effort.[236] Edward died in St. Louis on December 7, 1908.[237] He was eighty-eight years old and left an estate valued at a little over $8,500, a small sum compared to the immense quantities of silver specie and bullion he had transported across the plains and oceans during his youth.[238] At Calvary Cemetery, next to his wife, Edward was laid to rest. No stone marks his grave.[239]

NOTES

1.   These letters are included in Part III of this work.

2.   Glasgow family genealogy in Mullanphy Papers, Filed 1-26-1875, Missouri Historical Society (MHS), St. Louis, Missouri; and Eleanor Glasgow Voorhis Manuscript, William E. Connelley Coll., Manuscripts Department, Kansas State Historical Society (KSHS), Topeka, Kansas.

3.   Frederic L. Billon, *Annals of St. Louis in Its Territorial Days from 1804 to 1821* (1888; reprint ed., New York: Arno Press, 1971), 304.

4.   "A Golden Wedding," newspaper clipping (1868), Clark Family Papers, box 8, folder 2, MHS.

5.   Voorhis Manuscript, Connelley Coll., KSHS.

6.   Billon, *Annals*, 304; and "A Golden Wedding."

7.   "A Golden Wedding."

8.   As quoted in Billon, *Annals*, 140.

9.   John Mason Peck, *Forty Years of Pioneer Life: Memoir of John Mason Peck D.D.*, ed. Rufus Babcock (Philadelphia: American Baptist Publication Society, 1864), 84.

10. Billon, *Annals*, 305; and "A Golden Wedding."

11. Billon, *Annals*, 304. "Porter, Glasgow & Nivin" is among the names listed in a petition calling for a mail route between Louisville and St. Louis dated "St. Louis 5th December 1818," at which time William Glasgow was engaged in business at Belleville. At some point, Porter disappears from the partnership. The firm of "Glasgow & Nevins" is recorded in an 1824 St. Louis entry in an American Fur Company journal. Clarence E. Carter, ed., *The Territorial Papers of the United States*, vol. 15, *Louisiana–Missouri, 1815–1821* (Washington, D.C.: U.S. Government Printing Office, 1951), 469; and Fur Trade Ledgers Coll. (microfilm), MHS, Book K, Journal, American Fur Company, Western, 116.

12. William Hyde and Howard L. Conard, eds., *Encyclopedia of the History of St. Louis*, 4 vols. (St. Louis: Southern History Company, 1899), 2:900, 903.

13. Eleanor Glasgow Voorhis to William E. Connelley, May 2, 1907, and May 6, 1907, Connelley Coll. KSHS; and "A Golden Wedding."

14. Billon, *Annals*, 304–305.

15. Paul Wilhelm, Duke of Wuerttemberg, *First Journey to North America in the Years 1822 to 1824*, translated from the German by William G. Bek, *South Dakota Historical Collections*, vol. 19 (1938), 201.

16. Edward J. Glasgow, "Narrative of Some Events in the Life of Edward James Glasgow, Written for His Children," copy of typed manuscript provided courtesy of W. M. Glasgow, Houston, Texas; and Hyde and Conard, *Encyclopedia*, 2:903. William was still connected in business with John Niven at this time. The two announced the dissolution of their partnership in the St. Louis *Missouri Republican* of March 2, 1826. Sherida K. Eddlemon, *Missouri Genealogical Records & Abstracts*, vol. 1, 1766–1839 (Bowie, Md.: Heritage Books, 1990), 176.

17. *Ibid.*

18. Billon, *Annals*, 305; "A Golden Wedding;" and Ross & Glasgow advertisement, St. Louis *Missouri Republican*, March 25, 1828. See also entries for the firm of Ross & Glasgow in ledger books of American Fur Company and Bernard Pratte & Company, Fur Trade Ledgers Coll. (microfilm), MHS.

19. *History of Howard and Chariton Counties, Missouri* (St. Louis: National Historical Company, 1883), 548. I am assuming that these three men came to Missouri together, as all were from New Castle County, Delaware, and were business partners. The above history of Chariton County states on p. 515 that "the early business men of Chariton were the firm of John [James] Ross & Co., composed of John [James] Ross, William Glasgow and John Aull." And on p. 548 is an "Address" by a Mr. Cabell in which he says that Chariton's business "was largely augmented by the arrival of James Ross, John Awll [Aull], James

Glasgow." The first quote suggests that William Glasgow was involved with Ross early on, even though William was engaged in business elsewhere. See also Hyde and Conard, *Encyclopedia*, 2:902. John Aull, who later moved to Lexington, Missouri, was the elder brother of James and Robert Aull, prominent merchants of western Missouri who in the 1830s operated stores at Lexington, Independence, Liberty, and Richmond. See Lewis E. Atherton, "James and Robert Aull: A Frontier Missouri Mercantile Firm," *Missouri Historical Review* 30 (October 1935):3–27.

20. The firms in which they held interests were Ross & Glasgow, St. Louis; Charles S. Rankin & Co., Herculaneum; James Harrison & Co., Fayette; and Compton, Ross & Glasgow, Chariton. James Ross Estate Inventory, #936, Probate Court, City of St. Louis.

21. Billon, *Annals*, 305, gives the date of Mary Susan Glasgow's birth as November 19, 1828. Her tombstone in Bellefontaine Cemetary in St. Louis, however, gives it as November 14, 1829, which is the date I have used. Billon also states that the Glasgows had two additional sons, Charles and John P., who "died in infancy." A Glasgow genealogical chart that W. Merrill Glasgow of Houston, Texas, provided me records the deaths of Charles after living only two days in 1827 and John Porter at age three months in 1834.

22. George Catlin, *Letters and Notes on the Manners, Customs, and Conditions of the North American Indians* . . . , 2 vols. (1844; reprint ed., New York: Dover Publications, 1973), 2:29.

23. Walter B. Stevens, *St. Louis: The Fourth City, 1764–1909*, 2 vols. (St. Louis and Chicago: S. J. Clarke, 1909), 1:401. Also William Clark Kennerly, *Persimmon Hill: A Narrative of Old St. Louis and the Far West* (Norman: University of Oklahoma Press, 1948), 41–43.

24. James Neal Primm, *Lion of the Valley: St. Louis, Missouri* (Boulder, Colo.: Pruett, 1981), 136–137.

25. Hyde and Conard, *Encyclopedia*, 2:900, 903.

26. For a revealing look at both William and James Glasgow's ventures in steamboat ownership, see J & R Aull to E & A Tracy and William Glasgow, July 4, 1835, in James and Robert Aull, "Letters of James and Robert Aull," ed. Ralph P. Bieber, *Missouri Historical Society Collections* 5 (1928), 287–289. And for profit figures on tobacco investments of William Glasgow, Jr. (James Glasgow's son); William Glasgow, Sr.; and James Glasgow, see William Glasgow, Jr., to William Glasgow, Sr., December 13, 1837, Folder 12-15-1837, William Carr Lane Coll. MHS.

27. E. J. Glasgow, "Narrative."

28. *Ibid*. In a sketch of his life, dictated to his son, Edward stated that the merchandise for this venture was "brought from New York." Their shipment possibly included goods from Philadelphia and Europe as well. Edward J. Glasgow, autobiographical sketch dictated to William Jefferson Glasgow, April 21, 1907, Connelley Coll., KSHS.

29. President's message, July 9, 1840 (endorsed July 11, 1840), Nomination of Edward James Glasgow, Nominating Messages (SEN 26 B-A1), 26th Cong., Records of the United States Senate, Record Group (RG) 46, National Archives (NA).

30. E. J. Glasgow, "Narrative." Edward, in the above narrative, does not list his father as one of the partners in the firm. But it is apparent from the tone of the letters written by William to his son during this period that he was indeed financially involved.

31. See Ross & Glasgow advertisement in St. Louis *Missouri Republican*, March 25, 1828; and James Harrison & Co. advertisement in Fayette *Missouri Intelligencer*, March 14, 1828.

32. J. Thomas Scharf, *History of Saint Louis City and County*, 2 vols. (Philadelphia: Louis H. Everts & Co., 1883), 2:1264; and "A Golden Wedding." James Harrison (1803–1870) was a native of Kentucky who had come to Howard County, Missouri, in 1822. By 1828 he

was operating a mercantile establishment at Fayette, Missouri, under the name of James Harrison & Co. Both James Glasgow and William Glasgow had interests in this firm. Very little is known of Harrison's Chihuahua trip. A manifest of Harrison's goods taken to Mexico in 1831, can be found in the Hacienda Records, Mexican Archives of New Mexico (MANM), roll 14, frames 191–200. All of Harrison's biographers, who freely borrowed from one another, state that this trading venture lasted from 1831 to 1832. But in a letter published in the congressional record (U.S. Congress, Senate, *Documents Relating to the Bill* [S. 347] "to Establish Ports of Entry in the States of Arkansas and Missouri ...," S. Doc. 472, 26th Cong., 1st sess., 1840 [Serial 360], 9), Harrison stated that he had lived in Chihuahua "from the winter of 1832 to the fall of 1835, and was, during the whole time, actively engaged in the commerce of the country." This statement is questionable, as there is evidence that he was in Missouri as early as May 1835 and left shortly thereafter to open a store for the firm of Glasgow, Harrison & Co. in Hempstead County, Arkansas (see Complaint of John Harrison and Answer of James Harrison, both in case of *John Harrison v. James Glasgow & James Harrison*, St. Louis County Circuit Court, July Term, 1841, Abiel Leonard Coll., #3, folder 971, University of Missouri, Western Historical Manuscript Collection [WHMC]). In the late 1830s Harrison and James Glasgow were heavily involved in contracting with the U.S. government to supply foodstuffs to the Creek, Choctaw, and other Indian tribes (see U.S. Congress, House, *Report of Lieutenant Colonel Hitchcock, Respecting the Affairs of the Cherokee Indians, &c.*, House Ex. Doc. 219, 27th Cong., 3rd sess., 1843 [Serial 425]). Harrison moved to St. Louis in 1840 and continued to do business with the Glasgows until about 1846. He was later a member of the firm of Chouteau, Harrison & Valle, iron entrepreneurs.

33.   U.S. Congress, House, *Report on H.R. Bill 441: To Establish Ports of Entry in Arkansas and Missouri, and to Allow Debenture, &c.*, H.R. Rep. 540, 26th Cong., 1st sess., 1840 (Serial 372), 13.

34.   Valois's account of this expedition, as well as his observations on the mineral productions and trade of the state of Chihuahua, is published in *ibid.*, 14–16. Dr. Henry Connelly, Chihuahua trader and future partner of Edward James Glasgow, was also a member of the expedition and provided Josiah Gregg with an "interesting sketch" of the trip. See Josiah Gregg, *Commerce of the Prairies*, ed. Max L. Moorhead (Norman: University of Oklahoma Press, 1954), 334, n. 4.

35.   U.S. Congress, Senate, *Documents Relating to the Bill* (S. 347) "to Establish Ports of Entry in the States of Arkansas and Missouri ...," S. Doc. 472, 26th Cong., 1st sess., 1840 (Serial 360), 9; and E. J. Glasgow, "Narrative."

36.   William Glasgow to E. J. Glasgow, St. Louis, July 31, 1843, typescript in W. M. Glasgow Coll.

37.   James Boyd & Son(s) was located at 27 Merchants Row in Boston. See *Stimpson's Boston Directory* for the years 1840 to 1844. Daniel Boyd's passport application, dated July 11, 1840, states that he was thirty years old, 5 feet 10¾ inches tall, with a high forehead, prominent nose, oval face and round chin. His eyes were blue, hair brown, and complexion fair. Register of Passport Applications, November 14, 1834–May 8, 1843, 85, *Registers and Indexes for Passport Applications, 1810–1906*, NA Microfilm M1371, roll 1.

38.   U.S. Congress, Senate, *Documents Relating to the Bill* (S. 347) "to Establish Ports of Entry in the States of Arkansas and Missouri ...," S. Doc. 472, 26th Cong., 1st sess., 1840 (Serial 360), 6–7; and Manuel Alvarez in Sister Mary Loyola, *The American Occupation of New Mexico, 1821–1852* (1939; reprint ed., New York: Arno Press 1976), 16–17. This should not be taken to mean that the merchants handled only foreign goods; some American goods, especially domestic cottons, were more popular in the Mexican market than foreign products. "Your heavy American goods always outsells the British," wrote William Glasgow to

his son in 1841. Yet at the same time, the greater bulk and higher duties on U.S. textiles cut profits. To assure success, then, it was necessary for merchants to carry a good mixture of both American and foreign manufactures. Gregg, *Commerce of the Prairies*, 80; William Glasgow to E. J. Glasgow, March 8, 1841, typescript in W. M. Glasgow Coll.; and Alvarez, in Loyola, *American Occupation*.

39. It is unclear in Edward's "Narrative" if Boyd and Valois accompanied him on the voyage from New York or whether they rendezvoused with him in Mexico. His first mention of them as companions is in reference to their chartering a coach at Mexico City.

40. E. J. Glasgow, "Narrative."

41. *Ibid.*

42. *Ibid.*

43. William Glasgow to E. J. Glasgow, St. Louis, March 8, 1841, typescript in W. M. Glasgow Coll. In his reminiscences, Edward states that Harrison had already learned of Valois's indebtedness from a party of Chihuahua traders and had been "quite anxious in consequence." E. J. Glasgow, "Narrative."

44. E. J. Glasgow, autobiographical sketch.

45. "Consular Return of American Vessels Arriving at and Departing from the Port of Mazatlan from 1st January to 30th June 1841 Inclusive," *Despatches from United States Consuls in Mazatlan, 1826–1906*, NA Microfilm M159, roll 1. The *California* is recorded in the above return as having sailed from Philadelphia. Philadelphia is also indicated as the bark's home port. In 1845 the *California* was included in a published list of ships "owned in the city of New York." See *Merchants' Magazine, and Commercial Review* 13 (1845):477. I have been unable to identify the other ship used by the firm. Although Edward specifically mentions a brig and a bark in his "Narrative," a possibility might be the *Backus*, another bark shown in the above consular return as arriving in Mazatlan from Philadelphia six weeks after the *California*.

46. E. J. Glasgow, "Narrative." Parrott & Co. was organized by John Parrott, U.S. consul at Mazatlan, in 1838. Barbara Donohoe Jostes, *John Parrott, Consul, 1811–1884: Selected Papers of a Western Pioneer* (San Francisco: Lawton and Alfred Kennedy, 1972), 46, n. 14.

47. *Ibid.*, and autobiographical sketch.

48. William Glasgow to E. J. Glasgow, St. Louis, March 8, 1841, typescript in W. M. Glasgow Coll. Brazilwood (*Caesalpina echinata*) was used to produce a red dye. On his journey through Mexico in 1843, William Henry Glasgow noted that one of his meals was cooked with wood "from a Brazil tree, of which immense quantities are shipped from the Ports to England and the U.S. it is used in colouring or dying cloths &c." William H. Glasgow, "Memorandums of a Trip Through Mexico in 1842 & 1843," in W. M. Glasgow Coll.

49. "Consular Return of American Vessels Arriving at and Departing from the Port of Mazatlan from 1st January to 30th June 1841 Inclusive," *Despatches from United States Consuls in Mazatlan, 1826–1906*, NA Microfilm M159, roll 1. This return does indeed show the *California* leaving with a cargo of brazilwood.

50. E. J. Glasgow to John Black, Mazatlan, March 3, 1841, Box C 8.2, Correspondence Received, 1829 to 1841/1842 to 1844, U.S. Consulate General, Mexico City, Mexico, Records of Foreign Service Posts of the Department of State, RG 84, NA.

51. Edward stated in a 1906 newspaper interview that he had served as vice-consul at Mazatlan (see Appendix). Although I did not locate official documentation of Edward's consular service at Mazatlan, two letters written by Edward to consul John Black in

Mexico City in August 1841 support his statement. The letters, written during the absence of Mazatlan's consul, John Parrott, are requests for *cartas de seguridad* (safe-conduct passes, according to Max L. Moorhead, *New Mexico's Royal Road: Trade and Travel on the Chihuahua Trail* [Norman: University of Oklahoma Press, 1958], 144) for six American citizens then residing at Mazatlan. E. J. Glasgow to Black, Mazatlan, August 18, 1841, and August 31, 1841, Box C 8.2, Correspondence Received, 1829 to 1841/1842 to 1844, U.S. Consulate General, Mexico City, Mexico, RG 84, NA.

52. William Glasgow to E. J. Glasgow, St. Louis, October 28, 1841, typescript in W. M. Glasgow Coll.

53. *Niles' National Register*, December 11, 1841.

54. William Glasgow to E. J. Glasgow, St. Louis, February 12, 1842, typescript in W. M. Glasgow Coll; and E. J. Glasgow, "Narrative."

55. William Glasgow to E. J. Glasgow, St. Louis, February 12, 1842, typescript in W. M. Glasgow Coll.

56. E. J. Glasgow, "Narrative."

57. Petition of Glasgow, Harrison, Boyd & Co., July 3, 1841, Petitions and Memorials . . . , Committee on Finance (SEN 27A-G5), 27th Cong., Records of the United States Senate, RG 46, NA; and *Congressional Globe*, 27th Cong., 1st sess., vol. 10, no. 9 (July 7, 1841), 144. The *Globe* reported the petition as a memorial "praying that measures may be taken to encourage the importation of gold and silver bullion from the Mexican States." It should be noted here that for a period of time beginning at least as early as November 1841 and probably before, the ports of Mazatlan and Guaymas were the only Mexican ports at which gold and silver bullion could be *legally* exported. Other than these ports, the exportation of gold and silver "in bullion, ore, or dust" from Mexico was prohibited. This likely explains why the Glasgows were interested in establishing themselves in business at these places. See translation of the "General Arancel" of the maritime and frontier custom houses, issued by the Palace of the National Government in Mexico, April 30, 1842, in U.S. Congress, House, *Changes in Commercial Systems of Foreign Nations*, House Doc 29, 27th Cong., 3rd sess., 1842 (Serial 419), 251; Moorhead, *Royal Road*, 187, n. 7; and Gregg, *Commerce of the Prairies*, 297.

58. "Petition of Glasgow, Harrison, Boyd & Co., July 3, 1841," Petitions and Memorials. . . , Committee on Finance (SEN 27A-G5), 27th Cong., RG 46, NA.

59. U.S. Congress, Senate, *Report: The Committee on Finance, to Which Was Referred the Petition of Glasgow, Harrison, Boyd & Co.*, S. Rep. 271, 27th Cong., 2nd sess., April 27, 1842 (Serial 398), 1.

60. *Ibid.*

61. E. J. Glasgow, "Narrative"; and "Consular Return of American Vessels at and Departing from the Port of Mazatlan from the 1st January to the 30th June 1842 Inclusive," *Despatches from United States Consuls in Mazatlan, 1826–1906*, NA Microfilm M159, roll 1. Edward wrote in his "Narrative" that the vessel was also loaded with "several tons of pearl shell from the California pearl fisheries." The consular return cited above, however, does not list that commodity as part of the *California's* outgoing cargo.

62. Wiilliam Glasgow to E. J. Glasgow, St. Louis, February 12, 1842, typescript in W. M. Glasgow Coll.; and *Ibid.*

63. E. J. Glasgow, "Narrative."

64. Edward James Glasgow to Sarah Lane Glasgow, Valparaiso, Chile, August 20, 1842, Folder 8-20-1842, Lane Coll., MHS.

65. William Carr Lane to Mary Ewing Lane, St. Louis, September 12, 1842, William G.B. Carson Coll., MHS.

66. W. H. Glasgow obituary, Necrology IIC, 112, MHS; and Hyde and Conard, *Encyclopedia*, 2:903. Gay, Glasgow & Co., which was in business as early as 1839, was composed of James Glasgow; James Harrison; John H. Gay; William Glasgow; William Glasgow, Jr.; and Edward J. Gay. John Henderson Gay was a brother-in-law of William Glasgow, Sr., having married Sophia Mitchell in 1813. Edward J. Gay was John's oldest son. For about a year, Gay, Glasgow & Co. owned and operated the Belcher Sugar Refinery in St. Louis. Merchant License Application for Gay, Glasgow & Co., Dexter P. Tiffany Coll., MHS, Box 44, folder 4; Deed between John H. Gay et al. and James Glasgow et al., Deed Book T^2, 110, Recorder of Deeds, St. Louis City Hall, St. Louis, Missouri; *The United States Biographical Dictionary and Portrait Gallery of Eminent and Self-Made Men*, Missouri volume (New York: United States Biographical Publishing Company, 1878), 22–24; and Scharf, *History of Saint Louis*, 2:1243.

67. William H. Glasgow's "Memorandums" and the small diary book mentioned are both in the possession of W. Merrill Glasgow. Comparing the diary to the corresponding section of the "Memorandums" reveals that although William was faithful to his diary throughout, he did rewrite some passages and occasionally added information. At what period in his life he prepared his "Memorandums" is unknown. The last fourteen pages of the "Memorandums"are devoted to William Henry's experiences in 1846–1848, which are reproduced as Part II of this book. The summary of William's 1842–1843 trip is based solely on the "Memorandums."

68. A short biography of William Henry published in 1899 states that he quit the "wholesale grocery business" (probably meaning Gay, Glasgow, & Co.) in 1842 "to go on an exploring expedition to Mexico." Hyde and Conard, *Encyclopedia*, 2:901.

69. According to Max L. Moorhead, Jesús Maria is now known as Mineral de Ocampo. Gregg, *Commerce of the Prairies*, 293, n. 1.

70. William Glasgow to E. J. Glasgow, St. Louis, March 8, 1841, typescript in W. M. Glasgow Coll.

71. See Gregg, *Commerce of the Prairies*, 265, for mention of *guias*. Moorhead discusses the sandhills and the routes to El Paso in his *New Mexico's Royal Road*, 113–114.

72. The "Texan" expedition, which William and other members of his party had been alerted to in Chihuahua, was led by Charles A. Warfield, a trader who had received a commission as a colonel in the Texas republic in August 1842. By spring 1843, despite recruiting efforts in Missouri and the Rocky Mountains, Warfield had only twenty-four men at his side to menace the Mexican caravans on the trail and strike the settlements of New Mexico; see Nicholas P. Hardeman, "Charles A. Warfield," in LeRoy R. Hafen, ed., *The Mountain Men and the Fur Trade of the Far West*, 10 vols. (Glendale, Calif.: Arthur H. Clark, 1965–1972), 7: 356–357, 359. The limited size of Warfield's force proved to be a fortunate circumstance for members of William's train, who learned later from individuals traveling from Bent's Fort that the "Texian robbers" had spotted their caravan but did not attack it because it was so large. Another expedition of Texans, led by Colonel Jacob Snively, was also in the vicinity of the trail that year but not at the same time as William's party. See Louise Barry, *Beginning of the West: Annals of the Kansas Gateway to the American West, 1540–1854* (Topeka: Kansas State Historical Society, 1972), 478–479.

73. The murderers, including their leader, John McDaniel, were actually Missourians bent on plunder. Although McDaniel had been commissioned as a captain in the Texas service by Charles Warfield (see note 72) six months earlier, historian Marc Simmons accurately concludes that the entire band "were common highway robbers, not the legitimate

soldiers of fortune they would later claim to be." After robbing and killing Chavez, McDaniel's party failed to rendezvous with Colonel Warfield on the Arkansas as planned, and authorities in Missouri captured and tried several of its members for Chavez's murder. Two were eventually hanged, one of whom was John McDaniel. See Simmons's excellent *Murder on the Santa Fe Trail: An International Incident, 1843* (El Paso: Texas Western Press, 1987) for a complete history of the Chavez episode and its aftermath.

74. Jarvis Creek actually took its name from the murdered Chavez, Jarvis being a curious corruption of Chavez. Simmons, *Murder on the Santa Fe Trail, 70.*

75. William C. Lane to Mary E. Lane, January 17, 1842, Lane Coll., MHS. Although this letter is dated 1842, it is obvious that Lane accidentally misdated it. Mary Seematter of the Missouri Historical Society informed me of the existence of a journal Edward James Glasgow kept on his trip around Cape Horn. The journal was said to be in the hands of Glasgow descendants in El Paso, Texas. A letter from the superintendent of the Magoffin Home State Historic Site in El Paso, the old residence of William Jefferson Glasgow, states that the journal and other documents were tragically destroyed when improperly stored over the winter of 1986–1987 (Erich Brown to Mark L. Gardner, November 19, 1987). I have since learned through Bruce Dale of *National Geographic* (1991) that the above facts may not be entirely correct and that the journal may still exist. I have been unable to follow up this lead, however. There is one letter from Edward James Glasgow in the collections of the Missouri Historical Society that was written during his stopover in Valparaiso, Chile. See note 64 above.

76. E. J. Glasgow to Mary Susan Glasgow, Mexico City, June 25, 1843. The location of this letter is presently unknown. A photocopy exists at the Missouri Historical Society, through whose courtesy it was made available to me. See also E. J. Glasgow, autobiographical sketch.

77. William Glasgow to E. J. Glasgow, St. Louis, July 31, 1843, typescript in W. M. Glasgow Coll.

78. *Ibid.* Why Harrison "got sufficient to make him quite easy" and Edward and Boyd did not is not explained in the letter from Edward's father, nor is mention made of James or William Glasgow's interests. References in the correspondence between William Glasgow and his son suggest, however, that Glasgow, Harrison, Boyd & Co. was involved in other business ventures besides the Mazatlan concern. Unfortunately, the business records and correspondence of the firm, which would no doubt provide several revelations, are probably no longer extant.

79. E. J. Glasgow, autobiographical sketch; and William Glasgow to E. J. Glasgow, St. Louis, July 31, 1843, typescript in W. M. Glasgow Coll.

80. An "Henrique Connully" is listed as being with Alphonso Wetmore and bound for Chihuahua in a *guia* issued at Santa Fe August 22, 1828. David J. Weber, ed., *The Extranjeros: Selected Documents from the Mexican Side of the Santa Fe Trail* (Santa Fe: Stagecoach Press, 1967), 33. Connelly had apparently traveled to New Mexico in 1824 but then returned to Kentucky, where he attended the medical department at Transylvania University. Deposition of Henry Connelly, in *Condition of the Tribes: Report of the Joint Special Committee, Appointed Under Joint Resolution of March 3, 1865* (Washington, D.C.: Government Printing Office, 1867), 332; and William E. Connelley, *War with Mexico, 1846–1847: Doniphan's Expedition and the Conquest of New Mexico and California* (Kansas City: Bryant & Douglas Book and Stationery Co., 1907), 279, n. 65.

81. E. J. Glasgow to William E. Connelley, Governors Island, New York, August 13, 1906, Connelley Coll., KSHS. This letter is reproduced in Part III of this book.

82. Moorhead, *Royal Road*, 90, n. 32.

83. William Glasgow to E. J. Glasgow, St. Louis, July 31, 1843, typescript in W. M. Glasgow Coll.

84. "An Old Timer: Reuben Gentry a Pioneer Pays a Visit to the Scenes of His Youth," newspaper clipping in Dawson Scrapbook, vol. 37, "The Southwest," 145, Colorado Historical Society (CHS) Collections. Max L. Moorhead, in his *Royal Road*, 131, n. 22, identifies the English firm in Zacatecas as Kerford and Jenkins. Gentry later formed a partnership with the two individuals.

85. Philip St. George Cooke, "A Journal of the Santa Fe Trail," ed. William E. Connelley, *Mississippi Valley Historical Review* 12 (September 1925):245–247. On July 13 Cooke met thirteen wagons near Cottonwood fork "freighted by an Englishman for Chihuahua, via Santa Fe"; they were undoubtedly those of Reuben Gentry.

86. A manifest of goods introduced from the United States by "Enrique" Connelly is dated Santa Fe, September 4, 1843, and *guias* 73, 74 and 75 for Enrique Connelly with J. Haward (John Howard) and 116 for Reuben Gentry with Albert Speyer are dated September 26, 1843. MANM, roll 34, frames 1183–1184, 1212, and 1216.

87. St. Louis *Missouri Republican*, January 13, 1844.

88. William Glasgow to E. J. Glasgow, St. Louis, July 31, 1843, typescript in W. M. Glasgow Coll.

89. E. J. Glasgow to Black, Culiacan, December 12, 1843, Box C 8.2, Correspondence Received, 1829 to 1841/1842 to 1844, U.S. Consulate General, Mexico City, Mexico, RG 84, NA.

90. St. Louis *Reveille*, June 6, 1844. There is a possibility that Connelly may have been with this group when it reached St. Louis, as the *Reveille* reported that Edward's party included "other gentlemen, from Chihuahua and Santa Fe." If so, he would have to have overtaken them at some point on their journey, for a letter written by Connelly to U.S. consul John Black places him at Chihuahua on March 18, 1844, eight days after the departure date the *Reveille* gives for Edward's party. Henry Connelly to Black, Chihuahua, March 18, 1844, Box C 8.2, Correspondence Received, 1829 to 1841/1842 to 1844, U.S. Consulate General, Mexico City, Mexico, RG 84, NA.

91. Gregg, *Commerce of the Prairies*, 344 and 344, n. 18; James Josiah Webb, *Adventures in the Santa Fe Trade, 1844–1847*, ed. Ralph P. Bieber, Southwest Historical Series, vol. 1 (Glendale, Calif.: Arthur H. Clark, 1931), 25; and Barry, *Beginning of the West*, 504.

92. Barry, *Beginning of the West*, 527. Barry reports that the Connelly & Glasgow train, including merchant Francisco Elguea as well, contained approximately twenty wagons.

93. See Map 59 in Gregory M. Franzwa, *Maps of the Santa Fe Trail* (St. Louis: Patrice Press, 1989), for the location of Willow Bar.

94. *Niles' National Register*, March 22, 1845; and Webb, *Adventures in the Santa Fe Trade*, 107–108. Trader James Josiah Webb's version of the incident differs slightly from that of the *Register*. Instead of a snowstorm, he records Speyer as saying that it was a "very severe storm of sleet and rain" that killed his mules. He goes on to relate that Speyer lost "over seventy-five mules in one night of the storm" and that Connelly "reported that he had suffered about an equal loss with Mr. Speyer." See also James L. Collins, "Report on Winter Travel, 1852," in Marc Simmons, ed., *On the Santa Fe Trail* (Lawrence: University of Kansas Press, 1986), 14–15.

95. A manifest of Connelly & Glasgow's goods (241 bultos valued at over 30,000 pesos) destined for Chihuahua, Zacatecas, and Guanajuato is dated Santa Fe, December 13, 1844. MANM, roll 37, frames 504–517.

96. The inscriptions at Cold Spring are on private property in the Northeast Quarter of Section 4, Township 4 North, Range 4 East. See "Preliminary Report of Survey of Inscriptions Along Santa Fe Trail in Oklahoma," Chronicles of Oklahoma 38 (Autumn 1960):310–322; and Map 60 in Franzwa, Maps of the Santa Fe Trail (Franzwa's location of Cold Spring is slightly off).

97. Barry, Beginning of the West, 559.

98. Hacienda Records, MANM, roll 40, frame 265.

99. James W. Abert, Through the Country of the Comanche Indians in the Year 1845 ..., ed. John Galvin (San Francisco: John Howell, 1970), 21; and Barry, Beginning of the West, 551.

100. Connelley, Doniphan's Expedition, 281, n. 65.

101. William Glasgow to E. J. Glasgow, St. Louis, July 31, 1843, typescript in W. M. Glasgow Coll.; and William M. Lytle and Forrest R. Holdcamper, comps., and C. Bradford Mitchell, ed., Merchant Steam Vessels of the United States, 1790–1868 (Staten Island, N.Y.: Steamship Historical Society of America, 1975), 127. According to Lytle and Holdcamper, the Lexington, burthen 157 tons, was built in Pittsburgh. An 1897 report on Missouri River steamboat wrecks states that the sidewheeler operated between St. Louis and Weston, on the Missouri River, before it was snagged near Frankfort, Missouri, in 1845. See "Report on Steamboat Wrecks on Missouri River by Capt. H. M. Chittenden, Corps of Engineers," in U.S. Congress, House, Report of Missouri River Commission, Appendix D, House Doc. 2, 55th Cong., 2nd sess., 1897 (Serial 3636), 3884.

102. Ibid.; and Lytle-Holdcamper, Merchant Steam Vessels, 276. A W. H. Glasgow obituary states that "soon after he came of age he was made captain of a Missouri steamboat, and served in that capacity on various steamers until 1846." Necrology II C, 112, MHS.

103. Josiah Gregg, Diary and Letters of Josiah Gregg, ed. Maurice Fulton, 2 vols. (Norman: University of Oklahoma Press, 1941 and 1944), 1:200–201.

104. Moorhead, Royal Road, 74–75; and copy of Drawback Act in U.S. Congress, House, Report on the Petition of Manuel X. Harmony (hereinafter cited as Harmony Report), H. R. Rep. 458, 30th Cong., 1st sess., 1848 (Serial 525), 59–61.

105. Webb, Adventures in the Santa Fe Trade, 108, n. 151; Edward James Glasgow file, Applications and Recommendations for Public Office During the Administrations of James Polk, Zachary Taylor, and Millard Fillmore, 1845–1853, NA Microfilm M873, roll 33; and E. J. Glasgow, "Narrative." It is probable that Edward was first appointed U.S. consul and that the position was changed to commercial agent after the war broke out. According to Edward in his narrative, "the duties of this office are the same as those of Consul but as we were then at war with Mexico that country would not grant a Consular Exequatar." See also "Commerical Agents" in Regulations Prescribed for the Use of the Consular Service of the United States (Washington, D.C.: Government Printing Office, 1888), 6–7.

106. Following is a summary of the experiences of the merchants in New Mexico and Chihuahua from 1846 to 1848 as they pertain to the Glasgows. For an overview, see Moorhead, Royal Road, 152–183.

107. St. Louis Missouri Republican, August 3, 1846; S. W. Kearny to W. L. Marcy, Washington, January 10, 1848, and petition of Manuel X. Harmony, both in Harmony Report, 49–50 and 7, respectively; and Susan Shelby Magoffin, Down the Santa Fe Trail and into Mexico, 1846–1847, ed. Stella M. Drumm (New Haven: Yale University Press, 1926), 68–69.

108. W. H. Glasgow, "Memorandums"; and St. Louis *Weekly Reveille*, October 26, 1846. General Kearny implemented new duties shortly after his arrival in Santa Fe. Duties of four dollars each were to be collected for "wagons from the Arkansas or Chihuahua, with goods belonging to individuals, and not public ones," and two dollars each for "pleasure carriages, from the above places." Private carriages and wagons entering the plaza at Santa Fe were to be charged twenty-five cents. Order of General Kearny Regulating Licenses, August 27, 1846, in U.S. Congress, House, *Message from the President of the United States . . . Relative to the Occupation of the Mexican Territory,* House Ex. Doc. 19, 29th Cong., 2nd sess., 1846 (Serial 499), 24.

109. William H. Emory, *Lieutenant Emory Reports: A Reprint of Lieutenant W. H. Emory's Notes of a Military Reconnoissance,* ed. Ross Calvin (Albuquerque: University of New Mexico Press, 1951), 37; and deposition of Henry Connelly, Chihuahua, September 20, 1848, in "The Magoffin Papers," in Ralph Emerson Twitchell, *The Story of the Conquest of Santa Fe, New Mexico, and the Building of Old Fort Marcy, A.D. 1846,* Historical Society of New Mexico Publication No. 24 (Santa Fe: Historical Society of New Mexico 1923), 59–60.

110. Philip St. George Cooke, *The Conquest of New Mexico and California* (1878; reprint ed., Albuquerque: Horn & Wallace, 1964), 31 and 33.

111. Connelley, *Doniphan's Expedition,* 281, n. 65.

112. See J. W. Magoffin to W. L. Marcy, Santa Fe, August 26, 1846; Connelly deposition in "The Magoffin Papers," 43–44 and 59–60, respectively; and Report of the Citizens of New Mexico to the President of Mexico, Santa Fe, September 26, 1846, and Report of Gov. Manuel Armijo to the Minister of Foreign Relations, Interior and Police, Chihuahua, September 8, 1846, in Max L. Moorhead, ed., "Notes and Documents," *New Mexico Historical Review* 26 (January 1951):69–78. If Connelly did return to Armijo with a report that influenced his actions, he would have to have done some hard riding. Cooke's party did not reach Kearny until August 15. Armijo deserted his defenses at Apache Canyon on August 16. Rumors to that effect actually reached the Army of the West that same day. Henry Smith Turner, *The Original Journals of Henry Smith Turner, with Stephen Watts Kearny to New Mexico and California, 1846–1847,* ed. Dwight L. Clarke (Norman: University of Oklahoma Press, 1966), 141. On August 18 from Santa Fe, Connelly wrote (on behalf of General Kearny, according to Moorhead) to his "esteemed friend" Armijo, who was retreating to Chihuahua; Connelly encouraged him to return "with the troops and the close friends who accompany you, with the Armament which they carry and the Artillery," promising that no harm would come to him and that he would be able to choose whether or not he wished to become a citizen of the United States. Despite Connelly's entreaties, Armijo did not return. Henry Connelly to General Manual Armijo, Santa Fe, August 18, 1846, in Moorhead, "Notes and Documents," 82.

113. E. J. Glasgow to Sarah Mitchell Glasgow, Santa Fe, September 16, 1846, Wade Shipley Coll. (WSC), Lovington, New Mexico; and Connelley, *Doniphan's Expedition,* 66. Kearny had undertaken the expedition because of rumors that an army was being formed near Albuquerque to retake Santa Fe. Connelley, *Doniphan's Expedition,* 221; and Emory, *Lieutenant Emory Reports,* 59.

114. Emory, *Lieutenant Emory Reports,* 74; and St. Louis *Missouri Republican,* November 7, 1846.

115. E. J. Glasgow to Sarah Mitchell Glasgow, Santa Fe, September 16, 1846, WSC; and St. Louis *Weekly Reveille,* October 26, 1846.

116. Letter of Samuel C. Owens, Valverde, October 20, 1846, quoted in St. Louis *Missouri Republican,* December 8, 1846.

117. W. H. Glasgow, "Memorandums"; letter of Samuel C. Owens to his wife, Valverde, October 20, 1846, in George R. Gibson, *Journal of a Soldier Under Kearny and Doniphan, 1846–1847*, ed. Ralph P. Bieber, Southwest Historical Series, vol. 3 (Glendale, Calif.: Arthur H. Clark, 1935), 263, n. 390; and *ibid.*

118. See the sources given in note 117 as well as Moorhead, *Royal Road*, 163–164. José Gonzales, whom Moorhead (p. 158) describes as a "business associate" of Magoffin, had accompanied Magoffin and Captain Cooke's detachment to Santa Fe in August.

119. Letter of Samuel C. Owens, Valverde, October 20, 1846, quoted in St. Louis *Missouri Republican*, December 8, 1846.

120. Magoffin, *Down the Santa Fe Trail*, 161; W.H. Glasgow to Sarah Mitchell Glasgow, Valverde, November 2, 1846, WSC; W. H. Glasgow, "Memorandums"; and St. Louis *Weekly Reveille* December 21, 1846.

121. W. H. Glasgow to Sarah Mitchell Glasgow, Valverde, November 2, 1846, WSC; W. H. Glasgow, "Memorandums"; Cooke, *Conquest*, 96; W. H. Glasgow to William Glasgow, Valverde, November 18, 1846, WSC; and St. Louis *Missouri Republican*, January 1, 1847.

122. St. Louis *Weekly Reveille*, February 22, 1847; W. H. Glasgow to Sarah Mitchell Glasgow, Valverde, November 2, 1846, WSC; and W. H. Glasgow, "Memorandums."

123. W. H. Glasgow to William Glasgow, Valverde, November 18, 1846, WSC.

124. James W. Abert, *Abert's New Mexico Report, 1846–'47* (1848; facsimile reprint, Albuquerque: Horn & Wallace, 1962), 128; Connelley, *Doniphan's Expedition*, 276–279 and 83; Cornelius Davy to J. S. Phelps, Washington City, March 22, 1848, and Petition of Manuel X. Harmony in Harmony Report, 45 and 8, respectively.

125. Cornelius Davy to J. S. Phelps, Washington City, March 22, 1848, and petition of Manuel X. Harmony in Harmony Report, 45 and 80; Abert, *New Mexico Report*, 130–131; Connelley, *Doniphan's Expedition*, 279–282 and 83–84; and St. Louis *Weekly Reveille*, February 22, 1847.

126. Connelley, *Doniphan's Expedition*, 250–251 and 266.

127. Abert, *New Mexico Report*, 130. Abert states that he "learned" that Glasgow and "several other traders had started to Santa Fe." However, a letter from Santa Fe reprinted in the St. Louis *Weekly Reveille* of February 22, 1847, notes the arrival of Glasgow and Samuel Owens only, and Susan Magoffin (*Down the Santa Fe Trail*, 175) makes no mention of any other traders when she writes of their return on December 16. See also James W. Abert, *Western America in 1846–1847 . . .*, ed. John Galvin (San Francisco: John Howell, 1966), 68.

128. Abert, *New Mexico Report*, 131; petition dated Valverde, December 9, 1846, by Owens & Aull, M. X. Harmony, S. Houck, Fran'co Elguea, J. Calistro Porras, Thomas F. Macmaners [Macmanus], Alex. C. Ferguson, Hoffman & Barney, Kerferd & Jenkin, Corn's Davy, and W. H. Glasgow in Harmony Report, 46–48; and Abert, *Western America*, 69–70.

129. Abert, *Western America*, 70. Abert noted in his diary for December 9 that he "saw Mr. Glasgow's wagons pass by" while he was hunting quail below Valverde. This would have been William, as Edward was in Santa Fe at the time.

130. George [A.]F. Ruxton, *Adventures in Mexico and the Rocky Mountains* (1847; reprint ed., Glorieta, N. Mex.: Rio Grande Press, 1973), 183.

131. Connelley, *Doniphan's Expedition*, 86; and W. H. Glasgow, "Memorandums."

132. One of the reasons that the merchants were kept from preceding the army was a belief that the Mexican duties raised on their goods would assist the Chihuahuans in their war efforts against the United States. The merchants denied this possibility in their

petition of December 9, but George Ruxton, who had carried Governor Trias's circular to the traders from Chihuahua, states that

> it was a great object with the Governor of Chihuahua that they [the traders] should proceed to that city and pay the usual duties to him, which otherwise would have been payable to the customhouse of Santa Fé. The government being entirely without funds, and anxious to raise and equip a body of troops to oppose the advance of the Americans, the arrival of the caravan would have been most opportune, since, at the usual rate of duties, viz. 500 dollars for each waggon, the amount to be received by the government would exceed 100,000 dollars.

Ruxton, *Adventures in Mexico*, 157. See also D. D. Mitchell to M. X. Harmony, St. Louis, January 26, 1848, in Harmony Report, 44; and Gibson, *Journal of a Soldier*, 322.

133. Magoffin, *Down the Santa Fe Trail*, 175.

134. James Madison Cutts, *The Conquest of California and New Mexico* (1847; reprint ed., Albuquerque: Horn & Wallace, 1965), 77–78.

135. E. J. Glasgow to William Glasgow, El Paso del Norte, January 4, 1847, WSC.

136. Connelley, *Doniphan's Expedition*, 395.

137. Ibid., 386; and W. H. Glasgow to Mary Susan Glasgow, El Paso del Norte, February 3, 1847, WSC.

138. Connelley, *Doniphan's Expedition*, 97 and 398; and Gibson, *Journal of a Soldier*, 327–328. The train that eluded Doniphan was that of Kerford and Jenkins with partner Reuben Gentry. See "An Old Timer."

139. Connelley, *Doniphan's Expedition*, 397–398; and report of Colonel A. W. Doniphan in Harmony Report, 32.

140. Connelley, *Doniphan's Expedition*, 407–419 and 423–438; and statement of R. H. Weightman in Harmony Report, 36.

141. W. H. Glasgow, "Memorandums"; and statement of Calvin M. Jones in Harmony Report, 35.

142. E. J. Glasgow to Mary Susan Glasgow, Chihuahua, March 12, 1847, WSC; Frank S. Edwards, *A Campaign in New Mexico with Colonel Doniphan* (Philadelphia: Carey and Hart, 1847), 114; E. J. Glasgow to William Connelley, Governors Island, New York, November 27, 1906, Connelley Coll., KSHS; and M. B. Edwards in Abraham Robinson Johnston, Marcellus Ball Edwards, and Philip Gooch Ferguson, *Marching with the Army of the West, 1846–1848*, ed. Ralph P. Bieber, Southwest Historical Series, vol. 4 (Glendale, Calif.: Arthur H. Clark, 1936), 266.

143. Connelley, *Doniphan's Expedition*, 422.

144. Ibid., 445; Webb, *Adventures in the Santa Fe Trade*, 273; and E. J. Glasgow to William Connelley, Governors Island, New York, November 27, 1906, Connelley Coll., KSHS.

145. W. H. Glasgow to William Glasgow, May 6, 1847, WSC; W. H. Glasgow to Mary Susan Glasgow, March 23, 1847, WSC; A. W. Doniphan to David Waldo, Liberty, Missouri, January 10, 1848, in Ralph E. Twitchell, *The History of the Military Occupation of the Territory of New Mexico from 1846 to 1851* (1909; reprint ed., Chicago: Rio Grande Press, 1963), 328; and Connelley, *Doniphan's Expedition*, 107–108 and 450–451.

146. Edwards in *Marching with the Army of the West*, 275.

147. St. Louis *Missouri Republican*, May 12, 1847. See also Connelley, *Doniphan's Expedition*, 451.

148. W. H. Glasgow to Mary Susan Glasgow, Chihuahua, March 23, 1847. WSC. A Mexican version of the negotiations appeared in the *Republicano* and was later reported in the St. Louis *Weekly Reveille* of May 10, 1847. According to this account, Doniphan's proposal included the provision that the State of Chihuahua remain neutral but also required that Chihuahua pay an indemnity of $50,000 and allow the goods of the traders to be duty-free. "'It is not to be believed,' says the *Republicano*, 'that the sons of Chihuahua could consent to so disgraceful an agreement!'" It is doubtful that Doniphan actually proposed the last two conditions.

149. W. H. Glasgow to Mary Susan Glasgow, Chihuahua, March 23, 1847, WSC.

150. W. H. Glasgow to William Glasgow, Chihuahua, May 6, 1847. WSC.

151. Doniphan to Waldo, Liberty, January 10, 1848, in Twitchell, *Military Occupation of the Territory of New Mexico*, 327–329.

152. W. H. Glasgow to Mary Susan Glasgow, Chihuahua, March 23, 1847, WSC.

153. A. W. Doniphan to Brigadier General Wool, Chihuahua, March 20, 1847, in Connelley, *Doniphan's Expedition*, 454–455.

154. Connelley, *Doniphan's Expedition*, 108, 463; and Edwards, *A Campaign in New Mexico*, 132.

155. Harmony Report, 38.

156. W. H. Glasgow to William Glasgow, Chihuahua, May 6, 1847, WSC; and St. Louis *Missouri Republican*, June 22, 1847.

157. Decree of vice-governor Lauriano Muñoz, Parral, April 2, 1847, in Harmony Report, 39–40.

158. W. H. Glasgow to William Glasgow, Chihuahua, May 6, 1847, WSC.

159. Doniphan to Waldo, Liberty, January 10, 1848, in Twitchell, *Military Occupation of the Territory of New Mexico*, 328.

160. W. H. Glasgow to William Glasgow, Chihuahua, May 6, 1847, WSC; W. H. Glasgow to Mary Susan Glasgow, Chihuahua, May 7, 1847, WSC; and Connelley, *Doniphan's Expedition*, 467.

161. W. H. Glasgow to William Glasgow, Chihuahua, May 6, 1847, WSC; and Gregg, *Diary and Letters*, 2:104.

162. W. H. Glasgow to Mary Susan Glasgow, Chihuahua, May 7, 1847, WSC; and Gregg, *Diary and Letters*, 2:107.

163. Connelley, *Doniphan's Expedition*, 465–466.

164. W. H. Glasgow to William Glasgow, Chihuahua, May 6, 1847, WSC; and Webb, *Adventures in the Santa Fe Trade*, 277–278.

165. Gregg, *Diary and Letters*, 2:107; Magoffin, *Down the Santa Fe Trail*, 230; and Connelley, *Doniphan's Expedition*, 109.

166. Connelley, *Doniphan's Expedition*, 467; and Webb, *Adventures in the Santa Fe Trade*, 281.

167. W. H. Glasgow to William Glasgow, Chihuahua, May 6, 1847, WSC; and W. H. Glasgow to Mary Susan Glasgow, Chihuahua, May 7, 1847, WSC.

168. W. H. Glasgow to Mary Susan Glasgow, Chihuahua, May 7, 1847, WSC; and Connelley, *Doniphan's Expedition*, 468. According to a report from the St. Louis *Missouri Republican*, which had received letters from Chihuahua by James J. Webb, the terms of the treaty were that the "American merchants agreed to pay such Custom-House duties as were paid by the

Mexicans, and the authorities, on their part, guarantied the safety of the persons and property of the merchants." Nyle H. Miller, Edgar Langsdorf, and Robert W. Richmond, *Kansas in Newspapers* (Topeka: Kansas State Historical Society, 1963), 13.

169. W. H. Glasgow to William Glasgow, En Ramada, May 2, 1847, WSC.

170. W. H. Glasgow to William Glasgow, Chihuahua, May 6, 1847, WSC; and W. H. Glasgow to Mary Susan Glasgow, Chihuahua, June 3, 1847, WSC.

171. E. J. Glasgow to William Glasgow, Chihuahua, July 1, 1847. WSC.

172. W. H. Glasgow to Mary Susan Glasgow, Chihuahua, June 27, 1847. WSC.

173. *Ibid.*; and E. J. Glasgow to William Glasgow, unattached page, probably letter of July 1, 1847, WSC.

174. *Ibid.*

175. Aull, "Letters of James and Robert Aull," 296 and 302.

176. Reports had reached Santa Fe of the ill treatment of some Americans in Chihuahua, including imprisonment and confiscation of goods. The *Santa Fe Republican* cited these as justification for a campaign on Chihuahua in October 1847. Bieber, introduction in *Marching with the Army of the West*, 61.

177. St. Louis *Missouri Republican*, May 15, 1848; Aull, "Letters of James and Robert Aull," 306–307; and St. Louis *Reveille*, July 16, 1848.

178. O. C. Pratt, "Trip over Santa Fe Trail, 1848," diary entry for June 26, 1848, Coll. #1034 (microfilm), CHS. The original of Pratt's diary is in the Coe Coll. at Yale University Library.

179. Liberty *Weekly Tribune*, July 28, 1848.

180. E. J. Glasgow to Mary Susan Glasgow, Chihuahua, March 12, 1847, WSC.

181. An intriguing postscript to Edward J. Glasgow's Mexican War–era experiences is found in the U.S. census records for New Mexico. The 1850 census for Santa Fe, dated December 16, lists an Edwardo (or Eduardo) Glasgow, two years of age. His mother may be the young woman listed immediately above him by the name of Juana Gonzales. She was twenty years old. Both are shown as having been born in Mexico. They were living with several other Mexicans in the household of Hiram R. Parker, a North Carolinian. If the age for Edwardo is correct, he was probably born sometime in 1848 and possibly conceived early that year or in 1847. This corresponds exactly with the time period in which Edward J. Glasgow was in Chihuahua. Again, the child is recorded as having been born in Mexico. Did mother and child follow Edward out of Chihuahua to Santa Fe in 1848? Edwardo is found in the 1870 and 1880 censuses as well. In the 1880 census he was thirty-one years old and listed as a silversmith. More importantly, his father is listed as having been born in Missouri. Edward James Glasgow, although born in Illinois, was for all intents and purposes a Missourian, having lived there since a very young age. The trail of Edwardo Glasgow disappointingly ends with the 1880 census and I have been unable to discover any more about him. As would be expected, there is no mention of Mexican offspring, either legitimate of illegitimate, in any of the Glasgow records that I have examined. Seventh U.S. Census for New Mexico, Santa Fe, 346; Ninth U.S. Census for New Mexico, Santa Fe County, City of Santa Fe, 3rd Precinct, 332; and Tenth U.S. Census for New Mexico, Santa Fe County, City of Santa Fe, Enumeration District 40, 46.

182. St. Louis *Missouri Republican*, September 30, 1849.

183. St. Louis *Missouri Republican*, October 3, 1850, and October 5, 1850.

184. *St. Louis Directory* 1859 (St. Louis: R[obert] V. Kennedy & Co., n.d.), 164.

185. Irwin Switzler, "Missouri," in William F. Switzler, *Report on the Internal Commerce of the United States for the Fiscal Year 1889*, Treasury Department Doc. #1243b (Washington, D.C.: Government Printing Office, 1889), 405.

186. *Western Journal, and Civilian*, 11 (February 1854):362.

187. Thomas L. Rodgers, "Recollections of St. Louis — 1857–1860," *Glimpses of the Past* 9 (October-December 1942):117.

188. Rodgers, cited in *ibid.*, states, "There was quite a large amount of merchandise shipped from eastern points to Santa Fe and other places in New Mexico." He adds later, "A very large trade was done with Santa Fe and Albuquerque, New Mexico at that time. The trade of these places seemed to be largely in the hands of the Hebrew race."

189. Glasgow & Brother invoices and statements in the James Josiah Webb Papers, MHS, and José Felipe Chaves Papers, Coll. 10 P, in the Special Collections of the University of New Mexico Library, Albuquerque (UNM).

190. William J. Glasgow, "Edward James Glasgow, Notes," (typescript) dated El Paso, June 1, 1949, courtesy of Isabel Glasgow, El Paso, Texas.

191. See Webb Papers, MHS; Chaves Papers, Coll. 10 P, UNM; Felipe Chavez Papers, New Mexico State Records Center and Archives, Santa Fe (SRCA); Yrisarri Family Papers in the E. Boyd Coll., SRCA; and "Early Days of Southwest Trade Peril- Fraught," St. Louis *Daily Globe-Democrat*, March 11, 1906 (reprinted in the Appendix).

192. New Mexico, vol. 1, 364, R. G. Dun & Co. Coll., Baker Library, Harvard University Graduate School of Business Administration (BLHBS). In the Yrisarri Family Papers of the E. Boyd Coll., box 11, folder 180, SRCA, is an 1854 invoice book containing an invoice from Glasgow & Brother. This invoice, which shows goods purchased for Yrisarri in St. Louis by the Glasgows and items sold to Yrisarri from their own house, has been translated and appears in E. Boyd, *Popular Arts of Spanish New Mexico* (Santa Fe: Museum of New Mexico Press, 1974), 317–326.

193. As quoted in Marc Simmons, "A Humorous Incident of the Santa Fe Trade," *Westport Historical Quarterly* 7 (March 1972):3–4. Simmons found this story written on a "fragment of a letter" in the Amado Chaves Coll., SRCA.

194. Missouri, vol. 36, 196, and Missouri, vol. 37, 619, R. G. Dun & Co. Coll., BLHBS.

195. Eighth U.S. Census, City of St. Louis, Missouri, 6th Ward, 144.

196. Eighth U.S. Census, St. Louis County, Missouri, Central Township, 132. William had inherited a great deal of property through his first wife, Mary F. Wright. Her real estate was valued in the 1850 census at $50,000. In 1857 the Mercantile Agency reported that she was "said to be w[orth]. 300^{m} [$300,000]." Will of Mary F. Glasgow, July 4, 1854, copy courtesy of W. M. Glasgow; Seventh U.S. Census, City of St. Louis, Missouri, 3rd Ward, 361; and Missouri vol. 36, 196, R. G. Dun & Co. Coll., BLHBS.

197. St. Louis Genealogical Society, *StLGS Index of St. Louis Marriages, 1804–1876*, vol. 1 (St. Louis: St. Louis Genealogical Society, 1973); and Glasgow genealogical chart provided courtesy of W. Merrill Glasgow. Mr. Glasgow is the proud owner of a beautiful silver water pitcher bearing the monogram "MFG," which he states was probably a wedding present from William H. Glasgow to his wife. Mr. Glasgow believes that the pitcher, made by St. Louis silversmith Edward Mead, may have been produced from some of the Mexican silver the Glasgow brothers brought back in 1848.

198. Glasgow genealogical chart. According to this chart, William and Mary had lost a daughter, Mary, in January 1857. Their first son, William Wright Glasgow, had died in 1853. His death was reported in the St. Louis Missouri Republican of April 13, 1853. Lois Stanley, George F. Wilson, and Maryhelen Wilson, comps., More Death Records from Missouri Newspapers, 1810–1857 (March 1985), 38.

199. Frances Hurd Stadler, "Letters from Minoma," Bulletin of the Missouri Historical Society 16 (April 1960):253; and Hyde and Conard, Encyclopedia, 2:904.

200. StLGS Index of St. Louis Marriages; and Billon, Annals, 268.

201. St. Louis Directory 1860 (St. Louis: R[obert] V. Kennedy & Co., n.d.), 195; Stadler, "Minoma," 244, n. 13; and Elizabeth Kennerly Russell, "The Narrow-Gauge and Its Patrons," Bulletin of the Missouri Historical Society 6 (April 1950):278. The 1860 census shows that Edward and Harriet were also residing with Harriet's brother, William Clark Kennerly. William Henry's household contained his father and mother, sister Ellen and her children, and a Martha Jones, undoubtedly family friend "Miss Patsy Jones" (see note 17 in Part I).

202. See Missouri, vol. 37, 619, R. G. Dun & Co. Coll., BLHBS. Other firms were not so fortunate. According to James Neal Primm, "the number of commission and forwarding merchants in the city dropped from 109 in 1859 to 52 in 1864, wholesale grocers from 80 to 69, and dry goods wholesalers from 32 to 27." Primm, Lion of the Valley, 271.

203. James Thomas, From Tennessee Slave to St. Louis Entrepreneur: The Autobiography of James Thomas, ed. Loren Schweninger (Columbia: University of Missouri Press, 1984), 156.

204. The Glasgows' father was from a slave state, Delaware, and was a slave owner, as were his two sons. In the 1860 census William is listed as owning seven slaves and Edward is listed as owning four. A majority of these were probably household servants. Eighth U.S. Census, Slave Schedules for Saint Louis County, Central Township, 7, and 6th Ward of the City of St. Louis, 2. Edward freed a slave by the name of Cornelius Collins in November 1857. The manumission paper can be found in St. Louis Court House Papers III, no. 23, MHS.

205. William G.B. Carson, "Secesh," Bulletin of the Missouri Historical Society 23 (January 1967):119. Edward's old partner, Henry Connelly, governor of New Mexico Territory during the Civil War, was also loyal to the Union. "When the Texans invaded New Mexico in the spring of 1862," writes historian William A. Keleher, "Connelly helped to maintain the supremacy of the federal government." Keleher, Turmoil in New Mexico, 1846–1868 (Santa Fe: Rydal Press, 1952), 123, n. 38. See also Connelley, Doniphan's Expedition, 281–282, n. 65.

206. Primm, Lion of the Valley, 261.

207. Carson, "Secesh," 131 and notes.

208. Francis B. Heitman, Historical Register and Dictionary of the United States Army, 2 vols. (Washington, D.C.: Government Printing Office, 1903), 1:305.

209. Kennerly, Persimmon Hill, 245.

210. Missouri, vol. 37, 619, Missouri, vol. 44, 68, and Missouri, vol. 45, 154, R. G. Dun & Co. Coll., BLHBS. Besides changes in the partnership, the firm had by this time made changes in their address as well. According to St. Louis city directories (those of Edwards and Gould), they were located at 808 North Second in 1869 and 14 and 16 North Second in 1871. Their last move was to 415 and 417 North Second; they are listed at that location in 1878.

211. E. J. Glasgow, "Narrative."

212. Missouri, vol. 45, 154, R. G. Dun & Co. Coll., BLHBS.

213. Ibid.

214. E. J. Glasgow, "Narrative." It is possible that rumors of the Glasgows' financial problems were the impetus behind the lengthy report just quoted.

215. William J. Glasgow, "Edward James Glasgow, Notes."

216. Missouri, vol. 45, 154, R. G. Dun & Co. Coll., BLHBS. On March 21 the Mercantile Agency reported that William H. Glasgow had given a deed of trust on a portion of his real estate to obtain $66,860.00. According to the agency's report, Glasgow told them that "it is an individual matter [and] in no way connected with the bus[iness] of the firm, is not borrowed for the sake of improving the prop[erty] but declines to explain further." This action would be questioned later (see note 222, below).

217. Ibid. In the report of March 15, cited above, the Glasgows informed the Mercantile Agency that their eastern liabilities "at the present time are only 32[m] [$32,000]. The amt. is sometimes as high as 200[m] but is always represented by the coffee it pays for & [?] their lials [liabilities] here [St. Louis] are based on equally legitimate assets & are small in amt." Unless the Glasgows made some extremely large purchases after March 15, this statement compared with the later report of the Mercantile Agency suggests that the Glasgows were not being exactly truthful to the credit agency's investigator.

218. Ibid., 154 and 176.

219. Glasgow, Brother & Co. to Felipe Chaves, St. Louis, August 26, 1879, box 1, folder 39, Chaves Papers, Coll. 10 p, UNM. Translation by Marc Simmons.

220. Missouri, vol. 45, 176, R. G. Dun & Co. Coll., BLHBS. In referring to the bankruptcy, William J. Glasgow wrote in 1949 that "it was decided to settle for ninety eight cents on the dollar." He does not explain if this was to be a combination of cash and real estate, however. He may be in error, considering that he was a young boy at the time of the failure and that the Mercantile Agency did not mention that figure in their reports. William J. Glasgow, "Edward James Glasgow, Notes."

221. Glasgow genealogical chart.

222. The Mercantile Agency reported on August 15 that "WH Glasgow has never told what he did with the 66[m] raised on his RE in Mar last & he has since sold the store prop[erty] on 5th st to his wifes sister for less than its value, all of which is regar[d] as an injustice to cr[editor]s." Missouri, vol. 45, 176, R. G. Dun & Co. Coll., BLHBS. William J. Glasgow gives another reason why William Henry "had much more of this world's goods than my father." He states that William Henry won a lottery while in Havana, Cuba, on business. The prize was $60,000 in gold, "which at that time [?] was quite a fortune as gold was at a high premium compared with our greenbacks." Ten percent of the prize was kept by the firm he had asked to hold his ticket for safekeeping. William J. Glasgow, "Edward James Glasgow, Notes."

223. Gould's St. Louis Directory for 1882, 444, 1276, and 1490. William was a member of the board of directors of the Home Bitters Co. when it was organized in 1875 (another St. Louis firm had begun the manufacture of the bitters in 1868). By 1882 the Home Bitters Co. had evidently become the St. Louis Wine Co., the latter being listed at the address the former occupied the previous year (24 and 26 North Main). Another change appears to have occurred two years later, as William is listed in the 1884 St. Louis city directory as the president of the Home Bitters Co., with no mention of the St. Louis Wine Co. The Home Bitters Co. is listed in 1884 at 26 North Main. Camille N. Dry and Richard J. Compton, Pictorial St. Louis: The Great Metropolis of the Mississippi Valley (1875; reprint ed., St.

Louis: Knight Publishing Company, 1979), 89; and *Gould's St. Louis Directory for 1884*, 431 and 1231.

224. *Gould's St. Louis Directory for 1887*, 453.

225. Hyde and Conard, *Encyclopedia*, 2:904.

226. Estate Inventory of William H. Glasgow, #23361, Probate Court, City of St. Louis.

227. Necrology II C, 112, MHS. It was stated in another obituary that both William's daughters were ill with typhoid fever, one of them "in a dangerous condition." The *Manitou Springs Journal* of September 4, 1897, provides a different account, however. It reported under the heading "Prominent Man Dead" that William Glasgow had died "after a protracted illness, from which he came here several weeks ago with a view to recovering. Mrs. O'Fallen and Miss M. Susie Glasgow, his daughters, and some of his grand children have occupied a cottage in Engleman's canon all season and all were much improved by the climate, but the aged man's years are principally what caused his demise."

228. Personal visit to gravesite, October 1987.

229. Will and Estate Inventory of William H. Glasgow, #23361, Probate Court, City of St. Louis.

230. William J. Glasgow, "Edward James Glasgow, Notes."

231. Missouri, vol. 46, 255, R. G. Dun & Co. Coll., BLHBS. William J. Glasgow writes that "as time went on he became the executor of many of our Family's estates." William J. Glasgow, "Edward James Glasgow, Notes."

232. Twelfth U.S. Census, St. Louis County, 25th Ward, Enumeration District 378, 3.

233. Records of Calvary Cemetery, St. Louis, for Section 14, Lot #8, Card 1; and George W. Cullum, *Biographical Register of the Officers and Graduates of the U.S. Military Academy at West Point, New York, Since Its Establishment in 1802*, Supplement, vol. 5, 1900–1910, ed. Charles Braden (Saginaw, Mich.: Seemann & Peters, 1910), 468. A genealogical chart for the Kennerly family published by the Missouri Historical Society gives the year of Harriet Glasgow's death as 1899. Stella M. Drumm, comp., "The Kennerlys of Virginia," *Missouri Historical Society Collections* 6 (October 1928):115.

234. See T. B. Mills, "New Mexico," in Switzler, *Report on the Internal Commerce of the United States* , 565; and Glasgow correspondence in Connelley Coll., KSHS (reprinted in Part III).

235. Hyde and Conard, *Encyclopedia*, 2:803; and E. J. Glasgow to William Connelley, New York City, February 26, 1907, in Connelley Coll., KSHS.

236. See H. R. Bill 13714 in *Index to the Congressional Record: Sixtieth Congress, First Session, from December 2, 1907, to May 30, 1908*, vol. 42 (Washington, D.C.: Government Printing Office, 1908). There are no entries for Edward in the index to the second session of the 60th Congress (December 7, 1908 to March 4, 1909).

237. "Oldest Graduate of St. Louis U. Dies Here," *St. Louis Republic*, December 8, 1908.

238. Estate Inventory of Edward J. Glasgow, #36011, Probate Court, City of St. Louis.

239. Personal visit to Calvary Cemetery, St. Louis, Missouri, in October 1987.

PART I

LETTERS OF EDWARD J. GLASGOW AND WILLIAM H. GLASGOW

1846–1848

First page of a letter written by William H. Glasgow to his sister Mary Susan from "Camp Magoffin." (Courtesy of Mr. Wade Shipley, Lovington, New Mexico.)

Santa Fé August 22nd, 1846

My dearest Sue

Your letters by Major Lewis Clark were received at Bent's Fort and I believe remain unanswered as yet. Nothing of importance occurred that far except disagreeable and unprofitable detention by the "Army of the West". Thus far we have had no war, no blood shed, no dangers or perils which deserved the name.

As soon as our wagons passed over the Mountains this side of Bent's Fort, I left them in William's charge and rode on by fast as my mule could bring me towards this place — at the first settlement I heard that an engagement was to take place next day between Genl Kearny & Genl Armijo's forces and I travelled on as fast as possible to get up in time to see the fun — I overtook the Am. Army and travelled with them one day, when, as no enemy appeared I left them and came on in advance to Santa Fe where I found every body frightened out of their wits, Genl Armijo with his troops run away, the citizens leaving town with their families and all in confu—

First page of a letter written by Edward James Glasgow to Mary Susan Glasgow from Santa Fe. (Courtesy of Mr. Wade Shipley, Lovington, New Mexico.)

Camp Magoffin[1] Sunday Morning
24 [4 written over 5 in ms.] May 46

My Dear Sister [Mary Susan]

The Genl[2] [George Rogers Hancock Clark] yesterday rec^d a letter from Ellen and we rec^d a paper giving us the latest intelligence from "the seat of war", by this it appears that old Genl Taylor is doing very well and I only wish that he had killed 7000 in stead of 700 so that the war would be sooner ended.[3] I left the landing[4] (where we loaded our waggons) yesterday, and went out to the Generals quarters to pay him a visit. I remained with him until this morning, when after a good breakfast, (a thing I have not had since I arrived here) I rode down to my camp where I have taken up my quarters. Ja^s & my self have 17 Waggons loaded with goods Mr [Alexander C.] Ferguson[5] 4 — which are all placed in a circle (as you will see by Mr Greggs book[6]) and within 300 yards of Joe Magoffin's[7] fathers house. We are waiting for a provision waggon to be mended which we will load to morrow, Tuesday, we will go on to town, and On Wednesday morning cross the line of the state of Missouri and bid farewell to people, houses &^c for 60 days. Mr Clark and James will not leave for 2 or 3 days afterwards but will overtake us in one days ride after they start. The Genl looks a hundred per cent better already; he is at a very pleasant farm house with a nice grove of trees all around it, the yard full of roses & a fine breeze blowing all the time. The old Gentl^n said to him last night that his wife was afraid that George would feel a delicacy about asking for what he wanted and that he wished him to mention any thing that he would like to have and they would give it to him. but I told him that good living was what he was trying to get away from and that the poorest fare he could give him was what he wanted The gen^l never complains now of coughing, pains, aches or any thing else but is entirely satisfied and eats like a wolf.

Tell Ellen that her caution to him about exposing himself to danger from the Indians was not necessary for altho' the Genl "*talks*" a good deal his bump of *caution* is too largely developed to admit of his running much risk of his scalp Say to her That I will take care of her darling pet and not let the "*bob a sheeleighs*" catch him but will bring him back to her as fat as a bear and with more tales of adventures & hair breadth escapes than he can relate in 11 months. I am glad Mr Peake did not come up to accompany us, as Preachers

George Rogers Hancock Clark (1816–1858). A brother-in-law of the Glasgows, Clark accompanied them on their 1846 trip as far as Bent's Old Fort. He was traveling with the Glasgow caravan to improve his health. (Por-C, courtesy of the Missouri Historical Society, St. Louis.)

upon such a trip as this, are not "much account" and require too much waiting upon.[8]

Every thing about here is in a bustle & confusion. M^r [Manuel X.] Harmony[9] from N.Y. will leave to morrow with about 20 waggons[10] and will be some where in our neighbourhood all the way out. McManus[11] is loading his waggons and I think it more than probable will get ready in time to go with us. If so we will have a very pleasant party. Jeff[12] will not go out.

I write this, sitting in my "dug out" or carriage with the seat upon my knees for a table and can see the squirrels jumping about among the tree tops within 100 yards of me. Were it not Sunday I would soon have a few of them in preparation for dinner, but as it is I will grant them a furlough until to morrow morning.

Give my love to all my Sweethearts Sophy,[13] Cush,[14] little Magoffin, the fair Delia & last tho' not least Miss Mary J.[15] Remember [me] to all our Relatives & to Ellen & her brats, Ma Pa, Laura[16] Miss Patsey[17] Sylvia[18] Miss

Ilsey Gnesire [?] & every body Who may inquire for me & believe [me] Ever Your

Aff Brother W^m H.

Independence[19] May 27 1846

My dearest Sue

I received your welcome note to William and myself today, and I draw on the hours usually devoted to snoring to answer it. I have not written as often as I wished since coming up, because I have been perplexed and harassed getting ready for a start, and even now can hardly recall my scattered wits sufficiently to get a focus clear enough to scribble you a letter.

I wrote to Pa this evening before the mail closed. My letter was principally on business and notifying you that tomorrow I shall despatch the wagons and William for the plains and follow in two days with George to overtake them. I anticipate some delay on the Arkansas which will make the trip more pleasant and beneficial to George than if we were to go directly through. A month or two of exercise and plenty of Buffalo meat will make a hearty man of him. He has been kept running since he came up, and is now so greatly improved that he does not look like the same, hatchet faced croton oil customer that arrived a week ago.

In this good town everything is now alive with excitement. All the traders are busy, hurrying to get off, and the balance of the lords of creation are drumming up their courage and enlisting to go west and carry destruction and all sorts of balls and bowie knives into the humble village of Santa Fe. The Emigrants to Oregon and California are passing through daily in numbers, and it appears that very soon there will hardly be enough people left to take care of the town[20]

I am heartily rejoiced at the prospect of getting away soon and breathing the free air quietly as I have been run off my legs for the last ten days making my preaparations for leaving.

I hope to hear from you by every company that follows me out, as other modes of communicating are now closed. I also am in hopes that Laura will exercise a little industry in the same way. you will both have plenty of time before you "come out".

As regards that same "coming out", I trust that it will not be the immediately preceding ceremony to the ceremony matrimonial.

It will be better to remain at home a year or two in quiet enjoyment rather than be hurried from the school room into the matron's arm chair. Ellen can give you some advice on the subject. and even if your age were not too tender, there are very, very few young gentlemen in St. Louis to whom I would resign you. I hardly know of one.

I have been very desperately wounded myself by the darts from a pair of bright eyes up this Missouri River, but am recovering gradually.

I suppose William has written about it already, so I dont tell it in confidence.

And now before I retire to that "repose which waits on youth and beauty" let me urge you to let me hear from you as often as possible. If you knew how much I value your affection and your happiness above my own life you would not fail to demonstrate the strength of the first by frequent and free communications. Give my love to Ma and to all the folks at home and say I will return as soon as I possibly can, consistent with the proper attention my business demands, and my duty requires.

And accept for yourself the deep, heart felt unchangeable affection of the Brother who justly appreciates all your virtues and who loves you as brothers have rarely loved

James[21]

Wednesday 2'OClock 27 May "I believe

My dear Sue

Your note enclosed in Ellen's letter to the General I rec[d] yesterday evening and I suppose it will be the last until I reach Chihuahua or Santafé. I write now from about 300 yards from Camp Magoffin where my last despatch was started. We took up 10 of our waggons last evening to 1 Mile the other side of Independence and started the remainder this morning, when at this place the tongue of one of my waggons broke and I have encamped with it until I get it to town. The remainder of our waggons and every thing else are on their way to the City. A new tongue will be here this evening and I will probably get up to night. Our intention this morning, was to make the last start in the morning but my waggon breaking may detain us until the afternoon when we will toddle. We have been very much annoyed & detained by a man making our ox yokes — who failed to supply us until yesterday altho' they were to have been finished three weeks ago. We have now nothing more to detain us unless we break down again. Since last Saturday I have had the charge of our camp and have killed all the meat we have eaten The poor squirrels in the neighbourhood will doubtless appoint a day of thanksgiving now that we have gone and left them to mourn over their killed & wounded. I have become quite accustomed over more to a camp life and can sit upon the ground "tailor fashion" with my cup of coffee & tin plate before me and enjoy my fried middling & bread as much as if I had a good dinner. You would scarcely recognize me were you to see me as my face is very much tanned and I have shaved but once, since I left home. I have on a pair of old dirty pantaloons, a hickory shirt & neither suspenders vest coat or neck handkerchief. I write now lying upon the ground near my carriage and my only companion Charley Fergusson[22] is asleep upon the grass nearby while Señor "Santa Anna" of baker's bread notoriety is looking after my mule, which is grazing near.

Tell Aggy[23] that she could not have given him a great deal of information in the art of making bread, judging from the samples of his workmanship that I have seen; as it more particularly resembles putty than any thing else. However it makes but little difference as we make up in sharpness of appetite what we lack in quality of provision.

The General was down this morning for a few moments he is ready but will not start until Jim does say on Sunday or Monday. he looks very well and will return home without doubt fat & in good order. He told me that his letters were in [the] charge of Mr Fe[24] but they came, and of the gent we have seen nothing. I hope however he will make his appearance before Ja[s] leaves as I would be glad to have him along.

There is an escort or rather company of dragoons to leave soon for Santafé, which will prevent any trouble to us if the Mexicans were disposed to receive us otherwise than friendly but of this none of us have the slightest doubt.[25] About 20 waggons belonging to Mr Harmony of N.york left yesterday, about 20 more belonging to Mr [Cornelius] Davie[26] of Independence & [Manlius] Branham[27] of Columbia M[o] left to day. The two latter gent[n] appear determined to travel in company with us, which they will not do, if we can possibly avoid it, as our own company is abundantly large, for convenience and protection.

Thursday Morning

I left off writing yesterday evening to go out and kill something for Supper and ret^d in an hour with 3 squirrels which we stuck upon a Stick and cooked without either salt, butter or any thing else. so soon as I had finished supper my "Major domo"[28] made his appearance with a new tongue for my waggon and we were occupied until 9 oclock fitting it in, changing the irons &^{c}&^{c} This morning we devoted 3 good hours to prying the wheels out of the mud and I have just got it started for town. There is this morning quite an excitement in town in consequence of a Mr Meredith's having been shot yesterday by Mr Harper (son in law of Co^l Owens[29]) Mr M. is one of a party of young Gent from Baltimore going out to Chihuahua on a pleasure trip. he & Mr H quarreled at a "card table" when H shot him through the heart, he died instantly & without speaking a word. he is said to be a very fine young man and of good family in Balt.[30] I shall remain at this place until my Major domo gets up to town and sends me down a yoke of oxen to haul up my "*dug out*" and will leave town to morrow. Our waggons will leave some time to day. Give my love to Miss Mary J. Cush, Sophy and all my other sweethearts and tell Miss M. if she takes my advice she will not get married before I get back as she is yet *about a year too young.* Remember me to all at home Pa Ma Ellen & her brats Laura Miss [Patsy] Jones and [ms. torn at this point]. Am very sorry to learn that Sue Fergus [ms. torn, probably reads "Sue Ferguson"][31] no better. Any letters that you may write in, send them to Co^l Owens at this place and they will go out as there will be persons leaving all summer for Mexico Ever your Affe Bro W^m H.

Thursday 4 June
SantaFé road 16 miles from Independce

My Dear Ellen

As James & the Genl has doubtless informed you long ago I left Independence last Saturday about 10 oclock with our Waggons 19 in number & Mr Ferguson in Company with his 4. The first day we got but 3 miles from town with half our waggons the other half we left mired in devious & sundry mudholes strung along for a mile behind. On Sunday morng we started and got on pretty well until dark overtook us at Mr Barne's place[32] 8 miles from town[33] where we encamped and placed our animals all in his pasture. It commenced pouring down rain soon after dark and the next morning the roads were so slippy & muddy that we could not stir about 12 oclk however I rode over the road for 4 miles selecting good places to cross the mud holes and on Tuesday morning we got an early start and were getting on splendidly when in crossing a mud hole we broke both the hounds off the front axletree and were compelled to encamp in the prairie to put in new ones. This night it rained as fast as Water could possibly fall it cleared up a little on Wednesday morning and we started again to try and cross the big blue river[34] before the rains could raise the river but in half a mile we came to a hill which was so soft & slippery that our animals could not drag a waggon up it all & the rain came down faster than I ever saw it before So we were compelled to encamp again within half a mile of our old camp of the night before. We (as we did yesterday) turned our mules (112 in n°) & oxen (186 in n°) out to graze upon the prairie and it continued to rain splendidly all day. last night (as we did the night before) we drove a stake into the ground for every mule & horse & tied them to it & at dark placed the oxen in our "*corral*" and guarded them until day light, no pleasant business I can assure you as the mud is knee deep all around our camp & it rained all night. This morning it is still cloudy but has not rained As it is now 12 oclock we shall very probably have more rain. We are encamped within half a mile of the big blue river, which this morning *swam* the horse of our Major domo whom I sent to see how high the water was. We are now busy cutting down trees and filling up mud holes with them to enable us to cross the river as soon as the water gets down low enough not to run into the waggon beds.[35] You can form no idea of the roads we have here we have scarcely crossed a mud hole since we left Independence without hitching 11 to 12 yoke of oxen to each waggon and as our oxen were all foolish & not accustomed to work & our drivers were greener than the cattle we have had a sweet time of it as you may judge by the time (6 days) we have been in getting 16 miles 2½ *miles a day*. I have become a first rate ox driver in the morning when we start I wait & get all the waggons off then gallop on ahead to the first mud hole or hill and help the drivers over it. Then go on to the next & so on all day. five miles from this [place] we get onto a first rate road if it does not continue to rain and in 3 weeks I will have nothing to do but to hunt as we will have a good hard road from that on. James & your liegelord have not yet come out to us they were to have come yesterday but it rained so hard all day they did not. They will I suppose be out to day and I hope to hear from some of you by them. We will have as pleasant a time as any one can have in the prairies as we will have enough of us decent folks, to make the trip agreeable.

My Mare Lucretia is as fat as a seal & quite saucy, she will follow me like a dog any where & when I sit down come up & poke out her head for me to scratch it just like your ugly polk stalk of a husband. My Mule Mary Jane is a beauty & can out pace any horse or animal in our camp. They both, send their respects to you. The last I saw the Gen[l] he looked 50 per cent better than when he left home & he no doubt will return well if he stays long enough I am getting fat already. & altho' I was as wet as a drowned rat for 48 hours until this morning I never felt better in my life than I do now and after dinner am going down into the bottom to making roads again. A man has just come up from the creek & says it is falling a little so that if we have no more rain by Saturday or Sunday we will be able to get across. It is 4 miles from this to the last house and the state line. Give my love to all my Sweethearts & all enquiring friends All the folks at home Ma Pa Sue Laura Miss Patsey your brats &[c]&[c]&[c]&[c] & believe me ever you Affe brother William Henry

I wish I had Jack here to make an ox driver of him.

Pawnee Fork 9 July '46

Miss Mary Susan Glasgow
My Dear Susan

Since your note in Ellens letter which I replied to from Independence I have not heard from home. I will make myself think that you are all well until I hear something to the contrary I am however anxious to hear from Susan Ferguson & Mr[r] M[c]Pherson.[36] We are all here in a jumble about 400 men 150 waggons & 900 head of oxen & mules. The Indians have all decamped thinking I doubt not that we have come out to overhaul them for killing Mr Bents Cook who was killed about 1 mile from this place.[37] We are encamped upon the bank of Pawnee Creek about 5 miles above where it empties into the arkansas.[38] We feast every day upon green Buffaloe tongues, hump ribs, Buffaloe Sausages, marrow bones, fish & beans. The officers of Dragoons[39] are within half a mile of us and we are either in their camp or they in ours every day. They are as clever a set of lads as ever was. We arrived here on the 4th and had a grand blow out at the Dragoon Camp & another at our own the next day. Since then we have been quite rational and amuse ourselves spinning yarns hunting & fishing. Mr Fe is here and is a perfect specimen of laziness he has a horse & mule but is so poor a horseman than [that] he can do nothing with them. he has gone out hunting several times and fearing to shoot off his horse or mule, got down, when the animal invariably has left him to foot it 3 or 4 miles into camp. The first buffaloe hunt he took his mule took fright at them and ran into camp with him without his being able to stop him he says he tried to get a pistol out of his holster to shoot her in the head but she kept jumping so that he could not get it out. The Genl is in good health & spirits & if he does not get tired soon, will I think return entirely restored to health.[40] I would not be surprised to see Miss Jos[ephine] Magoffin any day as a Gent left Independence when I was there for St Louis with the consent of her Father to accomp[any] her, his intention is to return to Chihua^a this fall.[41]

I have not yet called upon Mrs [Susan Shelby] Magoffin[42] as she is encamped upon the other side of the creek & about 4 miles from this place, we are going over this evening or to morrow.

Tell Cush B[eaumont]. that her name must possess some particular powers as my mare (Lucretia) is as quiet as a lamb & as playful as a kitten with me & has invariably ran off with every other man in camp who has attempted to ride her. it may be because no one ever goes near her to feed, stake or water her except myself & I manage her when in the saddle more by speaking to her than by the bridle. We are all busy jerking buffaloe meat and around our camp is to be seen upon all sides frameworks of willow brush loaded with meat drying. how long we will remain here is yet a mystery not more than 2 weeks longer I hope.

2 Companies of volunteers have just come up[43] & we have had a meeting of all the traders[44] at our camp they have just left as well as Capt Moore of the Dragoons, who has given us all permission to go on to Bents Fort[45] he is going with us with 400 men there is about 500 more within 3 or 4 days march of us. we will go to Bents & wait for the ending of the war Co^l Kearny will catch up with us in about 12 days.

There are 2 Mexicans with us one a nephew of Gov [Manuel] Armijo[46] & Don Juan [previous word crossed out in ms.] Peo Sambrano[47] both frightened to death & thinking the army is going to eat Mexico & the

Mexicans. We recd a paper contg an account of the seisure of [Francisco] Elguias[48] goods in N.York but think it impossible that our government could be guilty of so mean an action.[49] If it should prove true Geo Doan may be in a bad way notwithstanding his English passport.[50] We hope to have a great deal of sport hunting at Bents Fort as the mountains are full of Deer, Turkeys & Bear and if we are detained there until Co[l]K takes possession of New Mexico we may have plenty of time. Some of the volunteers that came up to day are pretty sick of their "pleasure trip" they would now be content if they could get off to dispense with all the glory & laurels they expect to win — but they are in for it & will have to see the end of it. When Major M L [Meriwether Lewis] Clark[51] comes up with us I shall expect to receive letters from you all. until the ports upon the Mexican gulf are opened by F[t] Leavenworth is the most speedy route that letters can reach us as there will be expresses going continually between that place and Co[l] Kearneys army until their return.

Give my love to all my sweethearts & tell them I think of them particularly when standing guard at night watching for Indians.

Remember me to all my relations at home & tell them that I should be glad to hear from any & all of them at any time. Kiss Ellens brats for me & tell her we are making a man of her may pole as fast as may be Give my love to Ma Pa Miss Patsy Laura — Ellen the negroes & the babies & believe me ever your affectionate Bro

W^m H.

Remember me also to Miss "Coons".[52]

Santa Fe August 22nd 1846

My dearest Sue

Your letters by Major Lewis Clark were received at Bent's Fort and I believe remain unanswered as yet. Nothing of importance occurred that far except disagreeable and unprofitable detention by the "Army of the West." Thus far we have had no war, no blood shed, no dangers, or perils which deserved the name.

As soon as our wagons passed over the [Raton] Mountains this side of Bent's Fort, I left them in William's charge and rode on as fast as my mule could bring me towards this place.[53] at the first settlement[54] I heard that an engagement was to take place next day between Genl Kearny & Genl Armijo's forces and I travelled on as fast as possible to get up in time to see the fun. I overtook the Am. Army and travelled with them one day, when, as no enemy appeared I left them and came on in advance to Santa Fe where I found every body frightened out of their wits, Genl Armijo with his troops run away, the citizens leaving town with their families and all in confusion Genl Kearny arrived next evening [August 18] and marched into town without firing a gun. He made an address to the people stating that he took possession in the name of the U.S. and hoisted the American Flag over the Governor's palace. On the following day the civil officers of the town took the oath of allegiance and everything is as quiet and tranquil as if nothing had happened. The Mexicans have got over their fright and as they now understand that they are not to be molested nor robbed they already begin to rejoice that Uncle Sam has taken possession, as they say they are tired of belonging to so weak and vacillating a gov^t as that of Mexico which cannot even defend them from the incursions of the Indians. I have no doubt but the army will now move southward as far as the Paso del Norte and then march for California, but as Genl Kearny tells nobody what he is going to do, nobody knows on what to depend. We will start to the Paso del Norte ourselves in 8 or 10 days and remain there until Genl. Wool marches on to Chihuahua when we will proceed southward some farther if we are not prevented by the war. It will be impossible for either William or I to get home this fall but I am in hopes that we will be ready early in the Spring to return and I don't think I will be out here again soon. I have been so much bothered this trip by detentions of the army and other unpleasant circumstances attendant on the War that I am tired of them. Major Clark expects to remain here when the army moves on to California as the road is so bad that it will be impossible to transport cannon over it. All of the officers from St. Louis are well.

William will be along in two days with the wagons and we are compelled to make a halt here of about 10 days which will give our mules and men time to rest. You need not fear anything for our personal safety for I assure you that I have no fancy for hair breadth [e]scapes and as I come here to look for rhino and not in search of glory I intend to take care of No. 1. Give my love to all at home. I suppose George is nearly there by this time.[55] I am sorry he did not come this far with us. But I used all my eloquence to induce him on, and all in vain, so its no use regretting it now. Write as often as you can Your affte Bro

James

Santa Fé 29 August 1846

My Dear Sister [Mary Susan]

I rec^d your valued favour of 17 July yesterday by Mr [Charles] Bent[56] and was deeply grieved to hear of the death of poor cousin Susan.[57] I am glad to hear that Ellens health is improving so rapidly and hope upon my arrival home to see her about the size of Mrs Lane[58] and never more to hear of her innumerable aches & pains. her good for nothing husband is now doubtless at home, if not entirely restored to health he has to thank himself alone for it. As he was growing better all the time he stayed with us & if he had come on instead of returning when he did as we told him in 4 days he would be in the mountains where every morning & evening he would be compelled to wear his over coat & where he could have killed a deer in an hours walk at any time

We had a pretty rough trip from Bents Fort to this place as it is the most awful road that can well be imagined[59] the last 8 days it rained upon us nearly all day & night & for a week I had not on a dry stitch of clothes but did not Suffer any inconvenience from it as I have not been Sick at all since I left Independence and am now as fat as a bear & quite as graceful.

I was truly Sorry to hear by Mr Bent that Mr Swon [Swan] was killed by the Indians[60] upon his way in and hope it may have been a lesson for George & Mr Fé to be more careful how they strayed off alone from their camp. Poor Swon in coming out I cautioned him every few days about his imprudence and told him without greater caution he would not reach The Fort. the end has unfortunately proved my predictions to be correct. There is no danger upon the road when one is careful & upon the look out at all times, but under no circumstances aught a person to go out alone any distance from camp. You Say Mr M^cC. y had gone to Nashville & that the opinion of the folks was that they were engaged. If such be the case & they are married tell them I am sorry they were guilty of so great a piece of foolishness but hope they may be happy & not fight more than twice a day. For folks to marry, a man under

40 and a girl under 25 is most positive proof of their being demented and they should be placed under the wholesome restraint of a straight jacket at once.

As there is nothing like Speaking in time tell Mrs M^cC that I speak for her oldest *daughter* who will be ready to marry by the time I am and I do not wish to be disappointed as she will be my first love.

This town is quite gay the streets are full of soldiers, Officers, women, men & children of all sizes, the church bells are ringing, & the trumpets blowing every five minutes during the day. Night before last Genl Kearney gave a ball at the palace at which [were] present all the aristocracy of santa fé, they danced until about 2 o,clock when all went home very well satisfied, the ladies say it was a grand affair.[61]

How long we will be detained here we have no idea we hope however for permission to go on down in 10 or 12 days. We would start now if the Genl would let us as there is no more danger for us traders than in St. Louis but *he will* go before & as we are in the minority we are compelled to bring up the rear. Pete Morton[62] is getting along no better than usual. he has been under arrest pretty nearly ever since he got into the first settlements and is I fear incorrigible. he was placed under arrest yesterday again for absenting himself from the camp without leave I gave him some good advice but I fear it will not do him much good. he told me that he thought they would allow him to go home. I will see Genl Kearney & Maj Clark to day & endeavor to get him off & start him home in Company with Doct Craig next week. Doct Craig who carries this, is an old friend of James in Mazatlan and I hope you will pay him some little attention when he gets in as he is a fine man and a Gentleman.[63]

Neither James nor myself will be at home this winter as we will not reach Chihuahua before November and will then be compelled under any circumstances to wait for Spring before we can venture upon the prairies. Tell Cousin Sarah that I am truly sorry that I was not at home to play the agreeable to her lovely Cousins but am half glad that I was not as there is a Sort of fatality attending her cousins for me as I can never be with one of them without falling in love. I hope however they will pay her another visit after my return home.

Tell Cush She must not fall in love with Doc^t Marshall[64] or throw herself away upon Mr Dick — nor must She under any circumstances get married before I get home as no man shall have her without my permission & he will have to be Something better than I have Seen lately, if he obtains that.

Give my love to Ma, Pa, Ellen, Laura, Miss Patsey, Mary Ann Mrs MᶜC and all the balance of my relations not forgetting Miss Sophia (my Sister in law) say to Laura that I have recᵈ her numerous letters but as yet have not had time to answer them but will do So very soon. Gen K. will leave soon with 700 men for California. ML Clark will remain here. Write every opportunity you have and I will do the same ever your affectionate Brother

Wᵐ H. G.

Santa Fe' Septʳ 16" 1846

My dear Mother

Although very much occupied today in preparations to start towards Chihuahua, I have stolen a leisure half hour to write you, it being possibly the last opportunity that I will have for some time. I have just returned from a trip with Genˡ Kearny, as far down the River del Norte as the town of Tomé, and a very agreeable jaunt it was.⁶⁵

The first day's march was uninteresting enough; camped in the woods &c&c. the second day we reached an Indian village called Santo Domingo, we were met several miles from the village by a deputation of chiefs who accompanied us to their homes with demure faces, while the young men, decked out in fancy dresses, of feathers, buffalo horns &c&c capered around us on horseback, making sham fights with each other, firing guns, waving lances and looking as belligerent as possible. On arriving at their town we were liberally entertained with wine of their own manufacture, brandy, grapes, melons cakes and sundry other delicacies. The Genˡ made them a speech through an interpreter, and concluded by making them loyal American Citizens. From thence we passed on through another Indian Town called San Felipe, and were soon met by a committee from the Mexican Village of Algodones. The committee consisted of the Priest, the Alcalde and some of the most influential citizens, and we were invited to their houses and feasted as in Santo Domingo. The next halt was at Bernalillo whither we were also escorted by a committee of invitation and where we dined with a wealthy citizen,⁶⁶ and took wine with others of the vicinity at their different

Lithograph of the Pueblo of Santo Domingo as it appeared in 1846, after a sketch by Lieutenant James W. Abert. From H.R. Ex. Doc. 41, 30th Cong., 1st sess. (Serial 517). (Courtesy of the Colorado Historical Society.)

habitations, much to their satisfaction and our's also. From thence we visited another Indian Town called Sandia, where the Indians altho' very polite were too poor to give us much of a reception. Our next camp was at a small village called Alameda where we remained for the night. Here a number of the fairer portion of creation called on the Gen[l] at his camp; to see the great man and shake hands with him. They had come from several miles to gratify their curiosity and went home well pleased.

On the following morning we entered the town of Alburquerque, the residence of the Ex Governor Gen[l] Armijo; we were here received with kindness or at least civility. The citizens collecting on the houses and church firing rockets and guns in the air to welcome our approach. After being regaled at the house of the Priest, the General, Cap[t] [Henry S.] Turner, myself and a *select* committee of three others called on M[rs] Armijo the wife of the Ex Governor, who has ignominiously fled to Chihuahua and left his better half to take care of herself. She received us very kindly & even hospitably and although at first her manner was confused, at the presence of our renowned chieftain, she soon became composed and chatted very sociably. She, in common with the rest of the people of the margin of the River, had understood that all her property was to be confiscated, and half their throats cut, so that when they found no harm was to happen [to] them, they were delighted beyond measure.

We dined in Alburquerque with one of the rich proprietors, and then crossing the river took our supper and lodgings at the town of Padillas, where our entertainment was quite as good as at any other place. After breakfast at Padillas, we went to church, heard mass, and afterwards a sermon in which the priest extolled the Americans to the skies and prognosticated a happy era to the New Mexicans from the change of Govern[mt67]

From thence we marched to an Indian Town called Isletas where, we were invited to the Alcalde's house and while we were taking some of his wine and fruits, the priest arrived with burning candles and all the para-phernalia (or in other words, Tom-foolery) of the church, and invited us to go to church.

We went of course, heard a short mass; after which while we were all kneeling the Priest motioned to the General to follow him through the side door near the altar; Cap[t] Turner and I followed all wondering what was to come next. He took us through several rooms and court yards up a flight of stairs into a large room; where he had a table spread out and loaded, (not with chalices and relics of saints), but with good wines and every delicacy of the season — our repast being more savory from the company of some very pretty young ladies, no doubt *relatives* of the priest. After we had done justice to his good cheer, we returned to the church by the same way we came out; found all the congregation still kneeling, when the Priest gave them his benediction and we all retired. We then recrossed the river and stopped at Peralta where we were again feasted and where we dined and took up lodgings with another wealthy citizen,[68] who treated us more sumptu-ously than any one else had been able to do. Next morning after taking breakfast with him, we passed through Valencia and stopped for the night at Tomé. dined and took tea and lodgings at the Alcalde's and at night went to church to vespers, where the Genl. myself and several officers were invited near the altar and assisted in the ceremonies by holding long wax candles, and listening to chanting which was anything but musical. the chant was accompanied by the symphony of a fiddle, a guitar, and a bihuela:,(a kind of small Mexican guitar), and while they were in the midst of the Te Deum Laudamus, the musicians were sawing away at cotillions and country dances. We were glad to get out and I did not venture back again to church during our visit, as I was sick of the mockery of religion, and more sick of the stench of the throng of unwashed plebeians that crowded the church. At night we had fire works, rockets, and a kind of theatre, which the Genl attended, but could not understand the play from his ignorance of the language. He did not lose much however. The play was the conspiracy of Absalom to dethrone David. Absalom was dressed in a blue jacket with leather pants. David [was] in cotton domestic pants & shirt but no jacket. and had a red paste board crown. We were not sorry when we heard that Absalom was hanging by the hair in a tree behind the scenes for we were tired and sleepy & so took their word that King David was in no great danger for the present, and went to bed The next day a great Religious festival was celebrated — viz the Conception of the Virgin. Crowds of men, women & children from fifty miles distant were assembled. The Genl went again to mass. held candles and went through any quantity of mummery to gain the good will and quiet the fears of the people. I wisely went to sleep at my lodgings and left the priests to themselves. At night we had a great dance in which the priests all joined. There were many handsome ladies and the Officers were very well pleased.

Next morning we began to counter march towards Santa Fe, and the whole return trip was but a repetition of the trip down.[69]

The Indians whose villages we pass through are about half civilized — they have good mud houses with flat roofs, and no doors; to get in the house you ascend to the roof by a ladder and go down into the rooms through a trap door, by another ladder. They all speak their own language, have their own chiefs and magistrates, raise their own corn, grapes cattle &c, make their own wine, and are only under obligations to the Mexicans for their priest — for they are all catholics They are very good, harmless, lazy sort of people

Genl Kearny will leave for California in ten or 12 days. I will leave for Chihuahua in four or five, but I am only going a couple of hundred miles south, and then I will wait until I get news from Chihuahua of Genl Wool's arrival there.

The Chihuahua people say they are going to fight like fun, but every one who knows the citizens of that good city is aware that courage is not among their virtues and I am not at all uneasy about the result of Genl Wool's attack. I know that no force can [ms. torn, probably reads "be raised"] aised in Chihuahua to defeat him [ms. torn] if they had the inclination & courage.

Our mail closes this evening and leaves tomorrow morning, and I do not know when another opportunity will present [itself] of writing you. If any occurs I will not fail to let you know how I am getting on. William and

Lithograph of Valverde as it appeared in 1846, after a sketch by Lieutenant James W. Abert. From H.R. Ex. Doc. 41, 30th Cong., 1st sess. (Serial 517). Near the ruins of this deserted village, the traders remained camped from early October 1846 until the middle of December. (Editor's collection.)

I are both well & fat. Give my love to Miss Patsy, George the Girls, and all at home, including the darkies.   Your most affectionate and devoted Son

James

I have written Pa by
this mail

Camp at Valverde[70] 2[d] Nov[r] 1846.

My Dear Mother

The Mormon camp[71] is just going by us upon the other side of the river on their way to California & Lewis Dent[72] called by our camp to see us who says there will be an express go back to Santa fé to morrow & probably one to the U.S. soon. I consequently avail myself of this opportunity hoping that you may receive my communication not, that I have any news for you; but, merely to let you all know at home, that, if you have forgotten us, we have not forgotten you and think & speak of you all every day. The last letter we rec[d] from home was by Mr Bent, why we have rec[d] none since we cannot imagine as Lewis Dent says the mail leaves Fort Leavenw[th] for santa Fé every 2 weeks & 6 mails have reached St[a] Fe since Mr Bent. We rec[d] a week since a note from the Gen[l] upon his arrival at F[t] Leavenworth in which he said you were all well. M[r] [James] Aull[73] rec[d] a letter from his sister of 6 Sept in which she mentions that Uncle James was there, and as no mention is made of any of you being Sick I suppose you must all have been well at that time. I wrote home about 2 weeks ago, since which time, we have done nothing but lie in camp all day & chat & smoke. 2 days after I wrote you, we arrested 2 suspicious looking men upon the road as spies, as their movements were quite Singular & from all the information we could get, we thought there was a plan on foot in the Paso del Norte to raise a company of Mexicans to come up & endeavour to capture our wagons & take us prisoners & that the spies were sent up to get the people in the towns above us to raise and assist them. We detained the Gent a few days & moved our Camp 3 miles down the river and formed a Fort of our waggons 100 in number which 1000 Mexicans could not have taken and sent up an express to Capt [John Henry K.] Burgwin who with 200 regular Dragoons was 100 miles above us.[74] Capt Burgwin will be here with his troops in an hour or two, We have since rec[d] intelligence that all the troops they could raise in the Paso was 700 men who came up to Robledo about 90 miles & 100 miles from us & there not finding our waggons they mutinied & returned to the Paso.[75] The people above us here are too much afraid of the American Army to attempt a revolt as they told us all about the plan on foot & cautioned us to be upon the look out. I wrote you in my last letter that Connelly, [Francis] M[c]Manus, Geo. Doan & others were taken prisoners at the Paso & sent under guard to Chihua[a76] As according to our calculation Gen[l]. Wool must have entered Chi[a] several days since we are daily expecting the arrival of an express from below telling us to come on, and we care not how soon it comes as we are heartily tired out with the delays & detentions upon the road. It has now been more than 5 months that we have been living entirely out of doors & faring pretty roughly. We have the best of every thing the country affords, of the richness of this land you may judge, when I tell you what has been our only fare for a month back. We have flour, (with the bran included & no seives to clean it) poor Oxen & Coffee the latter we bought in santa Fe at 45[c] per pound this, with the exception of red pepper is the extent of our assortment of provisions; as we have neither, sugar salt, pepper, nor any thing else. We however are not troubled with City appetites and as we have less variety to eat, we eat the greater quantity of what we have and enjoy it about as well as you do Old Sylvias best dinners. We have nothing to do but lounge about Camp all day, spin yarns, smoke & eat, we cannot drink as there is not one drop of ardent Spirits in our whole Camp and we do not allow card playing. So we pass our time in listening to The tales of each other of what he is going to do when he gets back to the U.S. We are about 25 miles below the lowest settlem[t] (upon the Del Norte River) (except the Paso del Norte).

I suppose the Girls are just about making their first appearance or coming out & you will soon have your house filled with young Lawyers & Doctors & other *trash* of that kind, but I do hope they will have more sense than to fall *in love* for 4 or 5 years to come. In case they have already "*got it pretty bad*" tell them for me that this thing of love is all "*nonsense*" as I have found out by experience & that a few years hence, they will think so too: & that altho' they may think a great deal about marrying now, 3 years hence, their choice of a husband will be very different from that at this time. I hold, that the only time a person ever knows true enjoyment is before marriage & no one ought to marry until they have arrived at a mature age and "want some one to take care of them when they get old." I used to think differently but since Miss Mary Jane has *broken my heart* I have ceased to place confidence in woman and now do not intend to marry until I have the gout & require a Crutch — & someone to wrap my feet up in a warm flannel. Then, & not until then, will I make some woman happy. What a dreadful lonely time the girls of St. Louis must have had this summer as all the young Gent[n] of *any note* are away. It is a good lesson to them however & they will know how to appreciate them when they get back. Tell Sam Cuthbert[77] to give my love to Miss Ellen R__y & tell her that George Doan is a prisoner in the hands of the philistians and they have I hope shot him long ago. Remember me to all my relations & friends in S[t] Louis. Give my love to all the family seperately & individually black & white. Tell Cush B if she gets married before I get back I will give her a *spanking* or dance at her wedding I will, unless she marries that little pop eyed Dick. If you have not entirely forgotten us at home, please let us hear from you occasionally. I have written home every opportunity I have had since I left Independence & if I have not interested you with my letters it is because I have had no news to Communicate.

hoping soon to hear from you I remain as ever your Affectionate Son
W[m] H

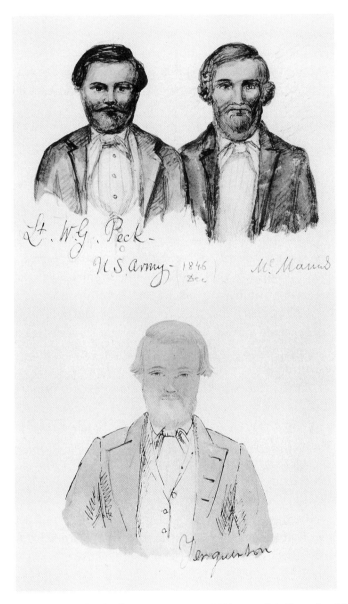

Watercolor portrait sketches by Lieutenant James W. Abert made in December 1846. "McManus" is probably Thomas Macmanus and "Ferguisson" is probably Alexander C. Ferguson, both merchants encamped with the Glasgows and other traders at Valverde. Lieutenant William G. Peck was, along with Abert, a member of the Topographical Engineers. From James W. Abert, *Western America in 1846–1847*, ed. John Galvin (San Francisco: John Howell, 1966). (Courtesy of the Colorado College Library, Special Collections.)

Ruins of Valverde 18 Novr 1846

My Dear Father

By Capt Burgwin, who left this place about one week ago for Alburquer-que, to go into winter quarters I sent several letters for yourself & the girls.[78] I have little news now for you, but as there is a man here who leaves to morrow for Santa Fé I write by him merely to let you know of our where abouts fearing my former letters may miscarry.

From the fact of Capt B'[s] having left us, you may infer that we do not consider ourselves in any danger at present from the Mexicans. We look for Co[l] Doniphans regiment here in a week at farthest as they were at the last accounts about 60 miles above us, awaiting the arrival of the Co[l] who had gone out with 2 comp[y's] to make a treaty with the Nabahoes. Since he went a party of the Indians came in to where his troops were encamped, bringing in with them 40 horses which they had stolen from Maj Jacksons Com-mand[79] and saying that they did not wish to fight any more. So we think that as soon as he got fairly into their country, he would only be detained a few days, to conclude a treaty of peace with them. So soon as this Regm[t] comes down they will go on to the Paso del Norte and we will follow on behind them. 2 days ago, a man returned from Capt Cooks command (of 500 Mormons) who brought letters for Capt Burguin and who stated, that all the animals of the Mormons had given entirely out and that finding it impossible to go on, Capt. Cook had determined to take possession of the Paso del Norte. in hopes to get some fresh animals & provisions.[80] This morning 2 wagons with 53 sick men from Capt Cooks com[d] passed up.[81] Should the Mormons continue on this winter, it is the opinion of every one that they will suffer exceedingly if many of them do not starve to death

James, yesterday paid a visit to Mr Elguia who is encamped about 15 miles below us at the entrance of the Jornada del Muerte from him he learned That. 2 days ago a Mexican (who went down as a servant with Mr Valdez[82] & who lives above us) had returned from Chihu[a] on foot. That he left Chih[a] 20 days ago and lay concealed 11 days in the Paso, awaiting an opportunity to slip out. This man, knew nothing of what was going on in Chih[a] he said the Am[n] merchants were there doing business. Mr Valdez was released from custody before his arrival in Chi[a] whether Connelly, Doan &[c] were still in confinem[t] he did not know as he lost no time in getting out of the place as soon as he was released.

He did not know whether there were any troops coming up from below or not, it was "reported" in the Paso that there were 1500 on the road. This "report" is like one of the thousand we hear daily as scarcely a day passes that we do not hear of some army coming up to recover possession of New Mexico. And as we have heard these reports almost daily for 2 months and none has yet reached here, we think it very probable that there never has been the slightest foundation for any of them.

This Mexican said, that Valdez & the others were prohibited from writing back and the people of the Paso had orders to stop all men from coming up here and to take prisoners all persons going down from above. But by our acc[ts] from Capt Cooks comm[d] he will be in the Paso in a day or two and will have no trouble in capturing the place, as there are no soldiers there.

Doniphans regim[t] can hold the place against any army that could be spared from below and we are anxious to get down there as we have pretty much used up the provisions from this neighbourhood and want at any rate to get a little farther south as the weather here is none too warm for persons who "live out of doors" and a cold rain would use our stock now pretty roughly. The grass around us is thick but very dry and contains but little nourishment for Animals. and we can get no corn without going back 25 miles to the first settlement and then paying about $1.[50] per bushel for it — which would be rather a costly operation. We have not killed our work cattle when we could buy others and consequently we have plenty of oxen yet. We pay 15$ for Beeves & from 5 to 7$ pr 100 [lbs] for unbolted flour which form all the articles of luxury we indulge in, in the eating line. We have coffee enough to last us a week longer, when we will be, on bread & meat alone.[83] But our fare troubles us but little and we would be content to live on bread & water if we could only — go ahead.

As to the business prospect you can judge of that better than us as there are now here 200 wagon loads of goods 40 of which were bought for the Zacatecas market[84] Should we get into Chih[a] soon we can do but little there with such an immense amt of goods which can not be sold until we are able to go below with them. We think that once in Chih[a] we can get on down and sell out before any goods can be brought in from the ports to compete with ours. As to duties, we will go into Chi[a] "after Gen[l] Woll" force; but goods can not be taken below without paying duties — what arrangem[t] we can make with the C. House there remains yet to be seen. We are not yet

discouraged however and hope in the end to be paid for our trouble, both
of mind & body which has not been a little, particularly of the former.
We are yet in the dark as to Gen[l] Wolls movements, as we have not yet heard
of his having started.[85] If you have heard one for every hundred reports we
have had here about insurrections &[c] you may have had some uneasiness on
our a/c, but of one thing you may rest assured, that we will keep you advised
of our Situation every opportunity we have. And as we are below all the
"intelligent correspondents" which your papers have in this country — They
can get no information from below unless we send it to them — as we "stop
all travellers on the highway" and do not let them pass if they bear any
communications to our [illegible] So that any news you may hear through
them, if unaccompanied by similar statements from us you may put down
as incorrect. There is but one road here and we watch that so that no one
can pass without our knowledge — and the bearer of any communications
for the country above, we always send letters by. Give my love to Ma, the
Girls Geo. & Ellen. Remember me to Uncle J cous W[m] & Mr Cuthbert. Y[r]
letters by Mr Grimm we have not yet rec[d]

                                                          your affe son W[m] H.

                                                      Santa Fe 10" Dec[r] 1846

My dearest Sue

        Your very welcome letter by M[r] [Norris] Colburn[86] was rec[d] a couple
of days ago also one from Ma for which I am truly thankful, I will start
down tomorrow to our camp about 180 miles south of this and will hand
over the letters to William who will be glad to hear from you.

        I am up here on a jaunt after news and your letters have paid me for my
ride. We had been so long without news and heard such accounts of the
sickness in St Louis that we were fearful some of you were sick, but your
letters brought the good tidings of the contrary. I hope by the time I get back
to camp which will be four days that Gen[l] Wool will have taken Chihuahua
and that we can move down

        Nobody in the United States seems to think Wool's movements worth
notice and at present we do not know whether he has left San Antonio or

not. We have waited at Valverde to hear from him until our patience has been exhausted.

We have been very well ever since we left home and have fine appetites but nothing to eat except bread and bull beef, and that very lean — fine diet aint it. I have got enough of travelling this trip and I think when I get back home again I will stay there, George Haywood[87] & Pete Morton are here, both well. Santa Fe is even a duller place than our camp — there is nothing doing here, nobody stirring, and being in the mountains it is very cold — our camping place on the contrary is very comfortable as regards climate. We have had no snow & very little unpleasant weather. We are camped on the bank of the del Norte in a thick grove of trees and have nothing to do except to make large fires, eat, drink sleep and smoke and the way we do that is a sin to Davy.[88]

M[r] Sam[l] Magoffin has his young Kentucky wife with him, she thinks travelling in the prairies and camping out in Mexico is not what it is cracked up for, and expresses an occasional determination to remain at home when she gets there. Tell Gen[l] Geo Rogers C. that I wish he would use a little industry in writing to folks, but I suppose the Gen[l] has not yet got done relating his Indian battles, perils by flood and field, hair breadth 'scapes &c &c

If he had come with us as we wanted him nothing would have happened [to] him. We have never been molested by Indians yet, but we do not omit caution on that account as it is the business of the trader never to be off his guard. Tell Ma I do not write to her because there is no news in this stupid country to fill one letter — much less two. As to her bet about my getting married, I have no time to think about it at present but I don't know what may happen when I get a little time to spare. I would do almost anything, even to committing matrimony to get to moving again, and if I were to take some Mexican girl, I suppose they might pass me for a citizen and let me go on down to Chihuahua with my goods.

[ms. torn] have lots of company at Valverde [ms. torn, probably reads "as there"] ere are about 500 persons including t[rad]ers and U.S. troops, but we are all getting stupid and tired doing nothing

If Co[l] Doniphan goes south with his troops as I suppose he will. I will move camp to the Paso del Norte and there wait for an opportunity to move on to Chihuahua

Tell Ellen I hope my Goddaughter is going to be very smart and handsome. I want her to teach her the 10 Commandments &c as soon as she can recollect them, and take her to hear the sermons &c I promised she should be edified with. I will write you again when I get to camp, but it will be some time before another opportunity will offer to send in any letters

Give my love to Miss Patsy and all at home including the darkies

Your Most afft Bro James

Paso del Norte[89] Jany 3^d 1847

Mrs Geo Clark
M. S. Glasgow &
Laura R. Mitchell.   My dear Sisters & Cousin

I last wrote you from above this 180 miles about 18 Decr since which time James ret^d from Santa Fe bringing me 11 letters from home and giving me several items of news that I had not heard before. I see by all your letters that you young ladies Sue & Laura have regularly come out and are cutting quite a swell among the beaux. You, no doubt put on all your consequence 3 days ago (upon New Years day) and drank wine enough to last you a year. Oh how I wish^d to be with you on that day — instead of that, I was perched upon the top of a big pile of corn in Donãna [Doña Ana] (a little town 60 miles above here) munching *peach pies* (what do you think of that) with *onions* in them. On Christmas day there was great doings near here — the Troops from Chih^a 500 in number with about 300 of the citizens of this place attacked our Missouri Volunteers as they were camping 30 miles above this place. The Missouri boys all laid down until the Mexicans gave them one fire and then rose and charged upon them killing 40 of them the balance of them "ab case" took to their heels and the last time we heard from them they were about half way to Chih^a & running still.[90] The troops took this place then without further opposition and as we walk the Streets here the Mexicans *take off their* hats to us. They are the most arrogant & cruel people in the world when they get once the advantage but whip them once and they are quite as servile & cringing I think now after so long a night that we can begin to see day breaking — as we have news of Gen Woll being within a weeks drive of Chih^a. We are now only awaiting the arrival of the Artillery from Sta Fe to go on to Chih^a and will probably start in a week. we will go down from here in 12 or 14 days. This will make our trip from Independence of only 8 months duration "very short, this, very indeed."

The weather for the last 10 days has been very cold at night and exceeding blustering during the days, and as there is no timber about here we have been put to it to keep comfortable it is however nothing like so cold as it is in St Louis. I wish you could see us sitting down to dinner our sole fare for a month back has been nothing but poor oxen and corn bread made of meal, we have ground, ourselves, in a Mill Ja^s bro^t out. We have however grown quite fat & saucy upon this diet and feel very well every day *after dinner.*

To E. Clark

By your last letters I learn that your snipe legged husband had reached home safely and had not "lost his hair" in the *many Indian fights he & Colburn had.* Strange they Saw so many more Indians than any body else. I Suppose the Genl has had enough of the prairies — well — so have I — I *think* — and would not try them again unless I had great inducements to do so. This life I think suits me better than most people and were it not for my relatives & friends at home I think I would Spend the remainder of my days some where in this country. for here every body attends to his own business and does not interfere with his neighbours affairs

To Sue & Laura

I am afraid from the tenor of my last letters from home that you young ladies are not going to "await your turn" in the matrimonial list, but are going to take advantage of the absence of Ja^s & myself to give us the slip. If you do, my dear Sister & Cousin I sincerely hope you may make a wise Selection and may find a Husband who will love you as truly as yr brothers Jas & W^m. I think however that you would do well to "wait a little while" and even if some Gent is *dying of love* for you & *cant wait* — would it not be prudent to try him for 12 or 18 months. be assured he will not die — and it is better to change y^r opinions before than after marriage. Recollect that ladies *can not nor do not know any thing* of the character of Gents from ever so intimate an aquaintance — you may think differently — but if so I hope you may never have reason to change your opinion. Oh could you s[ms. torn] poor human nature as I see it here in this poor degraded country every day you would look differently upon yr fellow beings — here every thing is vice — every body steals (ie the natives) not one in a thousand can read — & all live like hogs, with no idea of comfort.

I hope Soon to Write you from Chi^a Give my love to all the family Ma Pa Miss Patsey & all hands Remember me to my dear little Sister Cush & her

El Paso del Norte circa 1850, from John Russell Bartlett's *Personal Narrative of Explorations and Incidents* . . . (1854). (Courtesy of the Colorado College Library, Special Collections.)

Mother & Sister. Ellen give my love to yr ugly husband and yr Children Tell them all, that Uncle Willey would be very happy to see them and thinks about them every day that they must be good children until he comes back — when he will help spoil them himself. And now adieu I hope Soon to hear from you all.

Ever Yr Affe Bro. W^m H.

Paso del Norte Jany 4" 1847

My dear Father

I arrived here with all the wagons yesterday without having any accident or disturbance on the way. Co^l Doniphan with about 900 Volunteers are in town waiting for the arrival of artillery from Santa Fe which is daily expected.

As soon as it reaches this place the command will march on towards Chihuahua, All the traders will follow immediately after him.

We have advices here that Genl Wool was to leave Parras on the 19" ult^o for Chihuahua and I expect Co^l Doniphan will hurry down so as to take Chihuahua before Wool gets there so as to get all the laurels himself.[91] I do not know whether [Meriwether] Lewis Clark will come down in person or not with the artillery, as only one company is coming, but I expect he will. You have no doubt heard the Official report of the fight between Doniphan's volunteers and the Mexicans about 25 miles above this place — about 40 Mexicans were killed — none of the Americans were killed and only five or six wounded.

All the regular troops on the Mexican side bolted for Chihuahua, and could not be overtaken. I have no doubt in the world but that Doniphan will go into Chihuahua without any difficulty, as the regular forces there cannot exceed six hundred

I have no idea what prices we will get in Chihuahua, but at the lowest rates possible we must make something — there is so large an amount of goods going in that there must be a good deal of competition but if matters will admit of our going below I have no doubt we will do well. I am so heartily sick of this trip that I hardly think I could be induced to try it over. Lean oxen and corn meal is all we can get in the way of provisions and even that is very hard to procure.

In this beautiful city there is not a grain of coffee nor a pound of sugar for sale. Nothing in fact but corn and corn meal — for the latter we pay about $2^{75} [per] bushel.

There is no meat at any price, so we are eating up our extra oxen that we worked from Independence you can judge how fat they are.

However in three weeks we will no doubt be in Chihuahua and there we will make up for lost time in the provision line. Connelly and all the Americans in Chihuahua are at liberty except [James] Magoffin [ms. torn] last accounts. The people were getting very civil to them as the news of Wool's approach made them uneasy for consequences if they were molested. Nothing will be done to Magoffin they say.

I have rec^d the seal of the Com^l Agency, and will send on the last copy of the Debenture Certificates as soon as I get to Chihuahua and certify it there myself so as to make assurance doubly sure.[92]

William writes today and will give the other news. Love to all the folks at home Your Most Afft Son

James

Jany. 4th 1847
Camp 2 miles above the Paso del Norte

My Dear Mother

We reached this place the day before yesterday and yesterday I scribbled a letter to the girls. if they can make head or tails of it they can do more than I — for I had just gotten into town and learned that there was an express to Start immediately for Independence and sat down to write in a little room filled with people all jabbering, spanish, English, french & Dutch and had to Stop writing every moment to answer questions.

From this time forward, you may rest easy upon our account for if there was any real danger to be apprehended from the Mexicans some time ago, there is now none. Our troops have conquered the people of this place aided by all the force that could be raised in Chih^a and we have rec^d intelligence of Genl Woll's [forces] being with[in] 2 weeks march of that place At any rate Chih^a is whipped without Genl W. as the troops from that place aided by those of this place were so badly defeated near here. We hope by the time we reach Chih^a that peace will be established and we [will] be allowed to go on into the interior of the country. When we will get off for home, of course none of us can know yet. We have had a very perplexing & vexatious trip thus far, but are now considerably elated with the prospect of getting to Chih^a where our expenses will cease at any rate & in place of having 40 men to feed, we will have only ourselves to provide for.

Our fare for the last two months has been none too dainty, but we have always had plenty of either bread or meat altho' not always both together. It has been a good lesson for us and I think we will be none the worse for it. One thing we have learned beyond a doubt and that is "patience".

Since my last letter to you I rec^d the letters forw^d by Mr Grimm and was truly rejoiced to hear from home once more and to learn that you had passed safely through the sickly season. For your sympathy for me on acc^t of Miss Mary J$^{'s}$ marriage I am obliged but think that even without it I could have survived the event. You, at least, ought to know my character better but in case you do not I can tell you 2 things which are, firstly, That I have never had any idea of marrying any body & 2dly That if I ever had, I would be the *last* person any one would hear it from until all things were settled. So you may rest assured that when I "talk a great deal" about any young lady — (which you know I *seldom* do) It is not proof positive that I am in love with her. To be sure the desertion of all my sweethearts has gone very hard with me but *"tell Sue"* that I am in hopes that my *"darling Delia"* will prove constant and that in the end she will be rejoiced by having her, for a Sister whom she has so dearly cherished as a friend.

From devious insinuations in your letters I suppose that our two young ladies Miss Sue & Laura are not unappreciated in society. From all accounts Belcher[93] appears to have withdrawn his affections from Miss Mary J & placed them in [the] keeping of Miss Laura. Tell Laura — (if she is not married) that she shall not have Belcher unless she promises to make him bring home every night a pocketfull of candy for Ellens children. That without this, I wont give my consent. But joking aside I am very anxious to hear further from you, for I feel very deeply interested in the welfare of both Susan & Laura and do sincerely hope that in case, they do marry — They may find one, worthy of them. I think also, that if yet single they would do well to remain so, for a year or two. But if Belcher & L are married I will be rejoiced at it for he is a man that I like and I think Laura would do well, very well, to get him — Tis true he was rejected by Miss M J but in my opinion he is [ms. torn] trinsically worth a thousand McCrearys At any rate the girls ought not to be in too great a hurry, and in this above all other matters, should listen to advice, and not take men for Saints because they would persuade them that they are. Further more an affection that cannot last 12 months before marriage is scarcely strong enough to continue through life, afterward. Who, Sue's beau is I do not know unless it be Reynolds, but as he is not a marrying man I dont apprehend much danger from him. I hope she may yet be single when we get back. For her I have not so much fear as for Laura as I know she will do nothing contrary to the advice of her parents — but L I am afraid will be too much guided by fancy and too little inclined to listen to reason. I however hope for the best and will believe every thing so, until I learn to the contrary.

I am truly sorry to hear that Mary Ann & Mrs Hawk's[94] health are so bad, but hope they may speedily recover. for Mary A. cannot have a deeply seated disease. Ellen's description of Jno Gay's[95] going down to marry a "*rich girl*" was good. I think it no great wonder he came back without her as any woman that would marry him must be blessed w[ms. torn] "*pumpkin head*". Tell Cecilia I have not rec^d her letter yet & am waiting to answer it, that I will agree to pay the postage on it provided it only contains *one sheet* and that crossed and gives me a history of her beaux. Tell Mrs Sarah Irwin that I looked anxiously over the list of killed in Genl Taylors army but was sorry to find her husbands name not among them, but I have yet hopes of his getting pegged thro' the short ribs at San Luis Potosi.[96] And then I will make *her* happy. Remember me to her, Mrs B[eaumont]. & Cush & tell her I hope she will not be in so great a hurry to get married as not to wait for me, as unless Mr I. gets killed "she & Delia" are my only chances left, for escaping the happy estate of old batchelorhood. As I dont think I can ever raise energy enough to court another one and assuredly will never have any confidence in any one in [the] future if they desert me. Give my love to George Ellen & her children. To the Girls Miss Patsy & all hands in the Kitchen and be assured that I will be back with you, at the earliest moment possible and have but little idea of ever again leaving you for this country

                                                        Your Affect. Son W^m H.
Tell Pa Chihuahua is not in "*New*" *Mexico*. [written in left margin of first page]

                                                El Paso del Norte 3^d Feby 47
For Sue
My Dear Sister

      I wrote you from this place a month ago at which time I expected to be in Chihu^a ere this but the "fortune of war" willed it otherwise and I am still here. I am encamped 3 miles below the Plaza altho' the town runs 3 miles below me. James remains in town and I with the wagons. at first I was very lonesome but I opened a few trunks of goods and set up a store in my tent since which time my "store" has been crowded all day long with Gent^n & Ladies. I never was better treated in my life than I have been here. Whenever I go out to take a walk and pass by a house the lady belonging thereto always calls me in [and] gives me wine grapes & dried fruit and if near dinner time

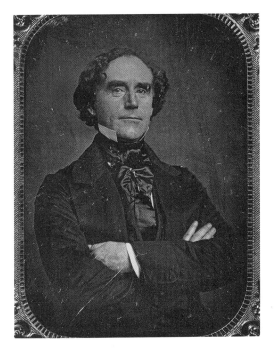

Meriwether Lewis Clark (1809–1881), from a daguerreotype by Thomas Easterly made in the 1850s. Clark was a family friend of the Glasgows. During the Mexican War he commanded the Battalion Missouri Light Artillery, which served under Doniphan. (Easterly 189, courtesy of the Missouri Historical Society, St. Louis.)

they are offended if I do not wait & eat with them. There is not an old woman within 3 miles of my camp who does not know Don Inlian as they call me. presents of wine, dried fruit eggs & chickens pour in upon me every day and I live like a fighting Cock

This morning an old Gen[t] who lives within 100 yards of my camp sent me up 5 gallons of first rate wine & another one asked me for a keg to fill. The wine of this place is very good and is about as strong as sweet cider in the U.S.[97]

The Artillery reach[d] here 3 days ago Maj Clark & his Mustachus 3 days before them. The Majors Mustach is about 2 inches long & red as fire. Tomorrow morning I leave for about 20 miles below where I will wait until the army "goes ahead".[98] They have abundant force to take Chihua without I think even firing a gun. It will be a glad day to me when I once more can see the steeple of the old church in Chih[a]

The presidio of San Elizario circa 1850, from John Russell Bartlett's *Personal Narrative of Explorations and Incidents* . . . (1854). At a camp near the presidio on February 11, 1847, the merchants and their teamsters were organized into two companies of infantry, forming what was called the Traders Battalion. (Courtesy of the Colorado College Library, Special Collections.)

By Genl Wool I expect to receive some letters from home. This we send back by santa fé. The Indians have been very bad here lately 2 weeks ago they stole from poor Old Mr Elguia 250 mules — 1 week ago 50 yoke of oxen from the Presidio 20 miles below & 3 days ago 20 yoke of oxen from the artillery store wagons.[99] We have not lost an animal yet nor do we expect to as we are always upon the lookout the Indians here seldom kill when they can avoid it but only rob.

I have so much business to close up to day that I must go back to camp & fix up for a start to morrow. Give my love to Ma Pa Laura Ellen the Genl Miss Patsy the children & ever body else black & white. Reme[mber] me to

Mrs Beaum^t Sarah & Cush & Believe me ever your Affectionate Brother
To Miss M.S. Glasgow

Wm H. Glasgow
Geo Hayward is within 20 miles of this place on his way here & is
as I learn in excellent health

Chihuahua March 12" 1847

My dearest Sister [Mary Susan]

A courier left a week ago for the United States by whom I wrote to Pa
but he left so soon after we arrived here that I had not time for any extra
correspondence and had to get William to do my part of the correspondence
as well as his own.[100] Another small company will leave tomorrow or day
after and make a bee-line for the U.S. via Texas and Ark^s and this may in all
probability reach you before the other.[101] The Battle at Sacramento was such
a glorious victory that the news of it must fly faster than my letters as it will
be old before my account could reach you.[102] An amusing incident occurred
during the hottest part of the engagement — one of my wagon drivers had
his wagon "stalled" in a small ravine, the oxen were so fatigued some of
them laid down, and the driver in despair droned out "well if any body can
git them oxens up he's smarter than me". No sooner had he spoken than a
cannon ball from a Mexican battery struck in a few feet of him, when he
sprang forward, caught an ox by the tail, stood him on his feet and giving
him a punch with his gun he looked around and remarked "I wonder what
the darned fools are shooting at me for, why don't they shoot at the soldiers"?

Indeed the coolness and courage with which our western militia
received the enemy's fire and marched up in the open field against the strong
fortifications of the Mexicans, is a circumstance hitherto unknown among
citizen soldiers, and for the future the United States will depend with more
than her usual confidence in the militia, in her struggle against any other
nation on the earth.

As for my individual self I am sick of war and its melancholy consequences and tired of Mexico in every way. The next time I return home will
be to remain there permanently.

"Battle of Sacramento, Feb. 28TH 1847, Terrific Charge of the Mexican Lancers."
This 1847 lithograph by N. Currier is based on a "sketch taken on the battle ground"
by Private Elihu B. Thomas, a member of the St. Louis artillery battalion. Note the
wagons at the middle right of the scene. These would represent the columns of
merchant and quartermaster wagons under the charge of the Traders Battalion
during the engagement. (Courtesy of the Library of Congress.)

The only man who fell on the Battle field (of the Americans,) was Maj^r
S.C. Owens, the best friend I had among the traders. He no doubt sought his
own death, as he was driven to desperation by family misfortunes.[103]

He died like a brave man and a patriot and his name will no doubt be
long remembered in the history of his country but he rushed on his death
unnecessarily and leaves a large family to feel his loss.

The Mexicans are yet fleeing from the towns distant 150 miles — an
universal panic seems to pervade them and none of them seems to consider
himself safe this side of Durango. Such are the people which the Republic
of the United States is waging war against. Such is the State of Chihuahua
against which Genl Wool was to be sent with 5000 men! All mercantile
business is of course paralyzed at present and I may very possibly be
compelled to remain here all this year to close up my business. However I
have been so long accustomed to delay and drawbacks that I have become
reconciled and have become quite a philosopher.

Whenever you can write me by way of Santa Fe, send your letters to care of J. Houghton[104] at that place and he will forward them to me.

W^m does not write today as he has written you all at length by [the] last courier. I have not written to Pa as I have nothing more to communicate than was contained in my letter of a week since.

Since I began my letter I understand the mail will be closed in the morning.

Commissioners have gone from here to make some kind of Treaty with the Govr of Chihuahua [Angel Trias] so that trade may be resumed. I hope they will be successful, but as yet we have heard nothing. Give my love to all the folks at home. Write as often as possible

My next letter will not be so hurried but I will have more time to take a longer chat with you. Kiss all the little folks at George's. always your most afft Bro

James

Chihuahua 23^d March 1847

My Dear Sister [Mary Susan]

Since my arrival in this place about 3 weeks since, we have written home by two conveyances all of which letters will I presume have been received long ere this reaches you. Since the battle all has been quiet and we are under no apprehensions of a repetition of our frolic at Sacramento. To us here it really looks strange, that an army of 1000 men (volunteers at that) should flog the troops of, & take possession of one of the wealthiest states in this Republic a state which in 1839 contained a population of 147.700 souls and must now number 150.000[105]

We have been in a great stew ever since our first entry, as Co^l D. said he would not remain here as the term of the enlistment of his regiment would expire 1st June & he would not have more than time to get home

For fear of being left behind, we trumped up a tale for the Mexicans & got Co^l D. to agree to make a treaty with "this state" by which we would be secure. Dr Connelly went down to Perral (200 miles below this) [and] had a conference with the Govr[106] The Congress held a Session & appointed Commissioners for the purpose They arrived here 1 week ago, but not being

City of Chihuahua, Mexico, from Cerro Santa Rosa. Photo by Ben Wittick, circa
1882. (Courtesy School of American Research Collections in the Museum of New
Mexico, Santa Fe.)

willing to obligate the State to remain "neutral" The treaty was not entered
into and our Commissioners will leave in the morning without having done
any thing

The merchants here, held a meeting and made a remonstrance to the
Co[l] against his going & all idea of leaving here for the present has been
abandoned Co[l] D. has sent an express to Gen[l] Woll & will abide by the orders
he will receive from him.[107] We hope that Gen[l] W. will order him to remain
here until his time expires & send some men to hold this place until peace
is made. A week ago we rec[d] the Mexican account of the battle between Gen[ls]
Taylor & Santa Ana — & Judge they must have had a desperate fight as Sant[a]
A[a] says in his official report that he fought Gen[l] T 40 hours without water
or any thing to eat except beef, but was unable to force Gen[l] T's position &
retired to Mataguala [Matehuala] to recruit his men & take care of his
wounded. His force was 20,000 men, That of Gen[l] T he says was 9000 but

from our latest advices from Genl T we know that he could not have had more than 6000. Santa Ana acknowledges that he lost of killed & wounded 1000 men. We think at the lowest his loss must have been 3000.[108] Of the revolution in the Capitol you have doubtless heard. Had Genl T's force been 15,000 he would have cut Sant^a A^s army to pieces & the war would have been over as there are no troops in this Country except those with him & at Vera Cruz. The Mexican army is without money, & provisions & could old Zac scatter them once, they could never be got together again.

Times here in Chi^a are exceedingly dull, there is not 1/4 the population of the town here, almost all the big bugs have toddled to Durango. And there they will doubtless remain until peace is made. We of course cannot sell our goods here unless somebody comes to buy them and no body is going to do that because they can't pass them through the C. Houses below here. So here we are for the present and how long a future the lord only knows. One thing we do know & that is, That, we are here until peace is made which will not be I suppose until after the next Presidential election when I hope the people of the U.S. will have sense enough to elect a *"man"* & not, an old granny.

I have not heard from home since my last letters were written, and am anxious to hear how you are all getting along & to hear whether you & Laura are going to wait your turn or not before you get married. You are both entirely too young to think of such a thing yet & Ja^s & I will promise not to keep you waiting long after we get back — for I have determined to get married immediately if not sooner (provided I get a chance to fool some young innocent) if for no other reason than to prevent me from ever returning to this confounded Country

I hope my darling *"DELIA"* will not prove faithless, if she does I will come back here, get married, & live here just to Spite her. How is that nice young Specimen of *"wit & intelect"* Mr Jno H. Gay J^r getting along, poor fellow he was like myself & couldn't come it with the Lit of Silou [?], sugar plantations &^c I hope however he has not *suffered* from the consequences as much as I. For had it not been for my confidence in my adored *"Delia"* I know not what I should have done. I certainly would not have dodged the cannonballs so often at Sacramento as I took occasion to do several times [previous two words crossed out in ms.].

I have begun to despair of finding any of my Sweethearts unmarried on my return if however any one of them is still languishing & grieving herself

to death about my abscense just tell her to hold on a little longer if she pleases
& I will buckle to as soon as I get home & put on a clean shirt & shave — the
latter I havn't done since I left Independence except on the upper lip. I think
my chance for making a fortune this trip looks rather bilious just now, but
I have had bad luck so long that I dont look for any other and would almost
be disappointed were it to turn out otherwise. One thing is also certain, that
I am not to [be] put down by ill fortune and am not a "goin to give it up
so Mr Brown" The word despair does not belong to my dictionary and if I
live long enough perhaps someday I may catch old dame fortune napping &
get the start of her. But I must bid you good bye I have spun out a good deal
of nonsense & said nothing. I have told you no news for I have none to tell,
the news factory here has gotten out of order since we came here, the
Mexicans not having politeness enough even to continue the mail to this
place. I merely write you because I have an opportunity to let you know that
I "dont know anything"

Give my love to Cush, Ellen & her brats, Laura Ma Pa the Genl Miss
Patsy & ever body else who thinks enough of me to enquire about me. Not
excepting my dearest Delia provided she is not married. Hollow my love
across the fence to Miss Coons will you and tell her that since I rec^d the love
she sent me in yr last letter I have been falling in love with her very fast

Your Affe Bro W^m H.

EnRamada 2^d May 1847

Dr Father

I am this far on my way to Saltillo with 1 wagon load of goods and have
just rec^d a courier from James with a passport from the Prefecto of Chi^a
telling me to return. The army left us so unceremoniously in Chi^a that we
could not get ready to leave with them with more than 1 load which I did
thinking that a little was better than nothing. Upon the road I could sell
nothing and now this morning I go back to Chi^a I will be there in 4 days
— being now only 145 [miles] below and having a good road all the way
back. Ja^s writes that you may all rest assured no harm will come to any of us
and we will do well I doubt not with our goods — do not be disappointed
if you do not hear from us as all communication with N Mexico & the lower

country in the hands of the Am forces will doubtless cease & we may not
have an opportunity for months of writing back.

You may rest assured that all will go well

Remember me to Ma Ellen the Girls &c I have not time to write you
fully as the Maj is waiting on me

Yr Affe Son W^m H G.

Chihuahua 6 May 1847

My Dear Father

James wrote home 8 days ago via Santa Fé[109] and 4 days ago I dispatched
a note by Maj Clark from Hacienda El Romada 140 miles below here and
upon the road to Saltillo.

The Army of the U.S. left us here in rather a forlorn condition. We
followed on from New Mexico to this place with the understanding that we
were to be *protected* by Co^l Doniphan's regiment, judge of our astonishment
3 days after our arrival here when we were informed that the aforesaid army
would remain in Chi^a 1 week and that the merchants would be allowed that
length of time to *Sell out* and be ready to go home as the army intended
returning via F^t Smith. As the am^t of goods thus introduced amt^d to *only*
about 1.000.000 $ it may readily be supposed that they could not easily be
disposed of particularly as the Congress of this State issued a decree (from
Parral where they removed immediately after the battle of Sacramento)
forbidding any one from purchasing any goods introduced by the army
under penalty of confiscation.[110] As one half the caravan was composed of
ox wagons, which barely made out to reach this place, we were in no very
pleasant predicament and the prospect for losing every thing was very bright
indeed.

Co^l D. said that if the Gov^t of the State would make propositions to him
to treat for the protection of the U.S. merchants he would agree to them,
accordingly Connelly & Don Felix Meceyra[111] our Prefecto set out for Parral
and brought up commissioners for the purpose. but our gallant Co^l fearing
to compromise himself, would not accept of their propositions nor would
he make any himself. They accordingly departed again and the army remained quiet a week or two. Our Gallant Co^l then thought he would go
down to Parral to root out the Mexican Congress &c he accordingly departed

Alexander William Doniphan (1808–1887), colonel of the First Regiment Missouri Mounted Volunteers in the Mexican War. This portrait of Doniphan was painted by Missouri artist George Caleb Bingham, circa 1850. (Courtesy of the State Historical Society of Missouri, Columbia.)

with one half his force and got 50 miles upon his way when he rec^d a letter from an Am^n merchant living in Perral (& who had just rec^d a Stock of goods from Durango & feared the competition of the Chi^a merchts) Stating that 5000 troops were upon their march from Durango to retake this place & he toddled back in double quick time frightened out of his wits.[112]

He then sent an express to Genl Wool and came very near not waiting for an answer indeed had it not arrived, upon the 1st of this month he would have left for F^t Smith. The express ret^d and contrary to the expectation of every one ordered Doniphan to "report to him at Saltillo as early as *practicable*" and Said "as to the Am merchts, they may at their option either remain in Chi^a or follow on under the protection of your columns to this place." Knowing that the army would certainly leave we had some days before the arrival of the express [and] induced our Prefecto to go down to Perral, state our willingness to pay duties &c to the gov^t and get from the vice gov^r an obligation to protect our persons & property after the army left in case we would guarantee the forces to leave the State within one month. 2 days before our express ret^d we rec^d a courier from our ambassador in Perral stating that the authorities there were anxious to enter into the arrangem^t and wanted to know if we were yet willing to make it we ret^d answer that we were and requested him to conclude the business.

The Prefecto was due here upon the 28th ulto. The express from Genl Wool arrived upon the 24th [23rd] and Doniphan immediately issued his orders to evacuate the town upon the "*next day*" and sent to each of us a copy of Genl Wools orders.

Conceiving that the orders did not require him to leave at once we represented to him again the State of our affairs and told him when we looked for the Prefect. and by dent of hard begging &^{c} we got him to order 400 men to remain until the *morning* of the 28th altho' we told him that Mr Meceyra our Prefect would not be here *until the afternoon of that day*. But he would not remain one moment longer upon any consideration. altho' we intimated to him that his orders to bring all the Am Merchts under the protection of his columns, who did not wish to remain here amt^d to an order to give them time to prepare to move. Thus were all hands left here to the mercies of the state authorities (when they should return) and to that of the populace until some one having authority should arrive to take charge of affairs.^{113} Meceyra did not arrive until the 30th when he came invested with full powers to make the best arrangem^t he could and to induce the merchants to remain here. About a half dozen of the traders had reduced their stocks very considerably and sold out the remainder to [José] Cordera of this place at 14c pr vara — as they were unable to move.^{114} As Ja^s & McManus had soon after there arrival here sold all th[e]ir Stock to the Q^t Master they had no teams & could not move I was in the same fix. They accordingly made up there minds that as they were unable to do any thing they would remain perfectly quiet & trust to Providence.^{115} Connelly advised me to leave with the army & take all the goods I could with me the balance he would claim as his property and being a Mex^n citizen he hoped it might all go right. I accordingly managed to scrape together 8 *mules* and put out with 1 wagon load of goods. I followed on with the army to El Ramada without being able to sell 1 vara of goods when I recd a courier from Ja^s here telling me that all was arranged and advising me to return immediately I accordingly did so and arrived here this afternoon. Every thing here now looks like old times. The old authorities are returning and all is quiet the people more civil than they have ever been known to be before. Our Prefecto is busily engaged in fixing up our documents and says all will go right and none of us have the slightest doubt but that we can now see our way clear before us and that we are just as safe here as we would be in St Louis

From the above statem^t of facts you may form some idea of what a state of anxiety & suspense we have been in for the last 2 months and can judge how much we feel relieved at present.

You will also see that the only obligations we are under to anyone are to the Mexicans and not our own countrymen, who have in this matter treated us all most shamefully. Maj Clark can tell you that we are under *particular obligations* to L^t Co^l D D Mitchell[116] for the hasty departure of the U.S. army as he never failed from the first day he entered this place to importune & harrass Co^l Doniphan to leave the place and not allow the interest of a *few paltry speculators* to influence his movements. He has left at last — and has been successful in obtaining one universal opinion from every foreigner in this place & That is — "a universal contempt for him as an officer & a most cordial hatred as a man." I have now a much better opinion of the Mexican character than I ever had before and a much smaller one of that of the people of the U.S. The soldiers of this country before the war doubtless thought themselves as brave as any one but now that they know they are not, They have ceased to make any pretensions and treat us with the most marked politeness. A day or two before Donipn left the influential men in this place held a meeting for the purpose of taking steps to have the peace preserved until authorities should return and concluded to raise 200 soldiers to act as Police

They have now only about 50 altho' there are here 200 who were formerly soldiers — and will not serve again as they say, that when they are seen parading and soldiering thro' the streets, the people will tell them "That they look [like] very brave and good soldiers and will continue to be so until the americans come again when they will run."

Business is yet dull here but so soon as we get all the authorities back again and things regulated as they were of old I hope we will soon be able to close up & return home. I now hope to be able to get home this fall. [Samuel] Magoffin packed off with the army with all his goods some 2 wagon loads. up to the time I left him he had not sold any of them upon the road and would pass through but 2 towns more of any consequence in this state   In both of which places I learn from Mr Capulard[117] (who has just come up from Monterey) the people are afraid to buy goods upon which no duty has been paid. M[r]. C. also told me that blea[ched] shirtings were retailing in Parras at 18[c] & in Saltillo at 12½ [c]. So that the prospect for getting first cost for goods below is bad.

All the goods now here are in the hands of but few men. Connelly, Macmanus, Jas Aull Elguia, Cordera & myself and we hope to be able to obtain pretty fair prices.

I yet owe Connelly & G. upon my outfit & Expenses to this place about 200$. The a/c is —

For Am[t] due for wagons freight & charges on goods at Indep[n]	$1211.90
" " my proportion of outfit of oxen provisions &c	1258.25
" " " " wages of drivers & herders	1134.13
" " " " of Expenses upon the road to Chi[a]	440.99
" " " " pd for corn & fodder for Stock	109.62
" " P[d] EJG, expenses going to Sta Fe for guia & for guia	180.00
	$4.334.89
By 1/2 amt rec[d] for Oxen Sold in Chia.	200.00
	$4.134.89

Upon acc[t] of the 8000 $ mentioned in your last letter I have not been able to pay them any thing as yet nor will I soon as I will have first to pay my duties here[118] Give my love to all at home

Yr Affe Son W[m] H

Chihuahua 7th May 1847

My Dear Sister [Mary Susan]

Since the 9th of Nov[r] '46 we have not heard from any of you, and now, since the Army of the U.S. has left us to take care of ourselves I know not when we will receive another letter from any direction.

The old Authorities having again taken possession of this town and New Mexico being in the hands of the U.S. forces I presume there will be no communication between that State & this, and as there is of course none below this, we may not hear from you for a considerable time. Mr [James Josiah] Webb (partner of Geo Doan) goes to morrow to Independence via

Santa fé,[119] when I will have another opportunity to write, is more than I can imagine as there will be no one left here who will probably be going to Sta Fe soon. So you need not be at all uneasy should you not hear from us again within the next 6 months. of one thing you may rest assured. That we will never let an opportunity pass without sending you word how we are getting along.

We have been deserted by our Countrymen at a time when we thought & so did they also — That if we remained here without some kind of a treaty's having been made to guarantee our safety that our property would be confiscated and ourselves either be mobbed or put into jail there to remain until the conclusion of a treaty of peace. They left us when they knew that provided they would remain 48 hours longer than they did The Prefecto of this city would be back from Perral (the present capital of this State) with full powers to make any kind of treaty in the world that would insure the army to leave the state. But they would not remain a moment and as all the principal merchants here were unable to remove their goods upon so short a notice as they received they concluded to remain with them and trust to the good faith and generosity of the Mexicans. By the advice of Dr Connelly & James I started with 1 wagon load of my goods all I could obtain transportation for and got down the country 140 miles when I rec^d an express from James Saying that all was right here and advising me to return to this place at once As I had in this place a considerable amount of goods and was unable to sell any where I was I accordingly did so and arrived yesterday.

In all the towns thro' which I passed on my return I was treated with marked politeness as well as by every one I met upon the road. I started back with a large company which consisted of Ralph Crabb[120] a Mexican servant 11 mules & myself. My Company gradually increased in size until the day I arrived here it amt^d to am^t [about?] 40 men, women, children, dogs, Jackasses &^{c} &^{c} all travelling with me for protection against the Indians. who kill them upon the road almost every day. To a person living in the U.S it is impossible to imagine the condition of the poor people of this country. They do not live as in our country scattered all over the world but in little ranchos or small towns the houses all close together & the farms all adjoining so that the country between each rancho & the one next to it is perfectly wild and filled with Indians At Hacienda of Gaoucillo [Guajoquilla] (where I stopped 3 days ago upon my return) about 10 days ago 40 Comanchee Indians rode into the plaza in the centre of the town about 10 oclock am, and halting, the greater part of them dismounted and visited every corral in the place and took out every mule. The inhabitants all shutting their doors and remaining perfectly quiet frightened out of their wits. At the same place 3 days afterward 5 wagons belonging to Jas & my old friend the Priest here, stopped there and turned the mules out to drive them to water at the river Conchas [Conchos] (distant not more than 100 yds when up rode a dozen bobbys and run off the whole lot of mules.

Chihu^a is herself again and we feel greatly relieved. as every thing was left to our Prefecto he returned with full powers to make a treaty with Co^l Doniphan, but finding him gone he said [that] as the merchts here had remained upon his pledge that he would make the treaty with them and published a proclamation to the people of the town & state ordering them to keep themselves quiet and to treat the citizens of all countries whatsoever with politeness & attention &^{c}&^{c}&^{c} which has been & is now done. I am at last done with the army and never want to hear another trumpet blow in the world. I am disgusted with my countrymen and had I not those whom I love most upon the earth living in the U.S. Never would I set my foot in that territory again. Of Maj Mitchell I am sorry to say that he used his utmost endeavors to ruin us all and had his advice been followed by Co^l D. we should have been left here long ago without the slightest provisions having been made for our security. But Providence has willed it otherwise and despite the exertions of Co^l D.D.M. we are now, as safe here as we would be were we in St Louis.

The next letter that I receive from home I expect will contain an account of the marriage of yourself & Laura but I hope you children will wait your turn.

I now hope to be able to return home this fall and hope that at least "*one*" of my sweethearts (which one I wont Say) may prove faithful if she does — I will "REWARD" her by making her "*happy*" for life. Give my love to Ma Ellen her children Miss Patsy Laura Mary Ann Cousin's Sarah Margaret & Susan Larkin[121] and all my other Relatives. Also extend the same to all my old sweethearts not forgetting the lovely Delia & Cushy Remember me also to Mrs Beaumont, Sarah, the Bishop & Mrs Hawks & Believe me ever yr affe bro W^m H.

"Chihuahua from the Casa de Moneda," photographed by William H. Jackson, circa 1883. (Neg. No. 7468, courtesy of the Museum of New Mexico.)

Chihuahua 3ᵈ June 1847

Miss Mary S. Glasgow
My dear Sister

By Mʳ Webb, who left this place for the U.S. nearly a month since I wrote some of you at home. I had then just retᵈ from below after having started for Saltillo. Chihuahᵃ is now herself again and it looks like old times here, all the marks of the Volunteers have been effaced. The Government has been reestablished here The people have returned to their homes and every thing goes on quietly, orderly & peaceably. The foreigners here are as well treated as if they were in their own country — not one of us has been insulted or treated in any but the most polite & friendly manner. But this we do not owe to *office seeking commanders* of the volunteers from the U.S. Young Zaloagers [Zuloaga's] father has not yet retᵈ from Durango.[122]

I suppose ere you receive this Maj M.L. Clark will have retd home,[123] if so give him my kindest regards and tell him that I congratulate him upon his having gotten rid of the annoyances he was subject to while under the orders of such men as Col's Doniphan & Mitchell. And in case he volunteers again I hope he will be more fortunate in having comd^g officers whom he can respect, if not for there official qualifications at least as *gentlemen*

I fear you may have been uneasy about our situation here after the army left us, but you need be so no longer for we are as safe here as if we were at home. last week I sold out all my goods & chattels to Connelly & James.

I have since bought from M^r [James] Aull a small stock of goods at *less prices* than I sold at — and in another week will be upon my road to the mining town of "huassa Parras" 300 miles west of this place and in the heart of the mountains

In that place I expect to remain until the latter part of February when I will return here in time to start home as early as practicable. James has gone to Parral 200 miles below here with some goods, but will be back again in about 4 weeks.

By Mr Webb we (all the foreigners here) sent a letter to Santa Fe to have all our letters there sent down to us by a man to be hired to bring them down, but they will not reach this [place] before I set out for the mountains. It is now more than 6 months since the date of my last letter from home and you may suppose we are anxious to hear from you — particularly how you Girls are getting on — Whether you have become tired waiting for Ja^s & I and are going to be married or whether you are disposed like *dutiful children* to wait your turns

I also want to know if any of my Sweethearts are yet constant or whether I shall find each and every one of them with a house full of brats of their own production upon my return

I have had such a rough time of it since I left home that I do not feel inclined to return to it until I go clear of debt and with something of my own. I made the best possible disposition of the goods I bro^t out and made a very handsome profit upon them, but not enough to pay me for the anxieties of mind & which I suffered the hardships I care nothing for — as soon as they were passed they were forgotten. I know I can make double the money here that I could at home and until next spring I shall try the mountains and the mines. After which I shall return to St. L. where I think I shall remain ever after. That is provided you don't let all my Sweethearts get married before I get back — for in 6 *weeks* after the day of my return I am going to buckle to any one of them that may prove faithful to "*reward*" her for her constancy. I suppose Leo Walker,[124] [William] Clark Kennerly[125] &^{c} &^{c} will take the shine off Jeff [Clark] & the *boys at home*, upon their return from the wars — if so turn about is fair play [but] the young lawyers and doctors will never have such another chance unless they can get up *another war.*

This is the first day of the feast of Corpus Christi and our square looks very pretty. The streets are all covered over with long sheds, of poles covered with green bushes — so as entirely to Shade the street and in every door there is a beautiful altar fined [?] up [and] adorned with flowers &^{c}

This morning a very large procession marched along the whole distance, composed first of the priests & their attendants and followed by at least 2000 ladies all splendidly dresd. This feast will Continue for 8 days In the meanwhile the shading of the streets will answer a very good purpose as in passing every door where there is an altar we of course take off our hats. and should any one of us be caught in the street while there is a procession on foot we might be compelled to walk across the square "hat in hand"

This letter I will send by Geo Doan[126] — when any one else [?] will be going up to Sta Fe is more than I can tell most probably not until spring This probably is the last letter you will receive until that time if so do not be at all uneasy as you must know there is no communication between this place and Sta Fé

Give my love to All my Relatives & friends To all the folks at home Ellen & her liegelord [?] and her "5" brats. To Mary Ann Cecilia Laura Cush & Believe me ever yr

Affe Bro W^m H.

Tell Cecilia, Cush & Laura that having so much idle time upon their hands I had hoped they could have spared 5 *minutes during the last year* to have written me — but I suppose they are all married and find more pleasant occupation in "nursing babies" than in writing letters to one they care nothing about. do not forget to give my love to Miss Patsy and Ellen dirty nosed brats.

Chi^a 27 June 1847

My dear Siss [Mary Susan]

Read all the other letters first as they were written some time ago.

Well, Our express arrived day before yesterday in the afternoon but our letters had all to go to the office of the "Administrador of the Correos" and we could not get at them until yesterday morning when our worthy & good Prefecto D^n Felix Meceyra sent to inform us that we could be accommodated. So about a dozen of us packed over to his office and "shuch a *readen* of letters you never did see" Jim & I got 15 and I need not tell you what a treat we enjoyed and how happy we were to hear that you were all getting on so finely at home. So you & Laura are cutting quite a Swell and Slaying the beaux right & left. Laura & her Page - de Lorvel who'd a tho't of it. You it appears have escaped scott free as yet are may be somewhat more — "sly" but hold on a little for I'm coming lumbring home next Spring & am goin to buckle to — immediately if not Sooner.

And you & Laura (the "*Linn-ite*") are dancing the Polka to Say nothing of little "Mrs Clark" & her herring g_tt_d & shad b_ll_d spindle shanked may pole who killed all dem Ingens last summer — but didn't bury 'em next mornin caus he couldn't find em. I reckon he was so savage that he ate em all as fast as he kill'd em & that accounts for the others not findin em. And Lizur Martin has got Letitia McKee stayin with her has she in your next [letter] please let me know who Miss Letitia belongs to, Where She comes from &^{c} as I never heard her blessed name before

Miss Coon hasn't been treed yet, well I'me werry sorry for her, poor thing as I think she was upon the anxious seat before I left and Delia my D. a is true yet, well if she's constant because nobody won't ax her she dont deserve much credit if she has had plenty beaux dyin about her and wouldn't take that kink out of her lip for em then do you just tell her to go to work on them ruffles & doins. I see by your account that the boys & gals are doin pretty well in the marrying line. they had better have closed all their trades before the warriors got back for then they'll be "nowhere." I'me happy to hear that Belcher has stood it so well, tell him I've not got well yet and am going farther away from Civilization into them mountains I was talkin about. And Mary Ann has got a lawyer the "image of his dad" you didn't say whether his head was bald or not but I suppose so of course. Tell her I wish her "much congratulation" and hope she may have a hundred more of em. The only drawback I had to the great pleasure hearing from you was in the bad health of dear little Cushie. Bud may break his leg & be dog^d. he's young & his legs will grow together again. I hope however when I hear from you again that C. may have entirely recoverd Give my love to her & Sarah and tell them & Mrs B that I long to go out to there house sleighing & will promise not to get tight upon Brandy peaches again. Cousin W^m has gone to Europe "I don't

believe it" the first sight of salt water will cure him as it did before Tell him
the next letter I write him will do him good. You made enquiries of me about
Certain persons renting a house in Sta Fe "building up the wall &ᶜ" The Gent
you alluded to, did have a room in which there was no door, the "apurture
sufficiently large to admit a man" was the window which reached near the
ground, he made no alterations in the house and as to his never leaving it I
think your informant was mistaken. That he played cards sometimes I know,
but not to the extent that you have supposed. He is now a much better man
than he gets credit for — his greatest fault with the world is — That what
almost all young & "old" men do *secretly* he does openly. I have never known
at any time 6 young men of my acquaintance who did not at times play cards
and were I to enumerate to you the gent in St Louis both married & single
who indulge in that vice you could scarce believe it possible. But enough of
this G is here an enterprising, "industrious" man & will make money if he
continues on as he is now.

He is not the man I would like to see you make an intimate friend of,
altho' he is a better man than many who boast of their morality &ᶜ. You will
no doubt be surprised after reading my former letters, to hear of my still
being in Chiᵃ. The cause is indeed a melancholy one. I boᵗ goods from Mr
James Aull and repacked them in his house. I had engaged an Arriero
[muleteer] to pack them out to Jesus Maria. On last Wednesday my packer
arrived with his mules ready for a start the next morning. About 6 oclock
the mornig following I was aroused from my bed by a negro belonging to
Mr Aull[127] who came bussting into my room saying that his master had been
murdered and robbed I went over immediately to his store and there found
him lying behind his counter stabbed 2 [twice] in the back once thro the
heart, both his hands horribly cut & his throat cut from ear to ear. he was
evidently murdered the evening before — as he was dressed and his bed had
not been slept on.[128] This was a horrible business and you could not imagine
the gloom it cast over us all We being here so few in number and one of us
to be so horribly mangled for the mere purpose of plunder

The murderers got 5000 $ in silver which I hope will lead to their
detection. This Circumstance aroused the whole town and the Authorities
have been actively employed in endeavoring to secure the murderers. They
have arrested 16 persons and last night sent off to arrest two who left 2 days
ago for Durango. We are certain they have 2 of the right men and it is pretty
certain the two they are in pursuit of are also guilty. Our Prefect & Judge both

say that as soon as they are convinced they have the right persons they will have them shot in front of the door where the murder was committed

This is the first affair of this kind which has ever occurred in this city and this was brought about by Mr Aull's own imprudence as he was in the habit of sitting in his store "alone" with the door open until 10 & 11 oclock at night. This is what no man in his senses ever would do in this country he had repeatedly been cautioned about it by persons who in passing have seen him thus, but he still persisted in it until too late. He occupied the store I did when Maj Clark was here. You need not be at all uneasy upon our a/c as we will never give any such opportunities as this. And this murder was done for the purpose of robbing and not upon a/c of his being a foreigner. Connelly has just come in and says they have found 2200 $ of the money in the house of one of the prisoners. Tell Ma we are very grateful to her for her solicitude about our comfort but as regards the clothes we can get any thing in the world in this place that we could get in St. Louis except those fresh Oysters the Gen¹ boasts so much about. We do not live very high as the Indians around here do not give the Beeves time to fatten and there are but few vegetables raised around here. We have however plenty & sufficient variety as we [?] care but little for what we eat.

I am sorry you do not get along with my little friend L. [illegible] she is however I suppose sorter "stuck up" with her own little consequence since she has come out a young Lady but I believe has a good heart. I should have liked to have seen Miss Fanny Thruston "set back & rack" in the Genls boots she must have looked as graceful as Miss Jule Davidson when she was "goin it on the Polka" in "my breeches". But enough of this nonsense I hope to be able to get my goods in a day or two and bundle off to Jesus Maria. The Authorities have not yet finished taking an account of Mr. Aull['s] effects. after they get through — they [illegible] of letters says he will turn mine over to me as soon as I establish the fact that I have never received them, which I will have no trouble in doing. This is I expect the last news you will get from us until you see us as there is now no one here who can possibly leave this [place] for N. Mexico before next Spring

Remember me to all my friends Give my love to every Member of the family both white & black. Kiss "D_a" for me And believe me ever yr Affe Bro Wᵐ H.

Chihuahua July 1st 1847

My dear Father

We sent word some time ago to Santa Fe instructing our friends there to hire an express rider and send down our letters. The Express reached us a few days ago and by him, William and I received a large pckge of letters with various dates from [the] latter part of Nov. up to 23 Feby. We were rejoiced to hear from you especially as your letters brought only good news. William has written you several letters and explained to you the state of his business affairs. He has done better by Selling out to us than he possibly could have done by holding on and he will make a very good profit considering the difficulties and delays we experienced getting here. Our own business C.& G. will take some time to close, as yet we have a large quantity of goods on hand. We bought in Santa Fe last year $16.000 worth of goods which we have paid for out of Sales and we have also paid a large part of the duties

These amounts and the large sums we were owing the wagoners (, which we paid on arrival), have made it impossible for us to make any remittances home; I have written by this conveyance to Mills and Siter, Price & Co.[129] that we will leave here next spring and will have funds to pay them on our arrival. I have determined that this will be my last trip to this country as I have been bothered so much this trip that I would not go through the same anxiety of mind again for any hopes of profits. I took a trip down to Parral a fortnight since with about 6.000 $ worth of goods which I sold on arrival for cash at good prices

Notwithstanding all our delays and expenses we will do well this trip, and if no more Am troops come here to interrupt the peace of the state we will be able to close up by commencement of the next spring with a nett profit on the adventure of, (I doubt not), from 18 to 20.000. I do not want to see any more volunteers while I am here, I have had enough of them. What with their escort, blockades impressments and protection, and finally dropping us here like a hot potatoe — they gave us a splendid chance for confiscation, which we however succeeded in avoiding. By a delay of three days Col. Doniphan might have made an arrangement with the authorities which would have left us and and our property in perfect security. This we represented to him in the most earnest manner that men could do who had perpetual bankruptcy staring them in the face — but some of his officers were tired of town and the good-natured politician could not lose 72 hours of such precious time.

Every one here speaks highly of Maj M.L. C_k [Clark], even the Mexicans. Every one speaks well of his officers and men. Of the balance of the Reg^t I cannot say as much. For the redoubted Co^l the general opinion is that he was a good-hearted good for nothing character, who did not want to do any harm and had not firmness or decision enough to do any good. — a perfect zero — a weather cock turned about by the breath of every man supposed to have any *political* influence. To Maj^r C-k both William and I are under a thousand obligations for the ten thousand favors we rec^d from him, and his unwearied kindness and exertions on our behalf. I do not believe there is a single trader who does not feel for him the warmest gratitude and respect. I almost believe that their good wishes for the Maj^r equal their contempt for Co^l Doniphan. Mr Zuloaga arrived here from Durango a few days ago; he says he wrote from there to Luis. He wishes you to keep Luis at St Louis at all hazards and keep him at School He says you must not be too delicate but do with him as if he were your own son. He wants him to remain there until his education is finished, and does not wish him at home at all — much less in the present state of affairs. I have given him a letter of credit to you for 500 $ which he will pay us here. For this purpose you can use the am^t of dfts. I sent from the Paso del Norte and some 275 $ which Maj^r Clark is to pay you for money we advanced him here. This will keep him going until I can send you some more.

Mr J. Magoffin is here. He has been acquitted of all charges against him and is now at liberty.[130]

We have all been well treated ever since Co^l Doniphan abandoned us here. We, (the Merchants) made a treaty on our own hook with the state Gov^t and they have rigidly adhered to it.

Maj^r Clark was afraid for us to trust to the word of the Mexicans, but we knew who we were dealing with and we are now very glad we remained.

George Doan will give you all the small news as my letter is growing very long and will not hold a great deal more. I received a long letter from

Cousin W^m which I do not answer as I suppose by this time he is beyond the seas, in the midst of his European tour.

Give my love to Ma and all at home

Your Most Affec Son
James

[Unattached page to William Glasgow, Sr., probably inserted in previous letter of July 1, 1847.]

A gloom has been thrown over our town by the death of Mr. James Aull of Lexington, M°. He was killed on the night of the 23 ult° by some men who perpetrated the act for the purpose of robbing him. He was in the habit of sitting in his store alone until a late hour reading; he had been told frequently that he was exposing himself but did not regard the admonitions. It appears from testimony that he was sitting alone about 10 o'clk at night reading when some men went in and stabbed him — afterwards robbing the house of about 5000 $. The men have been arrested and their trial is now progressing and I am in hopes they will get the reward of their crimes.[131]

All the authorities have been very active and have used the greatest exertions in securing his murderers & bringing them to justice.

William had purchased from him about 6000 $ worth of goods which were not yet delivered. As soon as he receives them from the authorities who have possession of them he will start to Jesus Maria and sell them. Ralph Crabb remains with us, as we will want some drivers here in our small freighting expeditions. He, William & myself will start home early next Spring. Dr. Connelly sends his regards.

Mr [James H.] Barney[132] who goes in with Geo Doan was one of our fellow travellers down here — if he comes in reach of your acquaintance I request you will show him some attentions, as he is a friend of mine whom I esteem very highly.

Mr. Grim has not yet paid the 15 $ — he is a grand scamp. Say to Geo. R.H.C. that we were delighted to receive his letter, but that the dozen others he mentions have not come to hand.

I am in hopes that some Germans here, (who speak of going shortly, will furnish me [an] opportunity of writing again. By them I will make you a remittance for Luis [Zuloaga]; Expenses for fear you Should be pressed for funds, as I know it is a Scarce article in St. Louis. I will try and find time to write George tomorrow. Love to all hands Your

Affec Son James

I have sent in money by Mr Barney to pay a note we owe to Wilson & Clarke[133] at Independence — Mr B. will take up the note for us and hand it to you

Chihuahua 29 March [1848]

My Dear Sister [Mary Susan]

Your Several favours, bearing dates from June to Oct came to hand a few days since and I need not say that I was happy to hear from you all again as my latest news up to that time was May 19. And now altho' my news is 5 months old still it seems to me but as yesterday. I observe what you say in regard to the increase of Wm Glasgow Jr's family and think myself that he had great need to have gone to Europe for "his health" if he had gone on to China I doubt not he would have had 4.

Mrs McCreery you say is grown into a sedate old woman, may be she intends throwing "dubs" too if so I don't wonder she is not very lively at present.

Your opinion of our Nobility here is badly founded upon the appearance of one poor little black doin's who makes a chimney of her mouth. What will you say when I tell you that as inveterate a chewer & Smoker as I have been for 11 years; last Christmas I made a vow to quit both and have fulfilled it up to this time and now do not feel the want of either Cigars or Tobacco.

You all take a great interest in young Mr Luis Zuloaga, what think you was the report handed in by him here. He brought no letters altho' Pa wrote that he sent some by him. He said that they turned him away from the schools in the U.S. because he was a Mexican That he was hooted at in the streets and at one time compelled to hide himself 2 days in the woods for fear of being murdered and that he was compelled to walk from Indep^e to Santa Fe his mule having given out in the early part of the trip. This is a sample of Mexican gratitude. I have changed my opinion since I wrote you last August and now would not incommode myself the least to save the life of any Mexican in this Republic except our old Prefect

Miss Cecelia says that if the girls now on hand are all getting married
there is a new lot coming on, please say to her that I do not like children
and that the suckling brats may hang at their Mammy's breasts — for I'll
[have] none of them. And poor Belcher is married at last purely a marriage
of convenience, well I doubt not he has taken the wisest course, Matrimony
is at best but a lottery and it is about as well to "go it blind" as any other
way. Love, and dying &ᶜ will do very well for school girls and old men, but
will not pass muster with any one in their sober senses. And all my loves
have proved faithless and when I get back I'll have to commence anew again.
I'll be dogged if I do. I'll buck up to Joe MᶜGoffin and if she says yes the way
we'll toddle back to this place again will be a caution. Sophy & Charley Tracy,
confound the brats they are neither of them old enough by 5 years, why
I'me older than Charley myself and the Lord knows I'me nothing but a boy
— his mother ought to have switched him & spanked the gal.¹³⁴

There was a fine fight 60 miles below here a few days since but which
I did not witness, as being out in the country I did not get here in time to
go down. The Mexicans fought well and had they been accustomed to the
use of fire arms would have killed ½ Genˡ Price's army. Price has taken the
laurels from Doniphan's brow and very deservedly. he marched from El Paso
to this place in 7 days (exactly 12 days less than was employed upon the
same trip by D[oniphan]) arriving here at 12 oclock at night and left the next
morning at 9 oclock in pursuit of Genˡ Trias army which he overtook that
night 60 miles below¹³⁵

We all hope peace will not be made until the U.S. [can] include this state
as well as New Mexico and we think the prospect for further continuance of
the war is good as we believe it will be impossible for the President to get
the Congress assembled upon a peace project every one believing that the
war is a benefit in place of an injury to the Republic. Tell Ellen I am glad to
hear she is getting on so well, and calculate young Wᵐ will be about 3 months
old upon my return home To the Genˡ you may say in this package he will
find an answer to all the letters & messages I have received from him and
furthermore that he may go to thunder. Give my love to all the family both
black and white and hoping to be with you in a month or two I remain
your affe Bro Wᵐ

Tell Geo Doan¹³⁶ that we are to have a nice little hanging spree in a few
days. 2 of the murderers of Mr Aull the other 2 got away.

Tell Cush B. she may go to thunder and that she needn't trouble herself making brandy peaches, for I'll not eat a single one of them nor any thing else she has touched a hand to.

Chihuahua March 31 de 1848

My dearest Sue

I have received a number of letters from you by various persons who came recently from Santa Fe along with the Army.

From the alarming accounts of the numerous marriages which have recently taken place and the number yet on the tapis [?] I am inclined to think that unless a new importation of young demoiselles [?] is made, there must be a scarcity of the single sisterhood equal to the late dearth of provision, in Ireland.

It is consoling to us here to know that you are all so well employed at home and in apparently such good spirits for I have no desponding letters yet from you except some written a short time before Mr Barney's arrival. And now that every thing is over I will confess that we have occasionally been in a little danger from our good friends the Mexicans and we were over joyed when Genl Price made his appearance in our city. Our valiant Governor General Trias did not fancy fighting Genl P. and so took the high road for the south as soon as he heard that the U.S. army was actually coming

Genl Price by making forced marches which are almost unparalleled, overtook Trias about 55 miles below and chased the latter into the town of Santa Cruz de Rosales where he fortified himself. The American force immediately began besieging the Mexicans who would not come out to fight the yankees, as there were about three hundred yankees and *only eight hundred* Mexicans with 8 pieces of artillery. The siege continued several days until the American artillery arrived when the ball opened and the Mexicans had to dance the same tune that they have practised at all other fandangoes of the kind. The fight commensed early in the morning with artillery firing on both sides, making the mud bricks fly about pretty lively and so continued during the greater part of the day — in the evening, the firing from town keeping up about as brisk as ever Genl Price got tired of that sort of work and dismounting his men charged up to the walls and drove out the Mexicans with carbines and sabres. Genl Trias and all the officers were made prisoners

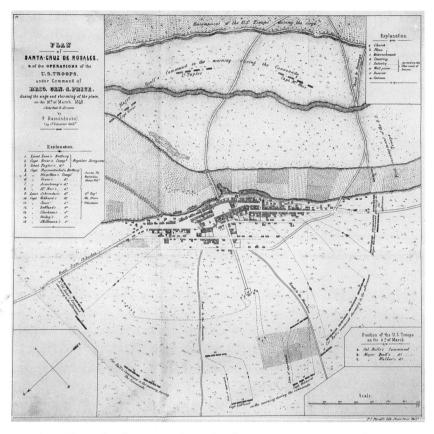

Plan of the Battle of Santa Cruz de Rosales, from H.R. Ex. Doc. No. 1, 30th Cong., 2nd sess. (Serial 537). Edward James Glasgow witnessed this engagement of March 16, 1848. (Courtesy of Colorado College Library, Special Collections.)

and a great many soldiers all of whom were immediately set at liberty on parole.[137] Every thing is now perfectly tranquil and as an armistice has been signed in Mexico I suppose there will be no more fighting for the present.[138] I do not believe that there will be any peace however for the Mexicans have not yet been whipped half as much as they require to be for this purpose. I heartily wish our country would either make peace or war. I care little which, but they are not fit to carry on a war and the Mexicans invariably beat [best?] them in diplomacy so that poor Bro Johnathan will be a greater sufferer in the end than Mexico.

As I had never seen but one small sample of a battle I went down to Santa Cruz and had a good chance to gratify my curiosity.

I left here late the day before the Action and rode all night, arriving at Santa Cruz just before day light. The battle began soon after and the firing was kept up incessantly for about three hours, when there was a cessation of a couple of hours owing to our men being ordered to assemble together to repulse a number of lancers who were erroneously stated to be charging from a wood near town.

I took advantage of this quiet "spell" to take a siesta, having been on horseback all the night before — and I had been asleep about an hour when I was awaked by a man calling out, "Lord God doctor what are you doing" and turning over I perceived the surgeon sawing away at a man's leg, and a short distance off some assistants dressing the stump of another's which had just been cut off. I did'nt feel sleepy again for some time. War is an ugly business, and I could not help thinking when all was over, that this thing of people's killing each other is the greatest nonsense extant. William and I will leave for home in about a month and if any body ever catches me in Chihuahua again I will give them leave to kick me all over town.

I am heartily tired of the whole country. the people are cowardly in the extreme and an old adage says that without courage there can be no truth and without truth there can be no other virtue. The Mexicans have perhaps fewer redeeming traits of character than any other nation; not excepting the Comanches nor the wild Arabs. I am now winding up my business — selling off and preparing to start, I will remain here a few weeks to close up as far as possible and then I will leave Connelly to settle the Balance[139]

Give my love to Ma Pa and all at home whom I do not write to. I will write another note or two before the man goes who takes this to Santa Fe. Always your most afft Bro James

NOTES

1. The Glasgows were camped on the farm of Santa Fe and Chihuahua trader James Wiley Magoffin. Judge Joseph Magoffin, a son of James Wiley, wrote in a letter to William E. Connelley that "in 1844 my father and family . . . left Chihuahua for the States, and my father settled near Independence, Missouri. He bought a farm there." William E. Connelley, *War with Mexico, 1846–1847: Doniphan's Expedition and the Conquest of New Mexico and California* (Kansas City: Bryant & Douglas Book and Stationery Co., 1907), 197, n. 39½. At my request, Independence historian Pauline Fowler diligently searched the land records of Jackson County and located the Magoffin farm site. It was situated astride the road that led from Blue Mills Landing, on the Missouri River, to Independence in sections 19 and 20 of Township 50 North, Range 31 West. The farm had previously

belonged to Harmon Gregg, father of Santa Fe trader Josiah Gregg, and it was from Gregg's widow and children that Magoffin began to acquire the estate in 1843. Four years later, after a total expense of $5,500, Magoffin became the sole owner of the 258.37-acre tract. In the 1850 census for Jackson County, Magoffin is listed as a "farmer" with four slaves and real estate valued at $6,000. The next year he sold the farm to his brother, Samuel Magoffin. Samuel and his wife, Susan Shelby, retained the farm until October 1852. Pauline S. Fowler, "History of Home and Lands of James W(iley) Magoffin and Wife, Dolores, in Jackson County, Missouri," unpublished paper, October 1989; and *Jackson County, Missouri: Census of 1850*, abstracted by Hattie E. Poppino (Kansas City: Hattie E. Poppino, 1959), 81.

2.   "The General" was apparently a nickname bestowed upon George Rogers Hancock Clark by the Glasgows. G.R.H. Clark, brother-in-law to the Glasgows, was a son of William Clark and thus a nephew of General George Rogers Clark of revolutionary war fame. G.R.H. Clark married Eleanor Ann Glasgow on March 31, 1841. Frederic L. Billon, *Annals of St. Louis in Its Territorial Days from 1804 to 1821* (1888; reprint ed., New York: Arno Press, 1971), 305. G.R.H. Clark was accompanying the Glasgows on this trip for health and sport.

3.   General Zachary Taylor had fought the battles of Palo Alto and Resaca de la Palma on May 8 and 9, respectively. See Justin H. Smith, *The War with Mexico*, 2 vols. (New York: Macmillan, 1919).

4.   This was Blue Mills Landing, known at that time as Owens Landing for trader Samuel C. Owens. Another river landing used by Southwest traders was Upper Independence or Wayne City Landing, further upstream and closer to Independence. Pauline Fowler to Mark L. Gardner, October 26, 1989. For detailed maps of the routes between the Missouri River landings and Independence see Gregory M. Franzwa, *Maps of the Santa Fe Trail* (St. Louis: Patrice Press, 1989).

5.   Ferguson's name appears on the petition submitted by the merchants at Valverde to Captain Walton dated December 9, 1846, and published in U.S. Congress, House, *Report on the Petition of Manuel X. Harmony* (hereinafter cited as Harmony Report), H.R. Rep. 458, 30th Cong., 1st sess., 1848 (Serial 525), 46–48. He is possibly the subject of the portrait found in the sketchbook of Lieutenant James Abert labeled "Ferguisson." (This portrait is reproduced in this book) Louise Barry's *The Beginning of the West: Annals of the Kansas Gateway to the American West, 1540–1854* (Topeka: Kansas State Historical Society, 1972) contains three references to Alexander C. Ferguson (pp. 530, 590, and 1149). On p. 1149 Barry quotes the 1853 diary of Celinda E. Hines in which "Mr. Ferguson, a Santa Fe trader," is mentioned and described as having "lived ten years in Mexico and crossed the plains six times." On December 22, 1857, he applied for bounty land based on his service in the Traders Battalion. According to his claim, he was thirty-eight years old and a resident of Natchez, Mississippi. He stated that he had served as a private in Captain Edward James Glasgow's company. Bounty Land File (BLF) 76953-160-55, Bureau of Pensions Correspondence and Pension and Bounty Land Case Files, Records of the Veterans Administration, Record Group (RG) 15, National Archives (NA). Another claim for bounty land, most likely fraudulent, exists for Alexander C. Ferguson; that claim is dated Santa Fe, April 2, 1858, and is included in the above file. Alexander C. Ferguson is found in the 1860 census for Natchez, Mississippi, as a forty-one-year-old banker, married, with real estate valued at $12,500 and a personal estate worth $26,000. His birthplace is given as Pennsylvania. Ferguson appears to have died sometime between July 21, 1866, when he executed a will, and February 28, 1867, when his will was recorded in the probate court of Adams County, Mississippi, and he is referred to as deceased. Eight U.S. Census, Adams County, City of Natchez, Mississippi, 41; and Will of Alexander

C. Ferguson, Will Book 3, 304–305, Adams County Probate Records, Natchez, Mississippi.

6. William is referring to Josiah Gregg's *Commerce of the Prairies; or, the Journal of a Santa Fe Trader, During Eight Expeditions Across the Great Western Prairies, and a Residence of Nearly Nine Years in Northern Mexico,* 2 vols. (New York: Henry G. Langley, 1844; reprint, ed. Max L. Moorhead, Norman: University of Oklahoma Press, 1954).

7. Although James Magoffin had a son named Joseph, additional references in the Glasgow letters indicate that William is referring to young Josephine Magoffin, a daughter of James. She, along with her sister Ursula, was living temporarily at the Visitation Convent in St. Louis under the guardianship of James Harrison. Connelley, *Doniphan's Expedition*, 197, n. 39½.

8. This was probably the Reverend Frederick F. Peake, who resided in Howard and Cooper counties from 1836 or earlier to 1839, when he moved to St. Louis and served at Christ Church. Peake may have contemplated accompanying the Glasgows to the Southwest for health reasons, as he is reported to have moved to Pensacola, Florida, shortly thereafter "in search of his health." Peake died there in 1849. *History of Howard and Chariton Counties, Missouri* (St. Louis: National Historical Company, 1883), 350.

9. Most of the information known about Harmony comes from the claim he submitted to the U.S. government shortly after his return from Mexico. Although a U.S. citizen, Harmony was a native of Spain and carried Spanish passports on this trip. According to his sworn statement of January 26, 1848, he had "resided in the city of New York for the last twenty years, and . . . [had] been a citizen of the United States for the last ten years." This was apparently his first trip to New Mexico. Harmony Report, 11 and 28; and St. Louis *Weekly Reveille*, September 14, 1846. Manuel X. Harmony, along with Peter Harmony, Leonard S. Suarez, Bernard Grahm and John Garcia, is listed in *The New York City Co-Partnership Directory,* for 1844 & 1845 (New York: John Dogett, Jr., 1844), 18, as a member of the shipping and commission firm of P. Harmony's Nephews & Co., located at 63½ Broadway. This firm imported goods for a number of "Mexican Santa Fe traders" in 1846 and continued to serve Hispanic merchants as agents, commission merchants, and bankers for several decades following the Mexican War. Harmony withdrew from this firm, however, on January 1, 1846, and appears to have been representing only his own interests on this particular trading venture. Harmony Report, 62; credit reports on P. Harmony's Nephews & Co. in New York City (NYC), vol. 365, 153 and 184, NYC, vol. 349, 916, 1100 sub p. 22 and 1100 sub p. 100; all in R. G. Dun & Co. Coll., Baker Library, Harvard University Graduate School of Business Administration (BLHBS); and Announcement of P. Harmony's Nephews & Co., New York, January 1, 1846, Manuel Alvarez Papers, reel 1, frame 523, New Mexico State Records Center and Archives, Santa Fe (SRCA). Like the other merchants on the trail that year, Harmony suffered numerous detentions by the U.S. forces in Mexico. He claims that while at El Paso in February 1847, he had decided to return north to New Mexico (some of Doniphan's soldiers reported that he "wanted to remain behind until our battle at Chihuahua and then come in a great friend to the victors"). Doniphan took armed possession of his train, however, and forced him to follow in the rear of the army. At Chihuahua he accepted back his wagons and goods under protest but then "abandoned" them to Doniphan shortly before he evacuated the city with his troops. Harmony had demanded that as his goods had been brought there against his will that Donipan should either protect them or "pay a reasonable and fair price for them." Back in the States, Harmony submitted a petition to the U.S. government requesting restitution to the amount of $102,956.89, stating that "by reason and consequence of the acts of the troops of the United States, his trading expedition has been utterly broken up, his expenditures rendered useless,

and his goods and merchandise wholly lost to him." The House Committee of Claims reported "a bill for the relief of the petitioner." Harmony Report, 6–12, 17–19, and 24–28; and M. B. Edwards in Abraham Robinson Johnston, Marcellus Ball Edwards, and Philip Gooch Ferguson, *Marching with the Army of the West, 1846–1848*, ed. Ralph P. Bieber, Southwest Historical Series, vol. 4 (Glendale, Calif.: Arthur H. Clark, 1936), 249–250. I have been unable to locate any evidence of this bill, and it may be that Harmony took action in the courts. Mercantile Agency reports for P. Harmony's Nephews & Co. reveal that a nephew, "not the firm," received a "verdict," the result of a suit against a "Captn in the U.S. Army for seizing wagons & g[oo]ds.," in his favor for 50 to 100 thousand dollars. See NYC, vol. 365, 184, R. G. Dun & Co. Coll., BLHBS.

10. By his own statement, Harmony left Independence with fourteen wagons, two of which were "chartered." Harmony Report, 7.

11. This is probably Francis (or Frank) McManus (or Macmanus), although a Thomas Macmanus was also on this expedition. Max L. Moorhead, based on information he found in Francis McManus's *carta de seguridad* (located in the papers of the Consulate General, Mexico, in the National Archives), gives his birthdate as about 1816. Max L. Moorhead states that McManus "was a Chihuahua trader from at least 1842 to 1847" (*New Mexico's Royal Road: Trade and Travel on the Chihuahua Trail* [Norman: Univeristy of Oklahoma Press, 1958], 157, n. 11). Louise Barry, in *Beginning of the West*, 1229, has a reference to McManus on the Santa Fe Trail as late as 1854. The Mercantile Agency has a report from 1871 for McManus Bro^s (Frank and George) of Chihuahua, dealers in general merchandise. According to this report, the brothers were from Pennsylvania and had been in business in Chihuahua for the past twenty-five years. Frank's age was given as fifty-five and George's as forty-five. Both were married. The Mercantile Agency estimated the "Reality of each party [at] One Million dollars." Another report exists on a McManus & Sons, Chihuahua bankers, dated May 6, 1881. No information is given, however, on the principals of this firm. New Mexico, vol. 1, 393; and Foreign Countries, vol. 2, 65; both in R. G. Dun & Co. Coll., BLHBS. Thomas Macmanus, possibly another brother of Frank, was one of the merchants who signed a petition to Captain Walton dated December 9, 1846 (his name is listed as "Thos. F. Macmaners"). He served as adjutant in the Traders Battalion. The portrait sketch by Lieutenant Abert labeled "McManus," apparently done at Valverde in December of 1846, is probably Thomas, as Frank was then being held in Chihuahua. (Abert's sketch is reproduced in this book.) Harmony Report, 48; and deposition of Edward J. Glasgow and William H. Glasgow, December 18, 1858, in Christopher C. Branham BLF 85000-160-55, RG 15, NA.

12. Probably Jefferson Kearny Clark, one of two sons from William Clark's second marriage and a half brother to George Rogers Hancock Clark. Jefferson Kearny Clark married Mary Susan Glasgow, sister of the Glasgow brothers, on August 8, 1849. Billon, *Annals*, 305.

13. Possibly Sophia Morton, the daughter of George Morton of St. Louis. Billon, *Annals*, 331.

14. This was Lucretia Beaumont (1827–1850), the youngest daughter of Dr. William Beaumont and his wife, Deborah. She married Herman Canfield on February 20, 1849, and died almost a year later, evidently from the effects of childbirth. See Mrs. Max W. Myer, "Sarah Beaumont: Her Life and Loves," *Bulletin of the Missouri Historical Society* 17 (October 1960):16–44.

15. This was Miss Mary Jane Hynes, daughter of a Colonel Andrew Hynes of Nashville, Tennessee. She wed St. Louis merchant Phocion R. McCreery of the wholesale dry goods firm of Crow, McCreery & Barksdale on October 8, 1846, at Nashville. William refers to this wedding in his later letters. Silas Emmett Lucas, Jr., ed., *Marriages from Early Tennessee*

Newspapers, 1794–1851 (Easley, S.C.: Southern Historical Press, 1978), 300; and *Green's Saint Louis Directory for 1847* (St. Louis: James Green, and Cathcart & Prescott, 1847), 123.

16.   Laura R. Mitchell, a cousin of the Glasgows.

17.   Miss Patsey (or Patsy) is wonderfully described by William Clark Kennerly, *Persimmon Hill: A Narrative of Old St. Louis and the Far West* (Norman: University of Oklahoma Press, 1948), 73–74:

> In some families a spinster friend or relative, a Miss Puss or Miss Patsy, would arrive for a short visit and remain for a lifetime, mothering the whole household, looking after the servants, and keeping an eye upon the older children when their mother was bringing more of them into the world.
>
> This good angel in the Glasgow family was Miss Patsy Jones, but none of the second or third generation even knew her last name. Miss Patsy was tall and very thin, her narrow face framed on either side by three white corkscrew curls and topped by a frilled lace cap with a little lavender bow. She was inherited by Jeff's wife, Susan Glasgow Clark, who gave her tender care until her death at ninety-two. In their home she lived, watering the plants in the Victorian flower stand, feeding the canary birds and the parrot, and carrying on animated conversations with "pretty Polly," mostly about a cracker.

18.   A deed of trust for October 1846 lists Sylvia as one of four slaves owned by William Glasgow, Sr., and his wife, Sarah. Sylvia is described as "aged about fifty Six years" and "Valued at One hundred dollars." Deed of Trust of William and Sarah Glasgow, Deed Book D^4, 358, Recorder of Deeds, St. Louis City Hall, St. Louis, Missouri.

19.   Edwin Bryant visited Independence that same May and described it as

> situated about six miles from the Missouri river, on the southern, or left-hand side as you ascend it. . . . Its population is about one thousand; and, at this season, every man seems to be actively and profitably employed. It has been for some years the principal outfitting point for the Santa Fe traders, and will probably so continue. Many of the houses around the public square are constructed of brick, but the majority of the buildings are frames. (Bryant, *What I Saw in California* [1848; reprint ed., Minneapolis: Ross & Haines, 1967], 13)

For a good account of the role Independence played in the Mexican or Santa Fe trade, see Eugene T. Wells, "The Growth of Independence, Missouri, 1827–1850," *Bulletin of the Missouri Historical Society* 16 (October 1959).

20.   A correspondent to the St. Louis *Republican* provided a similar description of the town in his letter dated "Independence, Mo., May 16, 1846":

> Since my last, the scene has entirely changed in our town. Instead of a great bustle of emigrants for Oregon and California, with their wagons crowding our streets, laying in their outfits for their journey across the plains, we have a great crowd of Mexicans and traders to Santa Fe and Chihuahua. It is supposed that we have at least two hundred Mexicans in the town and vicinity, at this time. . . . About forty wagons have left for Santa Fe and Chihuahua this week; and others are preparing to leave shortly. The late war news from Mexico does not seem to intimidate the traders. They are determined to push ahead, let what will turn up.

The letter was reprinted in *Niles' National Register,* June 6, 1846.

21.   Edward James Glasgow was called James by family members and also used that name himself until later years.

22.   Louise Barry notes that on October 3 and 4, 1846, a "Charles Ferguson, of Philadelphia," was among a group of men arriving in Independence from Santa Fe. They had left New

Mexico on September 9. Barry, *Beginning of the West*, 649. Ferguson, like several others that year, may have been accompanying the Glasgow train for purposes of recreation alone. What, if any, relationship he had with trader Alexander C. Ferguson I have been unable to determine. Yet Alexander was born in Pennsylvania (see note 5 above) and may still have resided there at the time of this trip. A survey of Philadelphia city directories from the mid-1840s failed to turn up a Charles Ferguson.

23. The deed of trust cited in note 18 above lists "a negro woman named Agnes aged about thirty years, Valued at Three hundred dollars" as the property of William and Sarah Glasgow.

24. Mr. Fe (or Fay), was identified simply as "an Italian" in an 1846 newspaper article published in the St. Louis *Union*. Dale Morgan, *Overland in 1846: Diaries and Letters of the California-Oregon Trail*, 2 vols. (Georgetown, Calif.: Talisman Press, 1963), 2:651–654. Fe was another one of the adventurers who accompanied the Glasgows. See notes 55 and 60 below.

25. William may be referring to George T. Howard's party, which included seven U.S. dragoons and approximately sixteen or seventeen Shawnee and Delaware Indians. Howard had been ordered to Santa Fe by Secretary of War William L. Marcy to alert the American traders on the trail and in New Mexico of the outbreak of the war. He left from near the Missouri border about June 1. Barry, *Beginning of the West*, 590; and Bieber's introduction in George R. Gibson, *Journal of a Soldier Under Kearny and Doniphan, 1846–1847*, ed. Ralph P. Bieber, Southwest Historical Series, vol. 3 (Glendale, Calif.: Arthur H. Clark, 1935), 28–29.

26. Cornelius Davy was born in Ireland about 1792. He was a merchant traveling the Santa Fe Trail from 1846, or slightly earlier, to 1851, when he died in Chihuahua. The 1850 federal census for Jackson County lists Davy as a resident of Blue Township with real estate valued at $15,000. His will, dated Chihuahua, September 26, 1851, is recorded in Record Book "GI" of the Office of the Probate Clerk of Jackson County. Trader David Waldo, also of Jackson County, was named as one of his executors. In 1868 a daughter of Davy, Cornelia, married Peter Connelly, son of Chihuahua trader Henry Connelly. Barry, *Beginning of the West*, 491, 956; Poppino, *Jackson County Census*, 33; Nadine Hodges and Mrs. Howard W. Woodruff, comps., "Jackson County, Missouri, Abstracts of Wills & Administrations 1849–1854" in *Missouri Pioneers: County and Genealogical Records*, (1969), 4:12; and Connelley, *Doniphan's Expedition*, 280, n. 1.

27. Manlius Branham (1819–1895) is listed in the 1850 census for Boone County, Missouri, as having been born in Kentucky. In 1860 he applied for bounty land based on his service in the Traders Battalion. According to his claim, he was forty years old and a resident of St. Louis. His brother Christopher Columbus Branham (1816–1890), a resident of Platte City, Missouri, was also a trader on this trip. Christopher applied for bounty land in 1858. His application gives his age as forty-one and his residence as Weston, Missouri. Both brothers apparently had different partners on this 1846 trip. A newspaper article that reported on the traders at Pawnee Fork listed the firms of Branham & Hickman and Branham & McCausland. Mark McCausland was a brother-in-law to the Branhams and a business partner of Christopher. As of 1934, Manlius and Christopher were both buried in Columbia Cemetery on West Broadway in Columbia, Missouri. Barry, *Beginning of the West*, 700; Seventh U.S. Census for Boone County, Missouri, District 8, 380; Manlius Branham BLF 95525-160-55 and Christopher C. Branham BLF 85000-160-55, RG 15, NA; St. Louis *Missouri Republican*, August 3, 1846; Columbia *Missouri Statesman*, December 24, 1890; and Mrs. E. E. Evans and Mrs. J. Frank Thompson, *Tombstone Records of Boone County, Missouri* (Columbia: Mrs. E. E. Evans & Mrs. J. Frank Thompson, 1934), 23 and 24.

28. This is derived from the Spanish, *mayordomo*. In a glossary of "Spanish or Hispano-Mexican words" included in the second edition of Gregg's *Commerce of the Prairies, mayordomo* is defined as "overseer." William's "Major domo" is actually his wagonmaster. Ruben Cobos, *A Dictionary of New Mexico and Southern Colorado Spanish* (Santa Fe: Museum of New Mexico Press, 1983), 108; Gregg, *Commerce of the Prairies*, 443.

29. Samuel C. Owens (1800–1847) was a respected merchant and Southwest trader of Independence, Missouri. A Kentuckian by birth, he was described by contemporary John C. McCoy as "a man of generous impulses — with a well cultivated mind — endowed with good common Sense & pleasing manners." Owens first entered the mercantile business at Independence in 1827 as a manager for a store belonging to James Aull of Lexington and eventually rose to become the sole proprietor of this same business. In 1846 he formed a partnership with his old employer to participate in the Mexican trade. They operated under the firm name of Owens & Aull. McCoy, "Early History of Col Sam¹ C Owens & James Aull," copy in the Jackson County Historical Society Archives, Independence, Missouri; James Josiah Webb, *Adventures in the Santa Fe Trade, 1844–1847*, ed. Ralph P. Bieber, Southwest Historical Series, vol. 1 (Glendale, Calif.: Arthur H. Clark, 1931), 42, n. 53; and Susan Shelby Magoffin, *Down the Santa Fe Trail and into Mexico, 1846–1847*, ed. Stella M. Drumm (New Haven: Yale University Press, 1926), 220, n. 91.

30. Shortly after William wrote of this incident it became apparent to the authorities and the community that John H. Harper had fabricated the initial story of a dispute over a game of cards and that the real reason for the killing was a supposed love affair that had developed between William Wirt Meredith and Harper's wife, Fanny Owens, the daughter of trader Samuel C. Owens. After an interesting escape from the law (aided by Fanny) and subsequent capture, Harper was tried for murder and acquitted in November 1847. One of his defense lawyers was none other than Colonel A. W. Doniphan, who had returned to Missouri from his Mexican War adventures in July of that year. Alfred S. Waugh, "Desultory Wanderings in the Years 1845–46," ed. John F. McDermott, *Bulletin of the Missouri Historical Society* 7 (January 1951):257–259; and Connelley, *Doniphan's Expedition*, 26–29. The other members of Meredith's party were two gentlemen by the name of Hoffman and Morris. Bryant, *What I Saw in California*, 17–18.

31. Mary Susan Ferguson was a daughter of John H. Gay and a cousin of the Glasgows. See note 57 below.

32. This was Jesse Barnes, who acquired property in sections 7, 8, 17, and 18 of Township 48 North, Range 32 West in March and October 1844. Barnes's residence was apparently located along the Santa Fe Trail in the southwest quarter of Section 8. Mrs. John Vineyard, ed., *Original Land Entries of Jackson County, Missouri* (Mrs. John Vineyard, 1971), 31; Sylvia D. Mooney, "Cave Spring: Historic Landmark on the Santa Fe Trail," *Wagon Tracks* 3 (November 1988):6; and Pauline Fowler to Mark L. Gardner, October 26, 1989. In 1850 Barnes was a sixty-four-year-old farmer with real estate valued at $12,000. He was at that time living in the household of his son, Sidney. Poppino, *Jackson County Census*, 5.

33. Susan Magoffin (*Down the Santa Fe Trail*, 2) writes in her diary that "the residence of Mr. Barns" was "some ten miles this side of that place [Independence]."

34. The Big Blue River is a tributary of the Missouri that runs in a northerly direction through the western portion of Jackson County.

35. The ford of the Big Blue River used by the traders was just north of present-day Red Bridge Road near Minor Park in the southern part of Kansas City, Missouri. See Map 15 in Franzwa, *Maps of the Santa Fe Trail*, where the ford is designated as Red Bridge Crossing;

and Mrs. Max A. Christopher, "Red Bridge," in *Vital Historical Records of Jackson County, Missouri* (Kansas City: Daughters of the American Revolution, Kansas City Chapter, 1934), 448.

36. William M. McPherson (1813–1872) came to St. Louis as a lawyer in 1841. He was apparently an in-law of the Glasgows, marrying a Mary A. Mitchell in 1843. Mary Mitchell may have been a sister of Laura R. Mitchell, who is mentioned in the Glasgow letters as a cousin (the 1850 census shows Laura and her husband, James H.P. Blackwood, living in the household of William McPherson). William McPherson and his wife were among the "select guests" at the fiftieth wedding anniversary of Mr. and Mrs. William Glasgow, Sr. The 1850 census placed the value of McPherson's real eastate at $80,000. In that same year, he was serving as a state representative. J. Thomas Scharf, *History of St. Louis City and County*, 2 vols. (Philadelphia: Louis H. Everts & Co., 1883), 2:1490; Seventh U.S. Census, City of St. Louis, Missouri, 3rd Ward, 297; and Thomas D. Shriver, comp., *Missouri General Assembly, 1812–1976* (Jefferson City: Office of Secretary of State, 1976), 60.

37. I have been unable to learn the identity of the unfortunate "cook." According to F. A. Wislizenus (*Memoir of a Tour to Northern Mexico, Connected with Colonel Doniphan's Expedition in 1846 and 1847* [1848; reprint ed., Albuquerque: Calvin Horn Publisher, 1969], 8 and 10), the man was killed in the latter part of May while accompanying the Missouri-bound Bent, St. Vrain & Co. train of twenty-two wagons. Lewis Garrard (*Wah-to-yah and the Taos Trail* [1850; reprint ed., Norman: University of Oklahoma Press, 1955], 28) tells us that he was killed when "imprudently going too far in advance of the train . . . [he] was charged upon and scalped by the Pawnees, in sight of his companions. Two others of the company had to run for it — just escaping." Louise Barry, citing the *Journal of William H. Richardson*, believes that the victim may have been R. T. Ross. Richardson came across Ross's grave near Pawnee Fork in September 1846. Barry, *Beginning of the West*, 589.

38. The mouth of Pawnee Fork, a tributary of the Arkansas River, is at present-day Larned, Kansas (see Map 38 in Franzwa, *Maps of the Santa Fe Trail*). Josiah Gregg estimated that it was approximately 303 miles from Independence (*Commerce of the Prairies*, 217). Wislizenus described the area a month before the Glasgows' arrival there as "an excellent camp. The short buffalo grass is rather dry, as everywhere else now, but there is plenty of timber, and fine running water, containing fish." *Memoir of a Tour to Northern Mexico*, 10.

39. Captain Benjamin D. Moore with two companies of U.S. dragoons had been sent down the trail on June 5 to overtake the caravan of trader Albert Speyer, which was reported to be carrying arms and ammunition for the Mexicans (see Part III, note 10). Moore and his detachment had traveled all the way to the crossing of the Arkansas in pursuit of Speyer, but they were unable to overtake him. The dragoons then backtraced to Pawnee Fork, approximately 89 miles distant according to Gregg, where the Glasgows found them. Moore had orders to halt all traders he encountered until Kearny could arrive. Letter of Benjamin Moore dated Pawnee Fork, July 10, 1846, in St. Louis *Weekly Reveille*, August 17, 1846; S. W. Kearny to W. L. Marcy, Washington, January 10, 1848, in Harmony Report, 49–50; St. Louis *Weekly Reveille*, June 15, 1846; and St. Louis *Missouri Republican*, August 3, 1846.

40. Captain Benjamin Moore wrote from Pawnee Fork that

> Among the traders, and those accompanying them, I have found some polite and courteous gentlemen; amateurs; some travelling for the sake of locomotion, some for pleasure, and some in the pursuit of health. Among the latter I have met an old friend, George R. Clark, of St. Louis. I am glad to say, his health is much improved. I have taken him into my mess, and by the time he reaches the base of the mountains,

and enjoys the bracing air, so celebrated for its efficacious influence in pulmonary and dyspeptic affections, I hope to see him perfectly well, and able to kill and butcher two buffalos, instead of one, (he mastered *one* a few days ago, on a hunt with me.) Letter of Benjamin D. Moore, Pawnee Fork, July 10, 1846, in St. Louis *Weekly Reveille,* August 17, 1846.

41. I have found no evidence of Josephine Magoffin's presence on the trail that year. It is probable that the outbreak of the war and James Magoffin's subsequent agreement with President James Polk to assist the Army of the West to obtain a "bloodless possession" of New Mexico changed whatever plans he may have had for his daughter. See "The Magoffin Papers," in Ralph Emerson Twitchell, *The Story of the Conquest of Santa Fe, New Mexico, and the Building of Old Fort Marcy, A.D.* 1846, Historical Society of New Mexico Publication No. 24 (Santa Fe: Historical Society of New Mexico, 1923).

42. Susan Shelby Magoffin was the nineteen-year-old wife of trader Samuel Magoffin, brother of James. Susan accompanied her husband down the trail that year and kept a diary of the trip that was published in 1926 under the title *Down the Santa Fe Trail and into Mexico.* It has since become a trail classic and gone through numerous reprintings. The diary covers Susan's experiences from June 1846 to September 1847, during which time she traveled with her husband's caravan to Chihuahua and beyond. It is an excellent companion to the writings of the Glasgow brothers.

43. A letter from the traders' camp written on the same day as William's and published in the St. Louis *Missouri Republican* of August 3, 1846, identifies the volunteer companies as those from Jackson and Clay counties, Missouri. These were companies A and C, respectively, of the First Regiment Missouri Mounted Volunteers commanded by Colonel Alexander W. Doniphan. The First Regiment, mustered into service at Fort Leavenworth during the month of June, consisted of eight companies totaling 856 men and formed the larger part of Kearny's Army of the West. Connelley, *Doniphan's Expedition,* 132–134.

44. The same letter cited in *ibid.* identifies the traders at Pawnee Fork on July 9 as being "Owens & Aull, Branham & Hickman, Branham & McCausland, F. MacManus, C. Davis [Davy], Bray, Ewing & Co., S. Magoffin, E. Leitensdorfer & Co., M. X. Harmony, and the Glasgows."

45. Bent's Fort was established in 1833 as a private trading post by Bent, St. Vrain & Co., Santa Fe and Indian traders. It was located on the north side of the Arkansas River approximately 6 miles northeast of present-day La Junta, Colorado. Kearny used the fort as a rendezvous point for the different components of his Army of the West. See David Lavender, *Bent's Fort* (Garden City, N.Y.: Doubleday, 1954).

46. This was probably Salvador Armijo, who evidently traveled to Independence in spring 1846. James and Robert Aull, "Letters of James and Robert Aull," ed. Ralph P. Bieber, *Missouri Historical Society Collections* 5 (1928), 292.

47. Don Pio Sambrano is briefly mentioned in the Report of the Citizens of New Mexico to the President of Mexico, Santa Fe, September 26, 1846, and described as "a merchant from Chihuahua." Max L. Moorhead, ed., "Notes and Documents," *New Mexico Historical Review* 26 (January 1951): 71. See also Barry, *Beginning of the West,* 580, where he is identified as Peo Semirane.

48. Although Francisco Elguea appears to have been heavily involved in the Chihuahua trade, very little is know of his background. Moorhead identifies him in his *Royal Road,* 166, simply as "a Spanish merchant of Chihuahua."

49. It is evident from documents in the Harmony Report that shortly after the outbreak of the war with Mexico, the U.S. secretary of the Treasury issued a circular halting the

exportation of goods to the Mexican ports, including Santa Fe and Chihuahua. Although many traders were already on the Missouri border making preparations to depart, there were several Mexican traders dealing with the firm of P. Harmony's Nephews & Co. in New York City who had not yet received their merchandise. The custom house at that port would not enter the goods for exportation to Santa Fe that P. Harmony's Nephews & Co. had imported for the traders. The firm presented its case to the secretary in a letter of May 30, 1846, stating that the goods had been purchased and were in the process of being imported, "in perfect good faith," before hostilities began, and that as the goods were selected specifically for the Mexican market, it would be "ruinous" if they were forced to send them somewhere else or had to keep them in New York. The secretary subsequently made a special allowance for these goods, and others consigned to the Philadelphia firm of Flemming & Marshall, to continue on their way to Mexico. Elguea's goods were probably among those temporarily detained, for he did go down the trail that year. Harmony Report, 46–47 and 62–66; and St. Louis *Weekley Reveille,* July 6, 1846.

50.   George Doan was the son of St. Louis merchant J. P. Doan of the wholesale dry goods firm of Doan, King & Co. and a partner in the Mexican trade with James Josiah Webb. Webb explains that Doan "was born and lived a few years of his early life in one of the British West Indies, and got a British passport from the consul at New Orleans." Doan was not at the traders' camp. He and Webb had left Independence on May 9, their train subsequently eluding the dragoons under Moore and entering Santa Fe closely behind the Speyer caravan. While in Santa Fe, Doan was injured from a rock thrown by an unknown assailant and was forced to remain there a short time to recover while Webb, in company with Albert Speyer, continued toward Chihuahua with their goods. Webb, *Adventures in the Santa Fe Trade,* 28, 175, 179–181, and 186–187.

51.   Meriwether Lewis Clark (1809–1881) was the first child of William and Julia Hancock Clark and a graduate of West Point. Before the Mexican War he worked as an architect and civil engineer in St. Louis and in 1836 was a member of the Missouri House of Representatives. From 1848 to 1853, Clark was Missouri's U.S. surveyor general. He moved to Kentucky about 1856 and after the outbreak of the Civil War served as a colonel in the Confederate States Army. During the Mexican War, Clark was a major commanding the volunteer light artillery battalion that had been raised in St. Louis. His battalion arrived in the vicinity of Bent's Fort on July 29. William Hyde and Howard L. Conard, eds., *Encyclopedia of the History of St. Louis,* 4 vols. (St. Louis: Southern History Company, 1899), 1:399; George W. Cullum, *Biographical Register of the Officers and Graduates of the U.S. Military Academy at West Point, N.Y., from Its Establishment, in 1802, to 1890,* vol. 1 (Boston: Houghton, Mifflin & Co., 1891), 459; Shriver, *Missouri General Assembly,* 19; Kennerly, *Persimmon Hill,* 105; Francis B. Heitman, *Historical Register and Dictionary of the United States Army,* 2 vols. (Washington, D.C.: Government Printing Office, 1903), 1:305; V. M. Porter, "A History of Battery 'A' of St. Louis," *Missouri Historical Society Collections* 2 (March 1905):4–5; and Frank S. Edwards, *A Campaign in New Mexico with Colonel Doniphan,* (Philadelphia: Carey and Hart, 1847), 36.

52.   William's Miss Coons was probably young Mary A. Coons, who is listed in the 1850 census as the twenty-year-old daughter (presumably) of Mary A. Coons, age fifty. The elder Coons is recorded as the head of the household and is estimated to be worth $60,000 in real estate. From the 1847 St. Louis city directory we learn that Mary Coons, widow, was living at 26 South Fourth, next to and on the same side of the street as the residence of William Glasgow, Sr., listed as 24 South Fourth. The elder Mary Coons appears to have been a partner in the St. Louis mercantile firm of Coons & Gallagher. She was also the mother of Benjamin Franklin Coons, a Santa Fe trader from 1847 to 1849 and early settler of El Paso, Texas. Seventh U.S. Census, City of St. Louis, Missouri, 3rd Ward, 415; *Green's St. Louis Directory for 1847,* 50 and 78; *Green's St. Louis Directory (No. 1)*

for 1845 (St. Louis: James Green, 1844), 41; and Rex W. Strickland, "Six Who Came to El Paso: Pioneers of the 1840s," *Southwestern Studies* 1 (Fall 1963):13.

53. According to a correspondent of the St. Louis *Weekly Reveille* who was writing from Bent's Fort on July 31, traders Edward Glasgow and Manuel Harmony had left Bent's Fort that day (presumably for Santa Fe) in company with three just-released Mexican "spies" who had been taken prisoner at the fort a few days before. Glasgow and Harmony had obtained Kearny's permission to make the journey, leaving their wagons behind to follow the army. Lieutenant Abraham Johnston's journal, however, only makes mention of Harmony's obtaining permission to travel to Santa Fe. Captain Henry Smith Turner's journal records under the date of August 2 that "Mr. Harmony who started for Santa Fe a few days ago has returned a little alarmed." Again, no mention is made of Edward, nor does Turner explain the cause of Harmony's alarm. If Edward did indeed leave with Harmony, he must have returned with him as well, as he here writes of being with his wagons until they crossed the Raton Mountains. St. Louis *Weekly Reveille*, September 14, 1846; Johnston in *Marching with the Army of the West*, 91; and Henry Smith Turner, *Original Journals of Henry Smith Turner, with Stephen Watts Kearny to New Mexico and California, 1846–1847*, ed. Dwight L. Clarke (Norman: University of Oklahoma Press, 1966), 67.

54. This would be either the small settlement near the junction of the Mora and Sapello rivers known as La Junta (present-day Watrous, New Mexico) or the town of Las Vegas, approximately 17 miles to the southwest. See Robert M. Utley, *Fort Union and the Santa Fe Trail*, Southwestern Studies Series No. 89 (El Paso: Texas Western Press, 1989), 28–29. Frank Edwards stated that the settlement on the Mora River was called the "Lower Moro." Edwards, *A Campaign in New Mexico*, 41.

55. George Rogers Hancock Clark left Bent's Fort for St. Louis on August 5 in a company consisting of about thirty men and "ten empty provision wagons." Besides the wagoners and a number of sick volunteers, Clark's party included Mr. Fay (or Fe); William Z. (or L.) Swan of Northampton, Massachusetts; Robert M. Ewing of Louisville, Kentucky; E. Hewitt; and St. Louis artist Alfred S. Waugh. St. Louis *Missouri Republican*, September 8, 1846; Morgan, *Overland in 1846*, 2:650–654; and Barry, *Beginning of the West*, 640. See also note 60 below.

56. Charles Bent, well-known Santa Fe trader and member of the firm of Bent, St. Vrain & Co., had left Independence on August 2 or 3. General Kearny appointed him governor of New Mexico Territory on September 22. He was killed in the revolt of the Pueblo Indians and Mexicans at Taos on January 19, 1847. Barry, *Beginning of the West*, 634; James Madison Cutts, *The Conquest of California and New Mexico* (1847; reprint ed., Albuquerque: Horn and Wallace, 1965), 65; and Michael McNierney, ed., *Taos 1847: The Revolt in Contemporary Accounts* (Boulder, Colo.: Johnson Publishing, 1980), 8–9.

57. The St. Louis *Missouri Republican* reported on July 11, 1846, the following: "Died, yesterday, after a long and painful illness, Mrs. Mary Susan Ferguson. Her funeral will take place from the residence of her father, John H. Gay, corner of Fourth and Myrtle streets This afternoon at 4 o'clock."

58. Mary Ewing Lane, the wife of Dr. William Carr Lane. The Lane's daughter, Sarah, was married to William Glasgow, Jr., a cousin of the Glasgow brothers.

59. William is probably speaking of that portion of their route over the Raton Mountains via Raton Pass, between present-day Trinidad, Colorado, and Raton, New Mexico (see Franzwa Map 78 and p. 160). It took Samuel Magoffin's train five days to traverse the pass, the difficulties of which young Susan Magoffin aptly describes in her diary. See *Down the Santa Fe Trail*, 78–84.

60. The St. Joseph *Gazette* of December 18, 1846, reprinted an article from the St. Louis *Union* that contained the following details of Swan's death (as quoted in Morgan, *Overland in 1846*, 653):

> When near Chouteau's Island, which lies in the Arkansas, Mr. Wm. L. Swan, a gentleman of the party, discovered that a horse belonging to him was missing. Taking a fine animal belonging to Mr. Geo. Clark, of this city, he mounted and went in pursuit. After returning on their trail some miles, he came up with the horse and returned with him to near where the main body was encamped. The shades of evening had closed in, and he had arrived within seventy yards of the camp, when the reports of two guns were heard. The persons in camp had no means of ascertaining the real state of affairs before morning, when Mr. Swan was found lying dead on his back, having been shot through the heart. The alarmed horse had apparently fled in the direction he had come, and there were the foot prints of four persons in pursuit. The horse eventually was taken by a wagon master, ninety miles distant, and returned to the party. Mr. Swan was buried in the plains. The persons who murdured him were believed to be Cheyennes, though they had attempted by signs to convey the impression that they were Camanches.

The above was not the only trouble Clark's party had with Indians during their journey. Sometime before Swan's death, at a place called Salt Marsh, Fay, who with a few others had separated himself from the main party, "had stopped to shoot a wolf, and suddenly found himself beset by two Cheyennes. They menaced, but did not injure him, as he was well armed." A Cheyenne village was nearby, and its inhabitants expressed friendship when the main party of travelers arrived there. After some trading, Clark's party left without incident. Another encounter with Indians occurrred at Cow Creek, just west of present-day Lyons, Kansas (see Franzwa Map 35), after Swan's death. Here the party was attacked in an attempt to drive off their stock. Three of Clark's mules were captured. One Indian was reported killed, and possibly two others died. Clark probably arrived in Independence about August 27 along with trader Norris Colburn, who had apparently overtaken their party at Pawnee Fork. St. Joseph *Gazette*, December 18, 1846; and St. Louis *Missouri Republican*, September 2 and 8, 1846.

61. Captain Henry Smith Turner wrote in his journal that the event "came off remarkably well — a great crowd of males and females," but there was so much smoking going on among the guests that the "General goes to bed sick in consequence." *Original Journals of Henry Smith Turner*, 74.

62. Peter G. Morton was a private in Captain R. H. Weightman's Company A of the light artillery battalion under Major Clark. He was the son of George Morton of St. Louis and a sister of Sophia Morton, who is mentioned in the Glasgows' correspondence. In Peter Morton's deposition taken for his bounty land claim, he stated that he was honorably discharged at Santa Fe on November 27, 1846, "upon Surgeon's Certificate of Disability, in consequence of lameness of the right arm." According to Billon, "he died unmarried in New Orleans, Sept. 9, 1853, aged 26 years." Connelley, *Doniphan's Expedition*, 577; Morton BLF 35763-160-47, RG 15, NA; and Billon, *Annals*, 331.

63. The St. Louis *Missouri Republican* reported on October 13 (Tuesday), 1846, that "Dr. Craig, of Kentucky, who has been residing in New Mexico and California for fifteen years past, reached this city on Sunday evening last. He left Mazatlan on the 1st of June, Chihuahua on the 15th of July, and Santa Fe on the 6th of September. Dr. C. brought in a mail, and despatches from Gen. Kearney to the Government, which he mailed at Independence." In 1841 Edward J. Glasgow had written from Mazatlan to U.S. consul John Black at Mexico City for *cartas de seguridad* for three Americans, one of whom was a Santiago L. Craig. Edward listed Craig as being thirty-eight years old with black (or dark) eyes and

black (or dark) hair. Louise Barry has two references to Dr. Craig but records him as James S. Craig. Glasgow to Black, Mazatlan, August 18, 1841, Box C 8.2, Correspondence Received, 1829 to 1841/1842 to 1844, U.S. Consulate General, Mexico City, Mexico, RG 84, NA; and Barry, *Beginning of the West*, 172 and 649.

64. Probably Dr. Alexander Marshall (1810–1875), a native of Scotland who first came to St. Louis in 1840. Scharf, *History of Saint Louis*, 2:1525.

65. Glasgow was one of only two American civilians known to have traveled with Kearny on this expedition. The other was James Magoffin, who did not return to Santa Fe with Kearny but continued on to Chihuahua "to smooth the way for General Wool." Magoffin was accompanied by José Gonzales (see note 76 below). "The Magoffin Papers," 44, 46, and 51; and Magoffin, *Down the Santa Fe Trail*, 107–108 and 178–179. All the towns and pueblos mentioned in Edward's letter are along the Rio Grande below Santa Fe, Tomé being the farthest at approximately 90 miles from the New Mexico capital. See T. M. Pearce, *New Mexico Place Names: A Geographical Dictionary* (Albuquerque: University of New Mexico Press, 1965), for exact locations. For accounts of this expedition by military personnel, see Turner, *Original Journals of Henry Smith Turner*; William H. Emory, *Lieutenant Emory Reports: A Reprint of Lieutenant W. W. Emory's Notes of a Military Reconnoissance*, ed. Ross Calvin (Albuquerque: University of New Mexico Press, 1951); and John T. Hughes in Connelley, *Doniphan's Expedition*.

66. This was Pedro Jose Perea (1784–?). Turner mentions that they stopped at the "large ranches of Mr. Perrea and his sons." Emory states that after they took "refreshment" with the "wealthy citizen" they "passed on to the house of our host's wealthy son, where we were invited to dine." This was probably either Juan Perea (1808–?) or José Leandro Perea (1822–?). According to a later account, while at this stop General Kearny offered Juan Perea the post of territorial governor of New Mexico. Turner, *Original Journals of Henry Smith Turner*, 76; Emory, *Lieutenant Emory Reports*, 67–68; W.H.H. Allison, "Colonel Francisco Perea," *Old Santa Fe* 1 (October 1913):213; Donald Dreesen, "Founders of Albuquerque, 17th and 18th Century," unpublished typescript, vol. 3, Special Collections, University of New Mexico Library, Albuquerque; and Margaret Leonard Windham, ed., *New Mexico 1850 Territorial Census*, vol. 4 (Albuquerque: New Mexico Genealogical Society, 1976), 6.

67. According to Lieutenant Emory, they breakfasted with Don José Chavez and heard the mass Edward describes in Chavez's private chapel. Chavez was a brother of Antonio José Chavez, who was murdered on the Santa Fe Trail by the McDaniel's gang in 1843. Emory, *Lieutenant Emory Reports*, 69; and Marc Simmons, *Murder on the Santa Fe Trail: An International Incident, 1843* (El Paso: Texas Western Press, 1987), 3.

68. Emory described their headquarters at Peralta as being "at the palace of Mr. Ortega, a spacious one store edifice, five hundred feet front." Emory, *Lieutenant Emory Reports*, 70.

69. Kearny arrived back in Santa Fe on September 11. The following day Edward visited Susan Magoffin. She wrote in her diary under the date of September 12 that "Mr. Glasgow — a trader — called this morning and soon talked away a half hour; he is quite an agreeable St. Louisan, and interested me with a description of the manner in which The Gen. was received in the lower settlements." *Down the Santa Fe Trail*, 126.

70. Valverde was near the northern entrance of the Jornada del Muerto, roughly 160 miles from Santa Fe. Here were the ruins of a Mexican village, which (according to James W. Abert in his official report) "were inhabited in 1820 and 1825, but constant depredations of the Apaches and Navahoes forced the people to desert their village." *Abert's New Mexico Report, 1846–'47* (1848; facsimile reprint, Albuquerque: Horn & Wallace, 1962), 125. In his original travel diary he wrote that "one can yet see the ruins of the old

acequia and the form of the town." Abert, *Western America in 1846–1847...*, ed. John Galvin (San Francisco: John Howell, 1966), 63.

71. This was the Mormon Battalion under Captain Philip St. George Cooke. It consisted of five companies of infantry that had been mustered into the service at Council Bluffs, Iowa Territory, in July of that year. Leo E. Oliva, *Soldiers on the Santa Fe Trail* (Norman: University of Oklahoma Press, 1967), 77–78; and Daniel Tyler, *A Concise History of the Mormon Battalion in the Mexican War, 1846–1847* (1881; facsimile reprint, Chicago: Rio Grande Press, 1964), 118.

72. Lewis Dent, son of St. Louis merchant Frederick Dent, Sr., was clerk to Major Jeremiah H. Cloud, an "additional Paymaster in the U.S. Army." Dent had accompanied Major Cloud to Santa Fe and was now traveling with him to California, Cloud having been ordered there by General Kearny. They were traveling with the Mormon Battalion. Lewis's sister, Julia, married Mexican War veteran and future president Ulysses S. Grant. Billon, *Annals*, 302; Lewis Dent BLF 78330-160-47, RG 15, NA; Heitman, *Historical Register,* 1: 311; and St. Louis *Weekly Reveille,* June 14, 1847.

73. James Aull (c. 1805–1847) had come to Missouri from Delaware in 1825, establishing himself in business at the Missouri River town of Lexington. In 1831 he formed the well-known partnership of James & Robert Aull with his brother. Their firm operated stores at Lexington, Richmond, Independence, and Liberty. In 1836 J & R Aull was dissolved. James continued to operate the Lexington store, however. Ten years later, James was on the trail as part owner of a train of goods, having joined with Samuel Owens under the firm name of Owens & Aull. This may have been James's first trip overland to Mexico, although as a Lexington merchant he had catered to many Santa Fe traders and is known to have sent goods to Mexico under the care of an agent in 1832. Aull, "Letters of James and Robert Aull," 268–269; and Lewis E. Atherton, "James and Robert Aull: A Frontier Missouri Mercantile Firm," *Missouri Historical Review* 30 (October 1935): 3–4 and 18. The Aull brothers, including their older brother, John, had been involved in various business ventures with the elder Glasgows. See Introduction, note 19; and James Aull Business Records, 1825–1851, Coll. #3001 (microfilm), University of Missouri, Western Historical Manuscript Collection (WHMC).

74. Burgwin's dragoons, originally part of Kearny's California-bound column, were camped near Albuquerque, having been sent back to New Mexico after Kearny learned from Kit Carson on October 6 that California was under U.S. control. Philip St. George Cooke, *The Conquest of New Mexico and California*, (1878; reprint ed., Albuquerque: Horn :& Wallace, 1964), 96; Connelley, *Doniphan's Expedition*, 270; and Cutts, *Conquest of California and New Mexico*, 180–181.

75. Another explanation given for the abandonment of the expedition was that it was "due to some difficulty about subsistence." This information was reported by a correspondent of the *Weekly Reveille*, who had obtained it from Edward Glasgow and Samuel Owens while they were in Santa Fe in early December. This same report stated that the Mexican force had marched as far as Doña Ana, approximately 10 miles south of Robledo. St. Louis *Weekly Reveille,* February 22, 1847. The *Missouri Republican's* correspondent at Santa Fe reported that this force was led by a militia colonel at El Paso and gave his identity only as "Col. Romano." The correspondent was probably referring to Ramón Ortiz, a priest at El Paso. In his official report, Lieutenant Abert mentions receiving information "that Ortiz, the cura of El Paso, had led the troops that came to capture the wagons of the traders." William, in his "Memorandums," also states that an El Paso priest was at the head of this force. While Doniphan's troops were at El Paso, Ortiz was looked upon with suspicion as the "head of the anti-American party" and considered dangerous. When Doniphan left El Paso he took Ortiz and others with him as prisoners, "fearing that he

would cause the people to raise an insurrection when we left." St. Louis *Missouri Republican*, January 1, 1847; Abert, *New Mexico Report*, 129; W. H. Glasgow, "Memorandums"; Gibson, *Journal of a Soldier*, 313, 324; and Connelley, *Doniphan's Expedition*, 97.

76. The letter William refers to has not survived. Connelly's party, which also included a Mexican trader named Valdez, was sent ahead by the traders to feel out the situation at El Paso and to make arrangements, if possible, to enter their goods. According to one report, they were arrested at Doña Ana and forwarded to "Col. Romano" at El Paso. Others say they were taken prisoner at El Paso. From El Paso they were then sent to Chihuahua, reportedly arriving there on October 18. Doan and Valdez were released, Doan because of his English passport (Doan continued south from Chihuahua, joining his partner James Webb at San Juan de los Lagos). Connelly and McManus were placed in the custody of two citizens of Chihuahua and were not released until after the Battle of Sacramento. According to James J. Webb, "Dr. Connelly being an American, and a Mexican citizen by naturalization, was looked upon with more suspicion, and suspected if not accused of treasonable designs." Letter of Samuel Owens, Valverde, October 20, 1846, quoted in St. Louis *Missouri Republican*, December 8, 1846; Samuel Owens to his wife, Valverde, October 20, 1846, quoted in Gibson, *Journal of a Soldier*, 263, n. 390; St. Louis *Missouri Republican*, December 30, 1846, and January 1, 1847; W. H. Glasgow to William Glasgow, Valverde, November 18, 1846, Wade Shipley Coll. (WSC), Lovington, New Mexcio; and Webb, *Adventures in the Santa Fe Trade*, 250 and note. James Magoffin and José Gonzales were a few days in advance of Connelly's party and were also taken prisoner. In a sworn deposition, Connelly stated that he was taken to Chihuahua in Magoffin's company. Moorhead, *Royal Road*, 164; and Connelly deposition in "The Magoffin Papers," 60. One St. Louis newspaper published a letter from Santa Fe that mistakenly included a Glasgow among the list of prisoners held at Chihuahua. Such reports were no doubt disturbing to family members at home, despite letters from the Glasgow brothers to the contrary. St. Louis *Weekly Reveille*, February 22, 1847.

77. Samuel Cuthbert is found in the St. Louis city directory for 1847 as a partner with William Glasgow, Jr. (a cousin of the Glasgow brothers) in the "St. Louis Chemical Works." I have not located any information on this firm. Cuthbert is also listed as boarding with William Glasgow. *Green's St. Louis Directory for 1847*, 53 and 78.

78. Samuel Owens and Edward Glasgow gave the following account of Captain Burgwin's stay with the traders to a correspondent of the St. Louis *Weekly Reveille* while they were in Santa Fe in December. It was published in the February 22, 1847, issue of the *Weekly Reveille*:

> Our friends Owens and [Edward] Glasgow report provisions very scarce in their camp. They say that when Capt. Burgwin was down with them, they essayed a dinner to him, but it presented rather a sorry aspect. The first course was lean beef and bread — the second bread and lean beef — and the third and fourth alternated in the same way. It happened that there were four bottles of claret in camp, the remains of some old stores of better days, and these had to suffer, of course. Col. Owens had one can of sardines left — not enough to be put on the table at the dinner — and this he begged Capt. Burgwin to accept individually. But if the fare was scant, there was any store of good feeling on hand, and the dinner was one of merriment and courtesy, as such affairs, in camps, at all times are.

79. Lieutenant Colonel Congreve Jackson. See Connelley, *Doniphan's Expedition*, 297.

80. The traders learned later that this information was false. Lieutenant Abert, who was then at Valverde, reported that "there was something about the man that excited suspicion, and the traders refused to furnish him with the mules which he said were necessary to

enable him to to carry Captain Cook's letters asking for reinforcements." Abert, *New Mexico Report*, 125.

81. The Mormon "invalids" were under the command of Lieutenant W. W. Willis and were on their way to Santa Fe. From there they traveled to Pueblo, on the Arkansas River, to winter. Willis wrote that they started with fifty-six men, "one big government wagon, four yoke of pour oxen, five days rations and two dressed sheep, as food for the sick." Cooke gives the number as fifty-five men. Willis quoted in Tyler, *Concise History of the Mormon Battalion*, 191–194; and Cooke, *Conquest*, 106.

82. Possibly Ignacio Diaz Valdez. In research conducted for the National Park Service, Susan Calafate Boyle has identified five *guias* for Valdez in the Mexican Archives of New Mexico (MANM) dating to the years 1843 and 1844. Boyle, "Comerciantes, Fiadores, Arrieros, y Peones: The Hispanos in the Santa Fe Trail," unpublished study, provided to me courtesy of the author.

83. Lieutenant Abert wrote in his diary under the date of November 16 that "we are all scant of provisions. Our traders have been at this place 40 days [and] in this time have consumed their provisions, for they made no calculation for such a prolonged trip. Sugar and coffee can be bought at Socorro, but at the rate of 50 cents a pound; beef, $15 a head." Abert, *Western America*, 63.

84. In addition to the wagons full of merchandise, there was probably a large number of personal carriages, or dearborns, and baggage wagons augmenting the traders' camp. Frank Edwards viewed the traders' caravan, apparently spread between camps at San Diego and Robledo at the southern end of the Jornada del Muerto, around December 22 and stated that he saw approximately 300 wagons. Colonel Doniphan reported that when he left El Paso on February 8, 1847, the merchant caravan numbered about 315 wagons. Edwards, *A Campaign in New Mexico*, 79; and Connelley, *Doniphan's Expedition*, 423.

85. Wool's column began its march to Chihuahua from San Antonio on September 25, 1846. At the time William wrote this letter, Wool was in Monclova, having passed through Presidio del Rio Grande, San Fernando de Rosas and Santa Rosa. Smith, *War with Mexico*, 270–273. For a map showing Wool's route, see Wislizenus's "map of a tour from Independence to Santa Fé, Chihuahua, Monterey and Matamoros" in his *Memoir of a Tour to Northern Mexico*.

86. Norris Colburn was a Santa Fe trader as early as 1843. According to historian Ralph Bieber, Colburn formed a partnership with William T. Smith of Santa Fe in 1845, operating under the name of Colburn & Smith. Colburn also appears to have been a member of the firm of E. Leitensdorfer & Co., which included brothers Eugene and Thomas Leitensdorfer and Joab Houghton. Colburn had married Josephine Leitensdorfer, a sister of Eugene and Thomas, on April 2, 1846. Colburn had gained some notoriety for his rapid trip from Santa Fe to Independence in August 1846, covering the distance in twenty-four and a half days. "This journey eclipses in speed any other ever performed between the two points," stated the *Missouri Republican*, "and shows that very soon it will be stripped of even the character of novelty." On October 1 he left Missouri again for Santa Fe on what was his second trip that year with Santa Fe–bound wagons, apparently the first time such a feat had been attempted. It was on this trip that he carried the letters from the Glasgow family that Edward speaks of. Colburn was murdered along the Santa Fe Trail in eastern Kansas on his return trip to Missouri, evidently by two (Sac?) Indians, in March 1847. St. Louis *Missouri Republican*, January 13, 1844, and September 2, 1846; Webb, *Adventures in the Santa Fe Trade*, 98, n. 143, and 41, n. 47; St. Louis Genealogical Society, *StLGS Index of St. Louis Marriages, 1804–1876*, vol. 1 (St. Louis: St. Louis Genealogical Society, 1973); Magoffin, *Down the Santa Fe Trail*, 62, n. 23; Barry, *Beginning of the West*, 647–648, 668–669, and 906; and Columbia *Missouri Statesman*, May 7, 1847.

87. A George A. Hayward is listed in Connelley, *Doniphan's Expedition*, 575, as a private in Captain R. H. Weightman's Company A, Battalion Missouri Light Artillery. This was also Peter G. Morton's company (see note 62 above). William Clark Kennerly, another member of this company, writes that "George Hayward, my close friend, who was even younger than I and no wiser in the science of medicine, was selected for hospital steward. I have often wondered how I lived through his heroic treatment for cramps, of which I had several attacks, for he gave me opium in large chunks; however, with an application of hot ashes and a merciful Providence, I managed to survive" (*Persimmon Hill*, 186). George A. "Haywood" is found in the 1850 census for St. Louis as a twenty-three-year-old "Santa Fee Trader." He is shown as having been born in Massachusetts. Seventh U.S. Census, City of St. Louis, Missouri, 3rd Ward, 353. See also references to George Hayward/Haywood in Barry, *Beginning of the West*, 876–877.

88. George Frederick Ruxton, who arrived at Valverde from Chihuahua about November 28, writes that

> The traders had been lying here many weeks, and the bottom where they were encamped presented quite a picturesque appearance. The timber extends half a mile from the river, and the cotton-wood trees are of large size, without any undergrowth of bushes. Amongst the trees, in open spaces, were drawn up the waggons, formed into a corral or square, and close together, so that the whole made a most formidable fort, and, when filled with some hundred rifles, could defy the attacks of Indians or Mexicans. Scattered about were tents and shanties of logs and branches of every conceivable form, round which lounged wild-looking Missourians, some cooking at the camp-fires, some cleaning their rifles or firing at targets. . . . From morning till night the camp resounded with the popping of rifles, firing at marks for prizes of tobacco, or at any living creature which presented itself. (*Adventures in Mexico and the Rocky Mountains* [1847; reprint ed., Glorieta, N.Mex.: Rio Grande Press, 1973], 174–175.)

89. The El Paso del Norte Edward and William visited is present-day Juarez, Mexico. Wislizenus wrote,

> The town is principally built on the right bank of the [Rio Grande] river; but few houses are on the left. Stretched out along the river to the length of many miles, all the houses surrounded by gardens, orchards, and vineyards, and rich settlements, with cornfields, as far as the eye can trace the stream, lining its green bank — such a scenery will always be attractive; but to a traveller, who has passed over the lonesome plains and through the dreary Jornada del Muerto, it appears like an oasis in the desert.

Wislizenus also stated that the population "of the town proper, which is but a small place, and of the long line of settlements that extend for 20 miles down the river, is estimated at from 10 to 12,000." *Memoir of a Tour to Northern Mexico*, 40–41. See W. H. Timmons, *El Paso: A Borderlands History* (El Paso: Texas Western Press, 1990).

90. This was the Battle of Brazito, fought on December 25, 1846. According to Colonel Doniphan's official report, his force consisted of approximately 500 men (not all his troops were concentrated at the time of the battle), and the Mexican force was 1,220. Half of the latter number, he reported, was from Chihuahua and the rest consisted of militia from El Paso. Forty-three Mexicans were killed. Doniphan's army had seven men wounded, who subsequently recovered. Report of A. W. Doniphan, Chihuahua, to Brigadier General R. Jones, March 4, 1847, in Connelley, *Doniphan's Expedition*, 377–378, n. 94. For other accounts of the Battle of Brazito, see *Doniphan's Expedition*, 370–378; and Cutts, *Conquest of California and New Mexico*, 77–79.

91. Wool and his army had left Parras on December 17, but not for Chihuahua. They were marching toward Saltillo, approximately 90 miles to the east of Parras, to join with Taylor's army. The decision had been made to abandon the Chihuahua expedition over a month before, Wool receiving orders to that effect on November 14. Smith, *War with Mexico*, 1:275–276 and 510, n. 22. Doniphan would not learn of this until his Missouri volunteers were about to leave El Paso for Chihuahua in early February.

92. Several requirements in the Drawback Act of 1845 had to be met before the overland traders could collect the drawbacks (rebates) on their duties. One of the more important was that they return the original invoice (or certified copy) of their goods showing the certificates (actually signed and certified statements) of the collector of customs at the port where the goods were entered for drawback, the inspector of customs at Independence (or Van Buren or Fulton, Arkansas, depending on what route was taken), and the consul or commercial agent at Santa Fe and Chihuahua. These certifications were given after an inspection of the goods and invoice was made by the above individuals. This was to ensure that the goods that arrived in Mexico were the same ones originally entered for drawback and that they had arrived in their original, unbroken packages, as required by the Drawback Act. As Edward was the newly appointed U.S. commercial agent at Chihuahua, it would be his job to check the goods eligible for drawback, including his own, and certify the invoices. These certificates would be sealed with the seal of the U.S. Commercial Agency at Chihuahua, which he had just received. See circular of instructions to collectors of the customs, forms for invoice certificates, and copy of Drawback Act of March 3, 1845, all in Harmony Report, 52–61.

93. This would have been either William H. Belcher (1811–1866) or his brother Charles Belcher. The brothers operated the St. Louis Steam Sugar Refinery, also known as the Belcher Sugar Refinery. See Scharf, *History of St. Louis*, 2:1243–1245; and *Green's St. Louis Directory for 1847*, 29.

94. This was the first wife of Bishop Cicero Stephens Hawks (1812–1868), whom Scharf identifies as "a Miss Jones, of Hillsboro', N.C., by whom he had one daughter." Cicero S. Hawks, a native of North Carolina, became the rector of Christ Church in St. Louis in 1844. He was appointed as the first bishop of Missouri by the Episcopal church that same year. The first Mrs. Hawks died in 1855. Scharf, *History of St. Louis*, 2:1715–1716.

95. John H. Gay, Jr., was undoubtedly a son of John H. Gay and thus a cousin of the Glasgow brothers. There is a record of John H. Gay, Jr., marrying a Caroline M. Page on November 23, 1848. He died at the age of twenty-six in August 1849. *StLGS Index of St. Louis Marriages*; and Lois Stanley, George F. Wilson, and Maryhelen Wilson, *More Death Records from Missouri Newspapers, 1810–1857* (March 1985), 37.

96. Sarah Irwin (1822–1913), the first child of Dr. William and Deborah Beaumont, had married Brevet First Lieutenant Douglass Simms Irwin in 1844. William's jest about Sarah's husband was almost certainly not well received back home. Irwin, then regimental adjutant for the Third U.S. Infantry, had been killed during the Battle of Monterey on September 21, 1846, which news reached St. Louis on October 14. William obviously had not yet obtained this information at the time he wrote his letter. Myer, "Sarah Beaumont," 17, 37, and 38–39; and Heitman, *Historical Register*, 1:564. I am indebted to historian Frances Hurd Stadler for assisting in the identification of Sarah Irwin.

97. El Paso was noted for its wines. Wislizenus wrote that the people of the El Paso area raised "an excellent grape, from which they prepare the celebrated 'el Paso wine,' and a liquor called by the Americans 'Pass whiskey.' The grape, which they cultivate extensively, is of Spanish origin; blue, very sweet and juicy, and produces a strong, sweet, southern wine of straw-color." Missouri volunteer John T. Hughes proclaimed that it

was "perhaps the richest and best wine in the world." Wislizenus, *Memoir of a Tour to Northern Mexico*, 41; and Connelley, *Doniphan's Expedition*, 392.

98.　William would be taking his wagons to a camp in the area of the Presidio of San Elizario. Near that place, on February 11, the traders and teamsters were organized into two companies, forming a battalion of infantry numbering approximately 150 men. Edward J. Glasgow wrote in 1906 that the battalion "numbered considerably over 200 men." This is not the number reported in contemporary accounts, however (see also Part II, note 5). Gibson, *Journal of a Soldier*, 326–327 and 332, n. 442; W. H. Glasgow BLF 78579-160-55, RG 15, NA; Connelley, *Doniphan's Expedition*, 98; Edwards in *Marching with the Army of the West*, 248; St. Louis *Missouri Republican*, May 18, 1847; and E. J. Glasgow to W. E. Connelley, Governors Island, New York, August 13, 1906, William E. Connelley Coll., Manuscripts Department, Kansas State Historical Society (KSHS), Topeka, Kansas (included in Part III).

99.　John T. Hughes, in camp with the army at El Paso, noted in his diary under the date of January 17 that "Algier [probably Elguea] & [Reuben] Gentry, two Traders, injudiciously moved their trains some 10 miles below out of the protection of the Army & thereby lost 280 head of their mules by the Apaches." (These two would later attempt to slip away from Doniphan's control, Gentry's train succeeding.) Almost two weeks later, in entries dated January 29 and 30, he noted "25 yoke of oxen stolen from the commissary teamsters near Donana; 20 yoke from the Mexican Algea." Connelley, *Doniphan's Expedition*, 93 and 95.

100.　These letters have not survived.

101.　Major John P. Campbell and approximately thirty-two men (possibly as many as thirty-eight) left Chihuahua for the United States on March 14 or 15. Campbell and several others of his party arrived in St. Louis in mid-May. St. Louis *Weekly Reveille*, May 24, 1847; Connelley, *Doniphan's Expedition*, 451; Edwards in *Marching with the Army of the West*, 275; and Gibson, *Journal of a Soldier*, 361.

102.　The Battle of Sacramento was fought on February 28, 1847. See William's account of the battle in Part II and Edward's account and map in Part III. For the official reports of Doniphan and his officers, see Connelley, *Doniphan's Expedition*, 423–438 and notes.

103.　Owens had taken part in the mounted charge on the Mexican position, which temporarily faltered when Doniphan's adjutant ordered a halt (accounts vary as to why) shortly after the command to charge had been given. Possibly not hearing the order, several men, including Owens, continued toward the entrenchments. Owens fool-hardily rode up to the rim of a redoubt and commenced firing his pistols on the soldiers within it until he and his horse were shot down. Mexican soldiers then left the redoubt and lanced the fallen trader. Edwards in *Marching with the Army of the West*, 263–264; Connelley, *Doniphan's Expedition*, 410–411, 415, n. 107, and 418, n. 108; *Niles' National Register*, July 3, 1847; and James Hobbs, *Wild Life in the Far West: Personal Adventures of a Border Mountain Man* (1872; reprint ed., Glorieta, N. Mex.: Rio Grande Press, 1969), 129. Edward was not the only one to suggest that Owens may have wished death. James J. Webb learned from one of Owens's employees that Owens had "shaved and dressed himself with care, saying he did not know what might happen. . . . He [one of his men] thought that owing to family troubles, he [Owens] courted death, as he told him he 'knew of no more honorable death than to die in battle.' " James Hobbs, whose work should be used with caution, provides even more dramatic insight into Owens's condition before the battle. He claims to have joined Owens at his carriage and had a drink with him. "I could see that Colonel Owens was greatly excited," Hobbs wrote, "and appeared to be in deep trouble. As we raised the cups to our lips, I noticed that Colonel Owens's was filled to the brim. Drinking it off, he said: 'This may be our last drink together, and probably is enough to carry me to perdition.' " He quotes Owens as saying, "All I want is to get in among the Greasers" to Colonel Doniphan, who noticed "that Owens was excited with liquor." Hobbs also blames "family trouble" for Owens's actions. (The family "misfortunes" alluded to by Edward, Owens's employee, and Hobbs may have been the shooting of William Wirt Meredith by Owens's son-in-law, discussed in William's letter of May 27, 1846.) There are other eyewitness accounts, however, that present Owens in a different light. George R. Gibson was with Owens a few minutes before the charge and described him as being "in the finest spirits and sure of a victory." Frank Edwards saw Owens as the charge began and wrote that he went "dashing past us . . . waving his hand in an exulting manner, and shouting out, 'Give it to them, boys! they can't withstand us.' " Webb, *Adventures in the Santa Fe Trade,* 274; Hobbs, *Wild Life,* 127–128; Gibson, *Journal of a Soldier,* 349; and Edwards, *A Campaign in New Mexico,* 114.

104. Joab Houghton (1811–1876), a Santa Fe trader since 1843, was a partner in the firm of E. Leitensdorfer & Co. The firm operated a store in Santa Fe, which, according to historian Ralph E. Twitchell, was located "on the corner of what was known as the Galisteo road and San Francisco street." Houghton had been appointed a judge of the superior court of New Mexico Territory by General Kearny in September 1846. Bieber in Webb, *Adventures in the Santa Fe Trade,* 45–46, n. 58; Ralph Emerson Twitchell, *The Leading Facts of New Mexican History,* 2 vols. (Cedar Rapids, Iowa: The Torch Press, 1911 & 1912), 272, n. 197; and Cutts, *Conquest of California and New Mexico,* 65.

105. Wislizenus reported that the population of Chihuahua in 1842 was 147,600 and "at present [1847] it is estimated at from 150 to 160,000 inhabitants." Wislizenus, *Memoir of a Tour to Northern Mexico,* 59.

106. According to the diary of John T. Hughes, Connelly left Chihuahua on March 8 and returned with three Mexican commissioners ten days later. Connelley, *Doniphan's Expedition,* 107–108. Dr. Connelly was accompanied to Parral by Chihuahua *prefecto* Felix Maceyra.

107. The express consisted of thirteen men and was commanded by James L. Collins, a Missouri trader who had been serving as an interpreter for Colonel Doniphan. Collins's party left Chihuahua on March 20 and returned on April 23. Connelley, *Doniphan's Expedition,* 108.

108. William is describing the Battle of Buena Vista, fought on February 22 and 23, 1847. Historian Justin Smith puts Taylor's force at 4,759 officers and men. Santa Anna's casualties in killed and wounded were "not less than 1800." Smith, *War with Mexico,* 1:386 and 397.

109. Edward's letter has not survived.

110. This decree, in both Spanish and English, is reproduced in the Harmony Report, 38–40.

111. In a letter written by Colonel Doniphan published in Ralph Emerson Twitchell, *The History of the Military Occupation of the Territory of New Mexico from 1846 to 1851* (1909, reprint ed., Chicago: Rio Grande Press, 1963), 327, the *prefecto's* name is reproduced as "Mesceira," and in an account published in the St. Louis *Missouri Republican,* June 22, 1847, it is "Maceyra." The latter is apparently the correct spelling. See Roy L. Swift and Leavitt Corning, Jr., *Three Roads to Chihuahua: The Great Wagon Roads That Opened the Southwest, 1823–1883* (Austin, Tex.: Eakin Press, 1988), 246 and 361, n. 44.

112. The expedition William speaks of left on April 5 and returned to Chihuahua approximately six days later. The American at Parral who sent the message of the approaching Mexican army is identified by John T. Hughes as "Hicks." This may have been Bethel Hicks, whom James Josiah Webb mentions in his memoirs as "doing business at about

150 miles below Chihuahua." Another possibility is Young E. Hicks, whose name is found in a list of Americans applying for *cartas de seguridad* through the U.S. consul at Chihuahua in 1842. Bethel and Young E. may have been related, as Webb mentions that a cousin of Bethel, a Mr. Hicks, was elected captain of the wagon train he was a member of in 1845. Wislizenus hints that the U.S. merchants in Chihuahua were responsible for the false report. He writes that the report was "invented, perhaps, in Chihuahua, by some persons whose interest it was to keep the troops there as long as possible." Whatever the source of the report and for whatever reason, the abandonment of the expedition was somewhat embarrassing to Doniphan's troops. M. B. Edwards wrote in his journal that "this is the first retrograde movement we have made, and the Mexicans are already laughing us to scorn; and even the women throw it at us, forgetting the example set by their own troops." Wislizenus, *Memoir of a Tour to Northern Mexico,* 62; Connelley, *Doniphan's Expedition,* 464; Webb, *Adventures in the Santa Fe Trade,* 133; Benjamin Riddells to John Black, Chihuahua, December 30, 1842, Box C 8.2, Correspondence Received, 1829 to 1841/1842 to 1844, U.S. Consulate General, Mexico City, Mexico, RG 84, NA; and Edwards in *Marching with the Army of the West,* 277.

113. According to Wislizenus, Doniphan

before he left, called the Mexican authorities of the place and made them promise to treat the American residents of Chihuahua in a decent manner, and threatened them, in case of disorder, with a return of the American troops and a severe chastisement. The Mexicans promised everything Many American and other foreign residents, however, had so little confidence in Mexican faith, that they preferred to accompany the army. (*Memoir of a Tour to Northern Mexico,* 62)

114. According to James Josiah Webb, traders Christopher C. Branham, Solomon Houck, and others (Webb does not identify these) had "decided to sell at almost any sacrifice." These merchants approached Cordero about buying their goods and

accepted his first offer, which was fairly liberal under the circumstances; but Mr. Houck, the old trader who considered himself the smartest of all, declined. A couple of days after, he concluded to accept the offer, but Mr. Cordero offered enough less to make the difference about $1,000, which was declined. The following day he went to accept the offer of the day previous, but was told that the offer was only good for the day, and he could now offer only so much, which was about $1,500 less than the day previous. The offer was accepted, and Mr. Houck was out about $2,500 by his smartness. (Webb, *Adventures in the Santa Fe Trade,* 227–278)

José Cordero was a prominent merchant of Chihuahua who deserves further study. He later served as governor of Chihuahua. John Russell Bartlett described him in 1852 as "a merchant and banker, the owner of a very large landed property, and is considered the richest man in the State." Bartlett, *Personal Narrative of Explorations and Incidents in Texas, New Mexico, California, Sonora, and Chihuahua . . .,* 2 vols. (New York: D. Appleton & Co., 1854), 2:427.

115. A letter from one of the merchants who followed Doniphan's army to Saltillo, dated May 22, 1847, was the basis for an article on the Chihuahua traders published in the St. Louis *Missouri Republican* of June 22, 1847. According to this article, the merchants who remained in Chihuahua were "Connoly, the two Glasgows, McManus, [James] Aull, [George] Wethered, [David] Douglass, and Archy Stevenson." It further states that "Mr. [Solomon] Houck, [Cornelius] Davy, [Christopher and Manlius] Branham, and several others, left for Santa Fe. Samuel and William Magoffin, [George] East, [Alexander C.] Ferguson, John Fristoe, [William] Messervy, [Benjamin] Riddells, and some new traders, went to Saltillo, having been forced to make heavy sacrifices to do so." This report apparently refers only to American merchants and even in this regard is not quite

complete. James H. Barney, for instance, also remained in Chihuahua for a short time after Doniphan's evacuation (see note 132, below). It is also important to note that some of the individuals named (Wethered, Douglass, Stevenson, Fristoe, Messervy, and Riddells) were already in the State of Chihuahua before the arrival of Doniphan's force. See Alfonso C. Anderson to John Black, Chihuahua, January 10, 1847, Correspondence 1845 to 1848, U.S. Consulate General, Mexico City, Mexico, RG 84, NA. John T. Hughes wrote in his diary that "10 [American?] Merchants remained in Chihuahua." Connelley, *Doniphan's Expedition*, 109.

116. David Dawson Mitchell (1806–1861), former American Fur Company employee and later superintendent of Indian Affairs at St. Louis from 1841 to 1844, was lieutenant colonel of the Second Regiment Missouri Mounted Volunteers under Sterling Price, which reached Santa Fe in October 1846. On November 17 Colonel Price directed Mitchell to open up a communication with General Wool, then believed to be near Chihuahua, and to "establish a reconnoitering party along the route to that city." Mitchell left for Chihuahua about two weeks later escorted by ninety-five men recruited from the ranks of the U.S. forces at Santa Fe. This detachment, called the Chihuahua Rangers, overtook Doniphan in the vicinity of Valverde and continued under his command to Chihuahua, participating in the battles of Brazito and Sacramento. After the Mexican War Mitchell again served as superintendent of Indian Affairs at St. Louis, filling that post from 1849 to 1853. Ray H. Mattison, "David Dawson Mitchell," in Leroy R. Hafen, ed., *The Mountain Men and the Fur Trade of the Far West*, 10 vols. (Glendale, Calif.: Arthur H. Clark, 1965–1972), 2:241–246; Barry, *Beginning of the West*, 437, 502, 630–631, 825, and 1147; St. Louis *Weekly Reveille*, February 22, 1847; Order No. 71, Headquarters, Army in New Mexico, Santa Fe, November 17, 1846, in Gibson, *Journal of a Soldier*, 371; and Edwards, *Campaign in New Mexico*, 71 and 75.

117. James Hobbs mentions a Frenchman by the name of Henry Cappilard as a freighter in Mexico in his *Wild Life*, 112.

118. William is here possibly referring to funds owed an eastern importer or wholesale house where he purchased his goods for this venture. Primm writes in a short biography of Henry Shaw that "in 1846, Shaw advanced funds to the brothers [Edward] James and William H. Glasgow for their celebrated trading expedition to Chihuahua and other Mexican cities during the Mexican War." I have been unable to confirm this, however, in the Glasgow materials I have examined, and a search of the inventories of the Shaw business papers by the archivist at the Missouri Botanical Garden in St. Louis failed to turn up anything that appeared significant. It is unfortunate that Primm's article is not footnoted. James Neal Primm, "Henry Shaw: Merchant-Capitalist," *Gateway Heritage* 5 (Summer 1984):8; and Martha Riley to Mark L. Gardner, St. Louis, January 25, 1991.

119. Webb and his partner, George Doan, had arrived in Chihuahua in early February with four wagonloads of goods, mostly sugar, which they had purchased at the fair of San Juan de los Lagos. Sometime before the Battle of Sacramento, the partners contracted to freight five loads of cotton to Queretaro. Doan accompanied this train with the intention of purchasing more goods for the return trip while Webb remained in Chihuahua to sell their remaining stock from the fair. Doan arrived back in Chihuahua with a new stock of goods after Doniphan's evacuation of the city. It was decided that Webb would take these goods to New Mexico and then continue to the United States, which furnished William Glasgow with an opportunity to write home. Doan remained behind in Chihuahua for a short time. Webb lost no time in reaching Santa Fe, departed that place about June 13, and arrived at Council Grove in company with a party of traders and discharged Missouri volunteers on July 7. Among the traders in the party were Solomon Houck, Cornelius Davy, and the Branham brothers, whom Webb had

joined with his teams at the Mora River. Webb, *Adventures in the Santa Fe Trade*, 255, 261, n. 262; 264–265; 281, 285, n. 275; and 287; and Barry, *Beginning of the West*, 699–700.

120. Louise Barry notes that during summer 1850, "Crabbe" was the "experienced" wagonmaster for a Santa Fe–bound train belonging to Dr. Henry Connelly. There is also a reference to a Mr. Crabb owning a rancho 16 miles above Fray Cristóbal (which would place it fairly close to Valverde) in 1854. Barry, *Beginning of the West*, 956; and W.W.H. Davis, *El Gringo; or, New Mexico and Her People* (1857; reprint ed., Chicago: Rio Grande Press, 1962), 208.

121. Susan Larkin (1811–1881) was a daughter of the Glasgow brothers' uncle, James, and the wife of commission merchant Thomas H. Larkin. Mullanphy Papers, Filed 1-26-1875, Missouri Historical Society (MHS), St. Louis, Missouri.

122. William Glasgow, Sr., was apparently overseeing a Luis Zuloaga, who was attending school in St. Louis. Luis's father may have been merchant Luis Zuloaga. Bartlett mentions a Zuloaga (he does not give the first name) as one of the "principal citizens" of Chihuahua he met in 1852. David A. Sandoval, "Gnats, Goods, and Greasers: Mexican Merchants on the Santa Fe Trail," in Mark L. Gardner, ed., *The Mexican Road: Trade, Travel, and Confrontation on the Santa Fe Trail* (Manhattan, Kans.: Sunflower University Press, 1989), 28; and Bartlett, *Personal Narrative*, 2:425.

123. Clark arrived in St. Louis on board the steamboat *Clarksville* in company with other officers and soldiers and "many trophies of the victory of Sacramento" on July 2, 1847. Connelley, *Doniphan's Expedition*, 500, n. 127; and St. Louis *Weekly Reveille*, July 5, 1847.

124. Lieutenant Leonidas D. Walker (1817–1866) was one of two adjutants for Major Meriwether Lewis Clark's artillery battalion. William Clark Kennerly described Walker as one of his "intimate friends" who accompanied him on a hunting expedition on the Great Plains with Sir William Drummond Stewart in 1843. Heitman, *Historical Register*, 2:71; Connelley, *Doniphan's Expedition*, 573; and Kennerly, *Persimmon Hill*, 144.

125. William Clark Kennerly (1824–1912) was a sergeant in Company A of Clark's artillery battalion. His account of his experiences during the Mexican War is published as chapter 10 in *Persimmon Hill*, 184–208. The Kennerly family was very close to the Clarks and the Glasgows. Jefferson Kearny Clark and William Kennerly were cousins. Jefferson was raised with William Kennerly after Jefferson's mother died in 1831. As noted in the Editor's Introduction, William's sister, Harriet ("Tea") Kennerly, married Edward James Glasgow. William Clark Kennerly is buried in the same plot as Edward and Harriet Glasgow at Calvary Cemetery in St. Louis. Kennerly's reminiscences, told to his daughter and published under the title *Persimmon Hill: A Narrative of Old St. Louis and the Far West*, provide an intimate, although somewhat romantic, look at the St. Louis and society of which he and the Glasgows were a part.

126. Doan apparently did not leave Chihuahua for another month.

127. Stella Drumm (*Down the Santa Fe Trail and into Mexico*, 24, n. 11) identifies Aull's servant as "Andrew." Yet the estate inventory for James Aull does not list an Andrew as part of his property (two slaves by the names of Frank and Jack are recorded). However, there is an account for an Andrew in the Owens & Aull invoice book for this venture. This may have been a slave by the name of Andrew Davis, who was originally owned by John Aull but apparently became the property of brother Robert Aull upon John's death in 1842. Unfortunately, Drumm does not provide any documentation for her statement. Estate Inventory of James Aull, October 30, 1847, and Will of John Aull, May 22, 1838, both in Probate Division, Circuit Court of Lafayette County, Missouri, Lexington, Missouri; and Invoice Book, February 14, 1846–1847 (Owens & Aull), 133, James Aull Business Records, 1825–1851, Coll. #3001 (microfilm), WHMC.

128. Aull was murdered on the night of June 23, 1847.

129. Siter, Price & Co. are listed as importers at 133 High Street in *McElroy's Philadelphia Directory for 1846* (Philadelphia: Edward C. & John Biddle, 1846), 328. This wholesale firm, composed of Quakers, was used extensively by Missouri merchants in the nineteenth century. Lewis E. Atherton, *The Frontier Merchant in Mid-America* (Columbia: University of Missouri Press, 1971), 63; and Aull, "Letters of James and Robert Aull," 283, n. 43.

130. James Magoffin was taken to Durango shortly before the Battle of Sacramento and held there as a prisoner. His situation was more grave than that of the other Americans retained at Chihuahua because of reports of his role in the U.S. occupation of New Mexico and some official correspondence meant for General Wool apparently found in his possession. Several accounts say that he was charged with treason, although historian Max L. Moorhead states that evidence indicates that he was not a naturalized Mexican citizen. Magoffin, *Down the Santa Fe Trail*, 169 and 214; Connelley, *Doniphan's Expedition*, 445; Connelly deposition in "TheMagoffin Papers," 60; M. B. Edwards in *Marching with the Army of the West*, 219; St. Louis *Missouri Republican*, February 19, 1847, and May 19, 1847; Abert, *Western America*, 66; and Moorhead, *Royal Road*, 84, n.18.

131. A few months later, Henry Connelly was appointed "Defender for the Estate" of James Aull and one of the Glasgows, probably Edward, was among the "securities." From the Owens & Aull invoice book it appears that the firm of Connelly & Glasgow purchased some of the remaining stock of the Aull estate in January 1848. Aull, "Letters of James and Robert Aull," 300; and Invoice Book, February 14, 1846–1847 (Owens & Aull), 43–44, James Aull Business Records, 1825–1851, Coll. #3001 (microfilm), WHMC.

132. James H. Barney was a trader from Baltimore who had served in Edward's Company A of the Traders Battalion. He was probably the "son" in the business of John Barney & Son, which is listed in the 1845 Baltimore city directory as "biscuit bakers" with an office in the "Exchange" on Gay Street. In the 1850 U.S. Census for Baltimore city we find James H. Barney, thirty-one years old, living in the same household as John Barney, sixty-five, and Esther A. Barney, thirty-six. Both John and James are recorded as merchants, however, not bakers. James H. Barney BLF 79009-160-55, RG 15, NA; *The Baltimore Directory, for 1845* (Baltimore: John Murphy, 1845), 14; and Seventh U.S. Census for Baltimore City, Maryland, 10th Ward, 86. In the Mexican trade, James was a member of the concern of Hoffman & Barney. Although there were several individuals by the name of Hoffman on the trail in 1846 and 1847 (see Barry, *Beginning of the West*), James's partner was probably trader J. Tilghman Hoffman of the Baltimore firm of Ricards & Hoffman, "Importers and Jobbers of Dry Goods" at 255 Market Street. The Mercantile Agency estimated Hoffman's worth in 1847 to be $20,000 to $30,000. He is reported to have died in December 1849. Hoffman did not remain in Chihuahua as long as Barney, leaving there for Santa Fe with a "Company of Traders consisting of 14 wagons and thirty men" on April 4, 1847. *Sheldon & Co's Business or Advertising Directory ... of the Cities of New-York, Boston, Philadelphia, Baltimore, &c., &c.* (New York: John F. Trow & Co., 1845); Maryland, vol. 7, 83, R. G. Dun & Co. Coll., BLHBS; and George Rutledge Gibson, *Over the Chihuahua and Santa Fe Trails, 1847–1848*, ed. Robert W. Frazer (Albuquerque: University of New Mexico Press, 1981), 9–10 and 14. Barney arrived in Independence about September 1 in company with trader F. X. Aubry. Aubry related information he had gained from Barney to the St. Louis *Missouri Republican*. Aubry reported that Americans were not allowed to leave Chihuahua. "Neutrals" could leave with their returns after paying a duty of 6 percent. Barney (who is called Barnum in the article) was able to depart by claiming to be an Irishman. George Doan, who apparently traveled with Barney as far as Santa Fe, no doubt left under his British passport. *Niles' National Register*, September 18, 1847.

133. Edwin Bryant, who was in Independence in 1846 preparing for a trip overland to California, purchased several items at "Messrs. Wilson & Clarke, who keep a general furnishing store for these expeditions." Bryant, *What I Saw in California*, 14.

134. Charles F. Tracy was the son of St. Louis merchant Edward Tracy, Sr. He married Sophia Morton. Tracy was appointed post sutler at Fort Dodge and Fort Larned in the late 1860s. Billon, *Annals*, 300; and Theodore Weichselbaum, "Statement of Theodore Weichselbaum, of Odgen, Riley County, July 17, 1908," *Collections of the Kansas State Historical Society, 1909–1910* 11 (1910):562.

135. The Battle of Santa Cruz de Rosales was the climax of Brigadier General Sterling Price's campaign on Chihuahua, which historians have questioned. Price had proposed to the War Department to advance on that state several months previous. After reviewing details of his plans, the War Department sent back instructions in November ordering him not to undertake such a campaign unless he should learn of a force in Chihuahua about to advance on New Mexico, and even then it was thought that he should not march there to attack it. But in early February, before these orders arrived, Price received information that an army of 3,000 men under General Urrea was marching north, and he immediately set his campaign in motion. Although Price learned at El Paso that the report was false, he determined to press on to Chihuahua and attack the army there under General Angel Trias. On March 7, before reaching Chihuahua, Price received a message from Trias informing him that a treaty had been signed ending the war and protesting his advance. Price doubted the report and boldly entered the town that evening, Trias having withdrawn his forces the day before. Price continued his pursuit the following morning, catching up to the Mexican army at Santa Cruz de Rosales, approximately 60 miles southeast of Chihuahua. Trias again insisted on the treaty, and Price postponed the attack to give Trias time to receive confirmation. This also enabled Price to bring up his artillery and other reinforcements. Price waited until March 16 and commenced his attack after Trias refused to surrender. The battle ended that night with Price's troops taking the town. According to the report of the secretary of war, Price's force numbered 665 men and Trias's 804, not counting officers. Price estimated the number of enemy killed at 238. The American loss was four killed and nineteen wounded. The Battle of Santa Cruz de Rosales was the last engagement of the Mexican War. The Treaty of Guadalupe Hidalgo had indeed been signed over a month before the battle. Bieber, introduction in *Marching with the Army of the West*, 61–68; Sterling Price to Brigadier General R. Jones, Chihuahua, March 31, 1848, and Report of the Secretary of War, December 1, 1848, both in U.S. Congress, House *Message from the President ...*, Ex. Doc. 1, 30th Cong., 2nd sess., 1848 (Serial 537), 113–119 and 77, respectively; and St. Louis *Missouri Republican*, May 12, 1848. Historian Justin Smith states, "One suspects that commercial interests were behind this campaign." Americans in Santa Fe had been pressing for just such a campaign. In a letter to the adjutant general in Washington, Price wrote that "Chihuahua taken and held is regarded by the American citizens here, of the utmost importance, and a measure effecting their interests to a great extent." Certainly an American occupation of Chihuahua meant a reopening of trade to that point. Smith, *War with Mexico*, 2:419; Bieber, *Marching with the Army of the West*, 61; and Price to Jones, February 6, 1848, as quoted in Bieber, *ibid.*, 63.

136. Doan had apparently got only as far as Santa Fe after leaving Chihuahua with James Barney in early July 1847. From there Doan returned almost immediately to Chihuahua in company with Joseph P. Hamelin, Jr.; Ebenezer Pomeroy; a Mr. (John?) Howard; and two others to assist them in settling the Aull estate (Pomeroy was a brother-in-law of Aull and Hamelin was Aull's employee). Doan probably left Chihuahua for St. Louis sometime in early 1848, as Robert Aull wrote from Lexington, Missouri, on April 4 that he had recently seen Doan. Aull, "Letters of James and Robert Aull," 296–297, and 305.

137. According to Price's official report on the battle, "General Trias and forty two (42) of his principal officers were made prisoners of war, and eleven (11) pieces of artillery, nine (9) wall pieces, besides 577 stand of arms fell into our hands." Price to Jones, March 31, 1848, in U.S. Congress, House, *Message from the President...*, Ex. Doc. 1, 30th Cong., 2nd sess., 1848 (Serial 537), 118.

138. The Treaty of Guadalupe Hidalgo had been signed on February 2. It was ratified with minor amendments by the U.S. Senate on March 10, and the Mexican congress ratified this revised version in the latter part of May. Ratifications were exchanged at Queretaro, Mexico, on May 30, 1848. Smith, *War with Mexico*, 2:240, 247, 251, and 474.

139. Edward James Glasgow traveled home in company with Ebenezer Pomeroy and Joseph P. Hamelin. According to the Liberty *Weekly Tribune*, their party left Chihuahua on May 14; the Santa Fe *Republican* reported that "Mr. Glasgow" arrived in Santa Fe on May 27. The men left Santa Fe for Missouri in early June. At La Junta, the small settlement near the junction of the Sapello and Mora rivers, Alexander Barclay wrote in his diary on June 7, 1848, that "Wells and Glasgow and Pomeroy's wagons passed to Santa Fe & U. States." The following day he wrote, "Glasgow & Pomeroy passed on to U.S., a cross hand left them and came for employment." Again on June 9 he wrote, "Glasgow on to States." Orville C. Pratt encountered their train at the Great Bend of the Arkansas on June 26. The three men arrived at Lexington, Missouri, on July 4, and on July 16 the St. Louis *Reveille* reported that "Mr. J. S. Glasgow, and several other gentlemen, recently from Santa Fe, arrived from Weston yesterday on the steamer *Whirlwind*." Aull, "Letters of James and Robert Aull," 306–307; Liberty *Weekly Tribune*, July 28, 1848; Santa Fe *Republican*, May 31, 1848; George P. Hammond, *The Adventures of Alexander Barclay, Mountain Man* (Denver: Old West Publishing, 1976), 158; Pratt, "Trip over Santa Fe Trail, 1848," diary entry for June 26, 1848, Coll. #1034 (microfilm), Colorado Historical Society Collections; St. Louis *Reveille*, July 16, 1848; and Barry, *Beginning of the West*, 762.

PART II

EXCERPT FROM WILLIAM H. GLASGOW'S "MEMORANDUMS"

Santa Fé August 1846[1]

About the middle of Augt 1846, I found myself once more in Santa Fé. That place having one week before been taken possession of by Genl Kearney for the use and benefit of the U. States. The order of proceedings I now found somewhat different from that existing during my former visit to that renowned city. Instead of the Iron rule of the Despot Armijo I found the rigid but just and equitable laws of Gen[l] K. in force.

Our prospects for money making, were however not very flattering. We found. War existing between Mexico & the U. States. Santa Fe & New Mexico in possession of the U.S. forces. Gen[l] Wool in the U.S. levying 5000 men to invade Chihuahua via Texas and expecting to reach Chihu[a] about October. Our goods having been selected for the Chihuahua market were of course unsaleable in Santa Fe. And we were consequently compelled to await an opportunity to take them on to that place (without danger of confiscation) before disposing of them. Our mules & oxen were in the mean while to be subsisted and as winter would soon be coming on we were compelled to move southward where the weather would be more mild & the grass more abundant. While the U.S. forces remained in N. Mexico we entertained but little fear of molestation from the Inhabitants and consequently about middle of Septr set out and journeyed slowly along often not going more [than] 3 to 5 miles per day. In this manner we soon reached the lower settlements of N. Mexico upon the Del Norte River 160 miles below Santa Fé. While encamped upon the bottom lands near this settlem[t] awaiting news of the arrival of Genl Wool in Chihuahua, we received information that the Mexicans in El Paso del Norte 140 below us, headed by a Priest [Ramón Ortiz] had organised a force of 600 men for the purpose of paying us a visit and possessing themselves of our wagons, mules & merchandise. This being rather an unpleasant state of affairs for us, we enquired into it a little further and at length succeeded in ascertaining, that a regular correspondence was kept up between the principal inhabitants of the lower towns upon the river and El Paso. That the inhabitants of these Towns were to join the forces from below and thus render our capture, certain and easy of accomplishment. We also learned that one of the emisaries employed in carrying communications back & forth, was to start down the day following and would doubtless pass our Camp during that night. Accordingly we notified each camp of this fact and placed a Patrol guard along the different pathways and roads and also among the hills to the distance of ten miles from the River.

The orders to our guards were to stop and take prisoner any and every one whom they might see when on their rounds To offer them no violence if they made no resistance. But to kill them in Case they should be unable to stop them otherwise. This night my post was in a small clump of Mesquite brushwood (about ½ mile from Camp) from whence I commanded a view of the road for about 100 yards, which road also passed immediately by me. I remained on guard about 3 hours without seeing any thing when I was relieved by the 2^d guard. Nothing passed until about 9 Oclk of the following night, when one of the companions of the man (for whom we were waiting) rode into our Camp. As the head quarters established for our "guard house" was at Co^l Owens encamp^t about 3 miles below we detained him in Conversation until we had saddled a couple of mules and one other person & myself escorted him down, where we soon placed him in arrest. We found no papers of any kind about him. His Companion did not pass near us and consequently escaped us.

The day following this arrest, for mutual protection all the different companies formed one general camp upon a plain near the ruins of the old town of Valverde where we formed a fortification with our wagons, which nothing but cannon could break through. From our Prisoner we learned that 2 of our Companions, who had left us a month before (for the purpose of making an arrangem^t with the authorities of Chihuahua by which we might introduce our goods without danger of confiscation) had been arrested as spies and were then in confinem^t in Chihuahua.^{2} As soon as we had completed our preperations for the reception of our enemies, we allowed our Prisoner to escape and he lost no time in getting down to El Paso and informing his countrymen that we were ready for them. He found them on their return from the expedition, their courage having failed them after having proceeded 60 miles upon their way.

At this encampment we remained inactive and expecting daily to hear of Genl Wool's arrival in Chihuahua until the 18th Decemb^r. At this date Col Doniphan with his regiment of 1000 Volunteers passed us on his way to join Genl Wool and we followed under his protection. On Christmas day at an encampment 40 miles above El Paso called Bracitto [Brazito] as this regiment was encamping news was brought to Co^l D. (who was amusing himself with a game of cards) that the Mexicans were in sight. The alarm soon becoming general in the camp, the companies were formed in as good order as undisciplined troops could be by officers entirely unacquainted with military tactics. That is in a straight line.

The Mexicans soon after came within musket shot and receiving the fire of the Am^n line, discharged their guns upon them and fled.

The American troops having been taken by surprise were unprepared to pursue them and they consequently got off with the loss of 3 or 4 men The Americans had 3 or 4 wounded — none killed.[3] Thus ended the celebrated battle of Bracitto.

The day of this engagement in entire ignorance of the doings of our countrymen, we were encamped 2 miles above Don Aña (25 miles above) grinding meal (for the purpose of making bread) from corn obtained at that village. The day following we proceeded on and overtook the army at El Paso, where they halted until the arrival of the Artillery under Maj Clark.

In this place they remained until the 5" [8th] Feby — when they took up their line of march for Chihuahua.

During the occupation of El Paso by Co^l D's forces all the trading Companies had encamped about 20 miles below that place for the purpose of grazing their stock and where they remained until they were passed by the army.[4]

As all the news received from Chihuahua confirmed a report we had received that the Mexicans in strong force intended to give us battle and as Co^l D's regiment numbered but about 1100 men. before leaving the Del Norte River 50 miles below El Paso, we formed our Merchants & Drivers into two Companies of Infantry and on the 11th Feby were mustered into the service of the U. States by Col. D.[5] Having had the honor of being elected 1st Lieut of Comp^y A of this Battalion I borrowed a sword (one of the trophies of Bracitto) of Maj Clark and felt myself very large while strutting about with an old sabre cracking my shins. Our Battalion was drilled 3 times, during those 3 Several drills I found my sabre of considerable inconvenience to me it having a singular propensity to entangle itself between my legs and on several occasions came near causing me to measure my length upon the ground.

We travelled on without any important occurrence until we reached the head of Lake Encenillas and encamped upon its banks one morning about 10 O.clk.[6]

While waiting for my breakfast, I saw a large column of smoke behind us and recognised the approach of a fire in the prairie which the volunteers had by their carelessness allowed to escape at our camp of the night before and which we left burning behind us. The ground upon which we had halted being coverd with long grass, we lost no time in driving up our stock and endeavouring to keep in advance of the fire, but during the course of the afternoon we found it overtaking us so rapidly, that 100 men were detailed to go on for half a mile & make a road 20 ft wide at right angles from the main road and extending from the road to the Lake. This they accomplished by digging up the grass with their Sabres We then fired the grass in advance of us, which in a few moments was all consumed to the new made road, and left us bare ground enough to stand upon which we lost no time in moving. Maj Clark however wishing still further protection ran his Artillery & Powder Waggon into the Lake.[7]

About dark the fire passed by us roaring & crackling most fearfully. This was by far the most grand, and beautiful as well as fearful sight I had ever seen upon the prairies. The grass being long and the wind blowing strong, caused one solid wave of fire 20 feet in height to extend from the road near us, across a plain 3 miles in width and to [the] top of a range of mountains to our left. The whole space intervening being one solid mass of flame.

Before camping this afternoon we saw at the distance of several miles in advance of us a large body of Mexican troops in full retreat. Two days afterwards we reached Rancho Saons [Sauz] & encamped within sight of their main body, which was drawn up in order for battle behind their entrenchments at Sacramento.

The next morning [February 28] after an early breakfast, with our forces disposed in battle order and a guard of 100 men thrown out in advance we moved on to the attack. The grounds selected by the Mexicans were admirably adapted for defence and the prospect for a nice frolic appeared quite brilliant. Their line of fortifications extended for half a mile along the road side and within 200 yards of where they thought us compelled to pass. Our approach to them for 10 miles lay down the slope of a level plain at the foot of which ran a creek with banks about 6 feet in height. Arrived within about 2 miles of their line of fortifications [when] we diverged to the right and digging down the banks of the creek, crossed in a gallop to the top of the plain upon the opposite side and about 1200 yds distant from them.

"The Battle of Sacramento," another lithograph by N. Currier made in 1847. This, however, is a highly romanticized and largely inaccurate depiction of the battle, particularly in regards to the uniforms of the Missouri Volunteers. (Courtesy of the Library of Congress.)

Here we halted our forces and opened fire upon them from our 6 pound guns, as they were rapidly advancing upon us, supposing from our change of position and rapid movements that we were retreating. A few shells however soon convinced them of their error and they immediately fell back within their entrenchments and under cover of the guns of their batteries. After a brisk cannonade for about an hour, from both sides and the loss upon our side only amounting to "5 oxen & 3 mules" our Bonaparte concluded to venture a little closer and accordingly ordered our whole line to advance. The Mexicans waited quite patiently until we arrived within 300 yards of them, when they fled in all directions pursued by our troops. One troop of about 300 Mexicans made an attempt to cut off our wagons and succeeding in placing themselves between them and the main body of our troops, were advan[c]ing rapidly upon us, but being discovered by Maj Clark (who with his battery of 6 pounders was about 100 yards in advance of us) he dispersed them by one round from his battery. At sun set we were all quietly encamped upon the battle field. Thus ended the great battle of Sacramento, which covered with glory & military renown the immortal Doniphan, who had about as much agency in producing the result of the engagement, as my old mule. The list of killed & wounded upon the side of our troops was 2 killed & about 30 wounded.[8] To say nothing of my own loss of 5 oxen which had their legs taken off by Canon balls.

Upon the part of the Mexicans 25 were killed and as many wounded. This account differs somewhat from that published by Col D in his official report to the Sect[y] of War in which he estimates the killed 300 & 300 wounded. His estimate must have been formed from the reports of his Soldiers after the battle each one of whom claimed to have killed with his own hand about 50. Such may have been the case, but if so they must Certainly have also eaten them for but 25 killed & mortally wounded could be found after the engagement and they fled rather rapidly to have carried many wounded off with them.[9]

On the 2[d] day after the battle we entered the City of Chihuahua and found it deserted by almost all its inhabitants.

x x x x x x x x x x x x x x x

Passing over a period of 13 months spent in Chihuahua, during which time we had been abandoned by our country men who, (although they fully expected us to be murdered by the Mexicans upon their surrender of Chih[a]) declined differing their departure 2 days in order to secure our safety and enable us to make preperations to accompany them with our merchandise. And the succeeding 12 months during which we were subjected to all kinds of insults and indignities from the Mexicans until the second invasion of Chihuahua by Gen Price in the month of March the following year. I found myself on the 6th April once more setting out for home having availed myself of the protection offered my [by] M[r] Collins[10] bearer of despatches to Washington City, who with a flag of truce left Chihua. upon that day escorted by 60 Dragoons under the Command of Capt [William N.] Greer [Grier] & Lieut. [John] Adams.[11]

1848   Our route for 20 miles after leaving Chihuahua led over a
Apl 6.   beautiful plain bounded upon either side by a ridge of mountains. It then passed for 7 miles through a gap in the mountains called the Cañon noted for being almost always frequented by Apache Indians, The road being very rough & hilly. The hills being covered with a thick growth of mesquite brushwood and in many places overhanging the road so as to render it a favorable place for the attack of

Indians upon travellers through this pass. 5 miles beyond we encamped at Hacienda Bachimba

7th   On the morning of the 7th we left Bachimba and journeying over a sandy plain overgrown with Mesquite brushwood at 20 miles distance passed through the town of San Pablo a neat village upon the bank of a river of the same name. Crossing over this stream at this place about 300 yds in width and 2 feet in depth in the deepest place, we halted upon the opposite bank to graze our horses for an hour or two. after which we proceeded on over a high sandy plain for 25 miles to Rancho Saoncillo[12] where we stopped for the night. This Rancho is a poor miserable place with about 200 inhabitants kept continually in a state of starvation by the frequent incursions of the Apache Indians, who rob them of all their stock, even going so far as to enter the town in day light and visit their stable yards for that purpose.

8th   Set out quite early this morning and rode along the fertile valley of the Conchos river for 15 miles to Rancho La Cruz[13] 3 miles farther at Las Garcias,[14] we crossed the river about 250 yds in width and in places 2 ft in depth [and] from thence to Santa Rosalia a distance of 10 miles our road lay over a succession of sandy ridges until we arrived near the town and crossed over a small creek which here discharges itself into the Conchas. Santa Rosalia is quite a considerable village, containing some few respectable houses. At the Southern extremity of the town and upon a height Commanding the country for a considerable distance around is built a very large fortification erected to prevent the advance of the army of Genl Wool upon Chihuahua. 25 miles farther we halted at rancho En Ramada at [and] pitched our tents.

9th   15 miles distant from En Ramada passed through Rancho Saons[15] containing but 2 houses, being nothing more than a dairy farm where is made large quantities of cheese from thence at the distance of 15 miles we entered the town of Guajuquilla where we remained a couple of hours laying in a supply of corn for our horses & mules After which we rode on 3 miles farther to hacienda de Dolores where we spent the remainder of the day in exchanging our old broken down horses for fresh ones

10.   Our route this day led over a sandy region not susceptible of much cultivation and through two deserted villages the inhabitants of which had been killed by Indians. at 52 miles distance we encamped upon the opposite bank of a small stream near the deserted village of San Blas

11.   Eight miles distant from San Blas we passed through San Bernardo & ten miles farther Sandoval both uninhabited on account of Indians 25 miles more brought us to Ojo San Jose or St Joseph's Spring a fine bold spring situated in the midst of a beautiful grove at the mouth of a gap thro' a ridge of mountains crossing the road, which forms the great "travessia" or pass used by the Comanchee Indians in their predatory excursions upon the Eastern Mexican Settlements. As we were approaching this place we saw several horses scampering off at full speed and upon arriving at the grove saw a number of moccasin tracks & other Indian Sign. After grazing our horses a short time we passed through this gap and after a 10 mile journey over a sandy waste encamped near a hole of water in the prairie.

12   Rode today for 35 miles over a high sandy plain destitute of vegetation and encamped at night near the town of Mapimi.

13.   On this morning we entered the town and encamped in the Public Square   Spent quite a pleasant day visiting among the inhabitants and enjoying a sumptuous breakfast and Dinner to which we were invited by a couple of Mexican Gent.

14   Two hours before day light this morning our bugle sounded the march and we were soon wending our way over a very rough road which led between 2 ranges of high hills which enclose the town. Soon after we entered upon a plain which continued about 25 miles where we persued our way for 5 miles through rich bottom land to the village of San Felipe from this place our road for the remainder of the day led through a fine wooded country the tree tops overhanging the road and the ground being covered with thick under growth. About dark we arrived opposite the town of San Lorenzo distant from San Felipe 20 miles   As we were crossing the creek and ascending the bank upon the side next the town we were fired upon by the inhabitants they having mistaken us for Comanchee Indians. Spurred up by the whistling of the bullitts around our heads we lost

no time in entering the public square, where we found all the inhabitants running for the Woods.

15. On Leaving this place we also left the fertile grounds behind us and entered upon a loose sandy soil arrived at 15 miles distce we halted upon the bank of a creek at the deserted town of San Juan. the inhabitants of this place had all been killed by Indians a few months previous 15 miles more accomplished and we encamped in the prairie without water.

16. Made an early start this morning and went to Rancho Poso[16] to breakfast, leaving soon after we rode over a high barren prairie until we reached the fertile valley of Parras and stopped at the hacienda of San Lorenzo belonging to Don Manuel de la Vara[17] distant from El Poso 30 miles This hacienda presents a better appearance for Comfort than any I had yet seen in Mexico. The Proprietor lives in the midst of the houses of his tenants — in a large fine looking mansion fronting upon an avenue 1 mile in length and ornamented by 6 rows of large trees and 6 rows or hedges of rose bushes its entire length. these hedges of roses are most beautiful being fancifully cut & covered entirely with bloom. He has 3 large vineyards from which he makes great quantities of wines & brandies. Like all other things in Mexico however this place has its drawbacks as while we were then stopping there Mr De la Vara was lying dangerously ill having been shot by some Indians two days before when persuing them for the purpose of recovering some stock which they had stolen from him.[18]

17. 20 miles from this place met a Pay Master of the U.S. Army on his way to Parras passing through Sieneca [Cienega] grande at 25 miles distance we encamped near Hacienda Casanuelo [Castañuela]. which we found occupied by a company of Texian rangers escorting a train on its way to Saltillo with corn.

18   At 1 oclock this morning our bugle sounded the Reveille and we set out in an hour afterwards. found the face of the Country much improved and the soil rich and fertile. after riding 25 miles we passed through Rancho Patos. 20 miles farther Rancho Vacas [and] 15 more and we entered upon the beautiful plains of Buena Vista the memorable battle field of Gen[l] Taylor. Over this ground we hurried faster than Santa Anna & his army as we were overtaken by

a most violent Thunder storm accompanied with rain, which compelled us to hurry on over ditches, old broken down redoubts, graves and every thing else and seek shelter from the storm in the hacienda of Buena Vista where were encamped the main body of Gen[l] Taylor's army

19. Remained at the encampment all the forenoon of this day observing the various Companies of Artillery, Infantry & Cavalry drilling. After dinner I went on 3 miles to Saltillo where I remained until 5 oclock when I left in an ambulance for Monterey. Did not much enjoy my ride this afternoon as it continued raining from the time we left until we broke down in a mud hole 34 miles distant from Saltillo and were Compelled to walk 2 miles further to Rinconada where we arrived wet, cold and hungry at 1 Oclock A.M. This town we found in ruins but one house in it being covered with a roof — the others having been demolished by the Soldiers of the U.S. Army on account of harboring Guerrilleros.

A company of Texian rangers occupied this house who allowed us to sleep in the room until morning but could give us nothing either for supper or breakfast. Were up by times this morning and

20. soon had our wagon mended and would have been compelled to proceed upon our way fasting had we not found a Mexican upon his way to Saltillo with two Jackasses laden with eggs. We bought 9 Dozen from him which we boiled in a borrowed Coffee pot and made a pretty fair breakfast for three. About noon we reached Monterey and spent the remainder of the day in making preperations for our further journey. At this place our escort left us and Mr Collins was turned over by Gen[l] Wool to the care of Lieu[t] [Clarendon J.L.] Wilson who was detailed to escort some wagons laden with bar

21   silver. Accordingly on the morning of the 21st we repaired to Walnut spring encampment where we joined the train just preparing to start. At 10 miles distance we passed through Agua Frio. 8 miles further Marin & continuing on for 5 miles more we encamped at Ramos. The houses in this place as well as those of the other two towns were unroofed & destroyed from the same cause as Rinconada. Passed to day the spot where a few months ago a train of 45 wagons were burned and the drivers & soldiers escorting them murdered by

the Guerrilleros. The bones of the murdered men were lying scattered along the road for half a mile.[19]

22   28 miles from Ramos we reached Ceralvo a considerable town then used as a depot for Gov[t] Stores and occupied by a regiment of Virginians. Here our escort of Dragoons were releieved and we were turned over to the protection of a dozen ragged cut-throat looking

23   Texians whom we could not get started the next day until about 10 oclock and consequently could not go farther than the camping ground of Ponte Aguarda[20] 15 miles distant from Ceralvo. We met this day a train of Gov[t] Wagons 250 in number on their way to Saltillo with provisions.

Setting out very early the morning of the 23[d] [24th], after a hot ride of 30 miles we reached the town of Meir [Mier] celebrated as the ground of a hard fought battle between the Texians (during their War for Independence) and Mexicans. In this place we found a tavern kept by an American Lady, where we obtained the first good dinner we had eaten since leaving Monterey. After dinner we moved about a mile down the river and encamped for the night

24 [25] Having grown pretty tired of Texian escort and mule back travelling. We set out at day light this morning and rode rapidly through a fine fertile country for 23 miles to Camargo, the head of navigation on the Del Norte River [Rio Grande] and the grand depot of Gov[t] Stores. Soon after our arrival our eyes were once more rejoiced by the most welcome sight of a Steam Boat which promised a more pleasant and Speedy mode of travel for the remainder of our journey

25. [26] At 10 Oclock this morng we left the city of Camargo behind and sped rapidly down the river, passing numerous farms & villages we arrived at Metamoras [Matamoros] on the eveng of the 25th [26th] and the next afternoon landed at the mouth of the river, where we remained until the day following when we rode over to Point Isabel 9 miles distant and found accomodation in an old Steam Boat converted into a Hotel

27.   At 5 Oclk this afternoon we left in the Steamer Fashion[21] and after a pleasant trip across the Gulf, on the evening of the 31st was once more rejoiced to find myself upon the Levee in N. Orleans.[22]

NOTES

1. As noted in the Editor's Introduction, it is apparent that William's "Memorandums" are based on diaries kept on his various trips. It is also evident that he did rewrite some passages and make other changes in the process of transferring his diaries to his "Memorandums." The account of his experiences for 1846 to 1848, however, which forms the last fourteen pages of his "Memorandums," is somewhat peculiar. The first portion of the account is written in a narrative style, more a recounting of events, with some comments and reflections that probably date to the time the "Memorandums" were prepared. The latter portion of William's account, however, when he begins his trip from Chihuahua to the Gulf, is written in the form of day-by-day entries (much like the 1842–1843 portion of his "Memorandums"). This section reads like a diary and is probably very close, if not a verbatim transcription, to one he kept. Why these two different styles in the same account? Did William lose the diaries he kept during the earlier period and then rewrite those experiences from memory? Did he perhaps not keep a diary at all during that time? Another curious aspect of William's account is that he does not once mention his brother Edward. In fact, very few individuals are mentioned by name throughout his "Memorandums." Yet the "Memorandums" excerpt is an excellent companion to the letters of the Glasgow brothers, revealing additional information about their Mexican War–era experiences and providing us with another opportunity to learn about William himself.

2. The two companions held in Chihuahua were Henry Connelly and Francis McManus. See Part I, note 76.

3. Doniphan placed the number of Mexican dead at forty-three. See Part I, note 90.

4. The traders were camped near the presidio of San Elizario, established in 1789. See W. H. Timmons, El Paso: A Borderlands History, (El Paso: Texas Western Press, 1990), 56.

5. Richard Cabeen, a private in William's company, wrote that "Col. Doniphan . . . seeing that he would have to fight before he could enter the City of Chihuahua told us that he had the power to press us all into the service but he would rather we would volunteer and elect our own officers which we did." The officers elected by the traders and teamsters were, for Company A: Edward J. Glasgow, captain; William H. Glasgow, first lieutenant; John Calvin Huston, senior second lieutenant; and H. C. Harrison, junior second lieutenant; and for Company B: Henry Skillman, captain; Manlius F. Branham, first lieutenant; John Howard, second lieutenant; and A. F. Francisco, junior second lieutenant. Samuel C. Owens was elected major of the battalion. Thomas Macmanus was adjutant, and Christopher C. Branham was a sergeant major. Richard Cyrus Cabeen to James W. Shaw, Aledo, Illinois, December 9, 1877, in Cabeen Bounty Land File (BLF) 75497-160-55, Record Group (RG) 15, National Archives (NA); U.S. Congress, House, Report on the Petition of Manuel X. Harmony, H. R. Rep. 458, 30th Cong., 1st sess., 1848 (Serial 525), 32; and deposition of Edward J. Glasgow and William H. Glasgow, St. Louis, December 18, 1858, in Christopher C. Branham BLF 85000-160-55, RG 15, NA.

6. Lake Encinillas, or Laguna de Encinillas, was approximately 171 miles from El Paso.

7. According to George R. Gibson,

    It was quite an exiciting scene: the teamsters urging their animals to the utmost speed; the rear, composed of commissary teams and traders, narrowly escaping; [and] the smoke, noise, and confusion being great. The fire no doubt having spread over such an extent of country by the rarification of the atmosphere greatly increased the wind, and it was traveling with a rapidity in the lake bottom which it was no easy matter to avoid, presenting a rolling flame ten feet high. Finally all were safe in the burnt spot. And to us in security, the spectacle was a magnificent one, the country enveloped in a dense smoke, and the fire visible for many miles in the mountains. (Gibson, *Journal of a Soldier Under Kearny and Doniphan, 1846–1847*, ed. Ralph P. Bieber, Southwest Historical Series, vol. 3 [Glendale, Calif.: Arthur H. Clark, 1935], 341)

See also Frank S. Edwards, *A Campaign in New Mexico with Colonel Doniphan* (Philadelphia: Carey and Hart, 1847), 109; M. B. Edwards in Abraham Robinson Johnston, Marcellus Ball Edwards, and Philip Gooch Ferguson, *Marching with the Army of the West, 1846–1848*, ed. Ralph P. Bieber, Southwest Historical Series, vol. 4 (Glendale, Calif.: Arthur H. Clark, 1936), 257–258; and William E. Connelley, *War with Mexico, 1846–1847: Doniphan's Expedition and the Conquest of New Mexico and California* (Kansas City: Bryant and Douglas Book and Stationery Co., 1907), 404–405.

8.   Doniphan reported that he had one man killed, one mortally wounded, and seven wounded who would "recover without any loss of limbs." John T. Hughes states, however, that there were eleven wounded, three mortally. The one man killed was Samuel Owens of the Traders Battalion. Connelley, *Doniphan's Expedition*, 436 and 416.

9.   Doniphan indeed estimated the Mexican loss at "about three hundred killed and the same number wounded." Some accounts gave higher figures. Frank Edwards wrote that "the enemy lost, in killed and wounded, about eleven hundred men." William's estimate is actually lower than that given by the Mexican commander, José Heredia. In his report of the battle, published in a St. Louis newspaper, Heredia stated that because of the "complete dispersion" of his troops, "it is impossible to give an exact detail of the number killed and wounded, but . . . they cannot be less than 80 to 100." Connelley, *Doniphan's Expedition*, 435–436; Edwards, *Campaign in New Mexico*, 118; and St. Louis *Weekly Reveille*, April 26, 1847.

10. James L. ("Squire") Collins (1800–1869) of Boonville, Missouri, and later Chihuahua, had been a trader to Mexico since 1826. In October 1846 he volunteered his services to Colonel Doniphan and traveled with him as an interpreter to Chihuahua, taking part in the Battle of Sacramento and later commanding the express sent to General Wool at Saltillo. When Doniphan evacuated Chihuahua, Collins apparently accompanied him as far as Monterey. At some point he started back for New Mexico "carrying dispatches from Wool's army to Santa Fé." A newspaper account states that he was taken prisoner "near Chihuahua." Edward Glasgow wrote to William Connelley that Collins was "arrested as a spy at El Paso and brought to Chihuahua for trial." He escaped from Chihuahua around February 1 (see Part III) and made his way to El Paso, where he met Sterling Price's troops. Collins traveled south with Price and at the Battle of Santa Cruz de Rosales served him as an aide-de-camp. After the Mexican War Collins lived in Santa Fe, where he was the publisher of the *Santa Fe Gazette* in the 1850s, the superintendent of Indian Affairs from 1857 to 1863, and the receiver of the Land Office and custodian of U.S. funds from 1866 to 1869. According to Edward Glasgow, he was "found one morning dead from a pistol shot in his office with the safe door open." Louise Barry, *Beginning of the West: Annals of the Kansas Gateway to the American West, 1540–1854* (Topeka: Kansas State Historical Society, 1972), 135; Collins BLF 77018-160-55, RG 15, NA; Ferguson in *Marching with the Army of the West*, 352–353; St. Louis *Missouri Republican*, May 12, 1848; E. J. Glasgow to W. E. Connelley, Governors Island, N.Y., November 27, 1906; Price to Jones, Chihuahua, March 31, 1848, in U.S. Congress, House, *Message from the President . . .*, Ex. Doc. 1, 30th Cong., 2nd sess., 1848 (Serial 537), 119; David Meriwether, *My Life in the Mountains and on the Plains*, ed. Robert A. Griffen (Norman: University of Oklahoma Press, 1965), 168, n. 5; and Donald Chaput, *François X. Aubry: Trader, Trailmaker and Voyageur in the Southwest, 1846–1854* (Glendale, Calif.: Arthur H. Clark, 1975), 191.

11.   The route for William's trip to the gulf was essentially the same as that taken by Doniphan and his Missouri Volunteers upon leaving Chihuahua in March 1847. Josiah Gregg and Frederick Wislizenus accompanied Doniphan's troops and left detailed accounts of the route that are useful for comparison. See Josiah Gregg, *Diary and Letters of Josiah Gregg*, ed. Maurice Fulton, 2 vols. (Norman: University of Oklahoma Press, 1941 and 1944); and Frederick Wislizenus, *Memoir of a Tour to Northern Mexico, Connected with Colonel Doniphan's Expedition in 1846 and 1847* (1848; facsimile reprint; Albuquerque: Calvin Horn Publisher, 1969), 62–82. See also Wislizenus's "map of a tour from Independence to Santa Fe, Chihuahua, Monterey and Matamoros," which accompanies his *Memoir*.

12.   Both Gregg and Wislizenus write this as "Saucillo." Wislizenus's map has it as "El Saucillo."

13.   Gregg calls this "La Cruz del Refugio."

14.   Both Gregg and Wislizenus record this as "Las Garzas."

15.   Gregg calls this "Rancho of Saucillo." Wislizenus makes no mention of it.

16.   Gregg has this as the rancho of "San Jose del Pozo." Wislizenus calls it simply "el Pozo."

17.   Gregg records the name as both "Don Manuel Ivarra" and "Ibarra," and Wilizenus, "Don Manuel de Ibarra." Gregg writes that the estate belonged to Manuel and his brother, "both of whom were educated at Bardstown, Kentucky, and speak very fair English, especially the brother: and possessed of enlightened, liberal, *American* principles, they were anything but popular with Santa Anna and his party." *Diary and Letters*, 2:91–92. Manuel was also the proprietor of El Pozo. See Wislizenus, *Memoir of a Tour to Northern Mexico*, 72.

18.   When Doniphan's troops were marching through the area in May 1847, Ivarra, or de la Vara, had enlisted Captain John W. Reid's help to attack a band of approximately fifty Indians who had recently stolen several hundred mules and horses and taken several Mexicans captive. Reid and some thirty men, including Ivarra, attacked the Indians at El Pozo, killing thirteen to seventeen (accounts vary) and regaining the stolen stock and the captives. Wislizenus, *Memoir of a Tour to Northern Mexico*, 71–72; Gregg, *Diary and Letters*, 2:123–125; and Connelley, *Doniphan's Expedition*, 476–477.

19.   Gregg offers this description:

      This was a most inhuman massacre, as the wagoners were butchered unarmed — and many, it was believed, burned alive! This cut-throat band was under command of Gen. Urrea — variously stated to be from 500 to 2000 in number. The wagons were rifled and burned. Besides some public property and money, there was a considerable amount of sutler's goods. It was many days after, before the murdered wagoners were buried; which was so badly done that the wolves had scratched many of the bodies up again, and their skeletons still lay bleaching on the plain! (*Diary and Letters*, 2: 139–140)

      An account of the guerrilla attack of February 24, 1847, as told by a wagonmaster in the train, is in Samuel E. Chamberlain, *My Confession* (New York: Harper & Brothers, 1956), 175–176. See also Edwards, *Campaign in New Mexico*, 152–153.

20.   Wislizenus and Gregg have "Puntiagudo."

21.   The *Fashion* was a large sidewheeler of 419 tons. Built in 1842 in New York, N.Y., it had been sold to the U.S. Quartermaster's Department in January 1847. William M. Lytle and Forrest R. Holdcamper, comps., and Bradford Mitchell, ed., *Merchant Steam Vessels of the United States, 1790–1868*, (Staten Island, N.Y.: Steamship Historical Society of America, 1975), 71.

22. According to an article from the New Orleans *Picayune* of May 4, 1848 (carried in the St. Louis *Missouri Republican* of May 12, 1848), the *Fashion* arrived in New Orleans on May 3, having left Brazos Santiago on April 30. William arrived in St. Louis on board the *Marshall Ney* on the evening of May 14, 1848. St. Louis *Missouri Republican*, May 15, 1848.

PART III

LETTERS OF EDWARD J. GLASGOW TO WILLIAM E. CONNELLEY

1906-1907

August 13, 1906.

Mr. William E. Connelley,

Topeka, Kansas.

Dear Sir:

Your letter of the 6th instant to Mr. Hargadine was forwarded to me here, where I am passing the summer, and I can probably give you more information about Dr. Henry Connelly than any person living.

In the year 1843 I went from Mazatlan, where I had been in business, to Chihuahua and formed a partnership with him to engage in the overland trade between that city and the United States, starting from Independence, Missouri. Dr. Connelly had already been in business several years in Chihuahua, was moderately well off and in good standing and credit as a merchant of ability, integrity and fair dealing, besides enjoying the personal friendship of many of the influential Mexicans and all of his own countrymen in that city. Our partnership continued until after the close of our war with Mexico in 1848.

To keep up our supply of goods we made yearly expeditions across the plains, transporting the goods in large wagons, and always at considerable risk of having our mules stampeded by thieving Indians at night.

As I was much the younger partner, most of the traveling devolved on me, while Dr. Connelly kept the store in Chihuahua and managed the business there, and was residing there when the city was captured by Colonel Doniphan.

When the war ended we both left Chihuahua, and Dr. Connelly located in New Mexico where he married Mrs. Chaves, a widow living at the village of Peralta, where he resided afterwards and continued in business several years in that Territory.[2]

He was appointed Governor of New Mexico during Mr. Lincoln's administration and died there, I think, about two years after his appointment.[3] I always understood him to be a native of Kentucky. He was educated for a physician, and was a man of intelligence. His step son, J. Francisco Chaves, a prominent politician, at one time delegate to Congress, was murdered about two years ago.[4] In the year 1846 war was declared against Mexico, just as I was leaving Independence with a large train of wagons loaded with our supply of merchandise for Chihuahua, and we accompanied the 1st Regiment of Dragoons under command of Colonel Stephen W. Kearny, as far as Santa Fe. At that time it was understood that General Wool was en route to occupy Chihuahua, and Colonel Doniphan was ordered to report to him there with his regiment. On arriving at El Paso, we learned that General Wool had joined his force with Taylor at Monterey and Buena Vista.

In consequence of this information and that the Mexican force at Chihuahua far outnumbered ours, Colonel Doniphan issued an order that all American traders and their wagoners should form into two companies of Infantry, elect their own officers, be mustered into the U.S. service and accompany him, which was done. The two companies numbered considerably over 200 men.

Henry Skilman[5] commanded one and I commanded the other, as Captains, and the battalion was commanded by another trader, Samuel C. Owens, as Major.

On nearing the Sacramento Ranch, about 16 miles from Chihuahua, it was found that the Mexicans had erected fortifications on the opposite side of the stream of that name, and on high ground awaited us.

Our wagons were then formed in four parallel columns, about thirty feet apart, the army being inclosed inside, and turning off the road, we crossed the stream nearly a mile distant and reached higher ground, when we turned toward the enemy and the fight began.

A few rounds of grape and spherical case shot soon drove back some cavalry which had come out from their works, when our whole force moved forward, with the result you know.

The Trader's Battalion has been badly treated by the Government, for although it participated in the battle and its Major, Samuel C. Owens, was killed in the engagement, none of us ever received any pay or pensions, the excuse given for refusal being that Colonel Doniphan had no legal authority to create any new companies of troops.[6]

Mention is made of this fact because you are writing a history of this Expedition.

My home is at St. Louis, but I will be here several months.

Yours truly, Edward J. Glasgow

TELEPHONE 6800 BROAD

GOVERNORS ISLAND
NEW YORK

Aug. 22nd 1906

Mr Wm E. Connelley
Dear Sir

Your favor of [the] 16th came duly. I am very willing to give you the information you ask for, but have to request some patience on your part, as my time is much occupied during this summer outing, and as I am in my 87th year I cannot write as rapidly nor as continuously as I could fifty years ago. My idea is from time to time, to jot down with a pencil the events as they come to mind and have them transcribed when completed.

I was born at Belleville, Illinois, thirteen miles from St Louis, in the year 1820, the year that Missouri was admitted to the Union of States on the claim that, although a census could not be taken, the population of the state was over 40,000.[7]

Our family came to St Louis (7) seven years later, which has been my home ever since, except for eight years passed in the Republic of Mexico.

I think there are some mistakes in the items of your letter

Mr. [Albert] Speyer[8] had charge of his own train. Gov Armijo had no train of goods that year.[9] Some time after Speyer had gone, a report became current that he was carrying powder to the Mexicans which report was afterwards shown to be erroneous.[10]

Col Kearny however sent a Compy of Dragoons from Ft Leavenworth, to stop Speyer, but the troops never caught up to him

They however stopped all other trains, our's included, until the army came up, and we followed in its rear

I was an intimate acquaintance of Mr Owens, (our Major of whom you write) and I dont believe he was desirous of being killed.[11] If his horse was white, it certainly was not the only white one.

I was conversing with him when the battle was beginning but have no recollections that there was anything particularly conspicuous in his appearance

Yours Truly
E J Glasgow

Governor's Island, New York,
November 2nd 1906.

Mr. Wm. E. Connelley,

921, Taylor Street, Topeka. Kansas

Dear Sir:

In reply to your request for information about the trade of New Mexico and Chihuahua for the period up to 1850, the goods dealt in were largely of brown and bleached cottonmanufactures and printed cottons or calico — some few silk goods and woolen cloth and cassimeres were included and the usual assortment of articles sold in dry goods stores, but the great bulk of the trade was in cotton goods. Up to the time of our war with Mexico these goods were sent in steamboats to Independence, Missouri, and there loaded in wagons of large size and generally drawn by eight or ten mules — oxen were occasionally used, but mules were preferred, being faster and better able to live on the short grass of the plains, to endure fatigue and the long stretches where water was not obtainable. No white people lived on the road between Independence and Las Vegas, — The plains were occupied by many tribes of Indians. Pawnees, Cheyennes, Arapahoes, Comanches, Kiowas, and Utes, — buffalo and antelope were plentiful and the chief subsistence for the traders and Indians. In New Mexico and Chihuahua the Apaches roamed and constant vigilance was necessary to protect the traders mules, there and on the plains from the Indians thieving. In New Mexico the trade was mostly in the hands of Mexicans.[12] In Chihuahua there were also several Mexicans, and among the Americans engaged in regular trade were James and Samuel Magoffin, Frank Macmanus, Connelley [Connelly] and Glasgow, and Owens and Aull. Other traders not regularly in the business were Webb and Doan of St. Louis, Barney and Hoffman of Baltimore, and Speyer of New York.

In 1846 while we were loading our train at Independence, news came that the war with Mexico had begun and thinking that goods would be scarce and high in Chihuahua, I left as quickly as possible, but was halted at Pawnee Fork, by Capt. Moore, who had been sent by General Kearney, from Ft. Leavenworth, with a troop of dragoons, to overtake a train which was supposed to be carrying powder to Santa Fe for Governor Armijo. He did not overtake it but caused all the traders to wait until General Kearney had passed with the U.S. Forces. We proceeded to Santa Fe with the Army, and all the traders went down the Rio Grande to Val Verde, where they formed a large camp and awaited the arrival of Colonel Doniphan, who had been ordered to report with the Regiment of Missouri Volunteers, to General Wool, who was supposed to be moving against Chihuahua.

On Doniphan's arrival, we proceeded with him to El Paso, where, learning that General Wool had gone to join forces with General Zach. Taylor, at Monterey, and that the Mexican force at Chihuahua far outnumbered ours, he issued the order for the American traders and their teamsters to form two companies of infantry, elect their officers, be sworn and mustered into the U.S. Service and accompany him with their wagons and goods to Chihuahua, which was done. The Captains of the companies were Henry Skillman and myself, the battalion being commanded by Major Samuel C. Owens, a trader also, who was killed at the Sacramento battle, a description of which I have written on another page. We were honorably discharged at Chihuahua, our assistance being no longer necessary.

Replying to some of your questions, I was in Chihuahua until the war ended and heard nothing of a confiscation of Mr. Harmony's goods. Ours were not seized nor those of the traders that I have named although they were Americans and our country at war with Mexico, and as Mr. Harmony was a Spaniard, I do not see what motive could exist for treating him more harshly or molesting him at all.[13] You ask for a description of my life, but it could not interest you much, as it has not been particularly eventful.

I was born at Belleville, Illinois in 1820. My father moved to Herculaneum, Mo. three years later, but as that town, unlike its namesake, was destroyed by water from overflow of the Mississippi river, we came to St. Louis, then a town of only 5000 people, in 1827, and that city has been my home ever since. In 1840, I went to Mazatlan, Mexico and engaged in business there, our goods being brought to us around Cape Horn in a vessel belonging to us, and remained there until 1843, when I formed the partnership with your relative, Dr. Connelley [Connelly] and engaged in the overland trade with Chihuahua, as previously written.

My letter is not written for publication in your book, nor with the care necessary for so doing, but merely for the purpose of giving some items of information to a relative of my former esteemed friend and partner in business.

Yours truly, Edward J. Glasgow

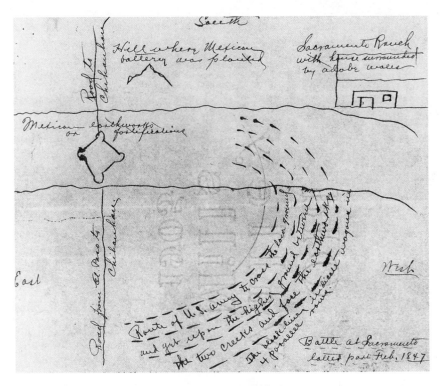

Edward James Glasgow's hand-drawn sketch of the Battle of Sacramento, which
accompanied his letter to William E. Connelley of November 2, 1906. Compare
this to the official sketch of the battle, which appears in the Editor's Introduction.
(Courtesy of the Kansas State Historical Society.)

The fortifications or earthworks thrown up by the Mexicans extended across
the road leading from Santa Fe and El Paso to Chihuahua, and were on high
ground between Sacramento creek and the bed of another dry creek. On
arriving within a mile of them Col. Doniphan, ordered all the wagons of the
traders and Army, (about 160 in number), to be formed in four parallel
columns, about 30 feet apart, the Army placed between them, when they
turned off the road and crossed the dry creek nearly a mile to the west,
coming up on higher ground, when they turned and faced the enemy. It
looks as if the Mexicans thought that Col. Doniphan was avoiding a battle
and possibly seeking shelter in the buildings and walls of Sacramento Ranch,
as they sent out a large body of cavalry to attack. When they came near our
artillery opened fire on them with solid shot and spherical case shot some

of which bursted among the cavalry causing confusion and a rapid retreat to the main body. Doniphans force formed immediately and moved rapidly towards the earthworks under a fire of musketry and artillery. On coming near the Mexicans broke and fled in several directions, pursued by our men, and leaving their artillery and stores behind. The wagon columns kept up their formation and moved as rapidly as possible and as near the Army as possible, making a kind of moving fortification, as in case of a repulse, our troops could have fallen back between the wagons which could have been corralled into a fort.

From the best information I could get the Mexican forces numbered about 3000 and Doniphan's force, including the Traders and Teamster's Battalion about 1100.

Governor's Island, N.Y.,
November 27th 1906.

Mr. William E. Connelley,
      Topeka, Kansas.
Dear Sir:

Replying to your letter of the 19th instant, I feel certain in thinking that Peter[14] and the old survivors are mistaken about any confiscation of Dr. Connelly's property at any time. He and I were partners from the beginning of 1843 till the end of the war with Mexico and previously to that time he always had the friendship of the officials. He and other Americans were in Chihuahua at the time of the Sacramento battle. They were not allowed to leave the city until the battle was over but were not imprisoned. In regard to Mr. James Kirker; he was an Irishman by birth, a large, strong athletic man who had been with the fur company for some years among the Indians. He was employed by the State of Chihuahua to drive out the Apaches and for that purpose employed a number of Delaware and Shawnee Indians. I was told that he received a stipulated sum, $40.00 each, I think, for the scalps of the men and half price for those of the squaws and children and succeeded in ridding the State of Apache annoyance. He met Doniphan above El Paso and offered his services as scout and guide against the Mexicans. Doniphan accepted the services but regarded him with suspicion as he had been living with his family in Chihuahua and employed as above stated, and although he led the scouting parties in advance, men were watching him, ready to put a bullet in him in case of treachery. He proved faithful however to the end.[15] Mr. James L. Collins was living in Chihuahua when I first went there. He came from Boon-ville, Mo. While the war was going on he was arrested as a spy at El Paso and brought to Chihuahua for trial. Mr. Pomeroy[16] of Lexington, Mo., employed a man to throw a rope over the prison one dark night by which Collins climbed over.[17] He went to the livery stable, took out his mule and escaped and met Sterling Price's force coming down for the last battle of the war, where General Trias was defeated at Santa Cruz sixty miles south of Chihuahua. He was afterwards made depository of government money at Santa Fe and was found one morning dead from a pistol shot in his office with the safe door open.

I have no recollection of Major John P. Campbell[18] of whom you make inquiries. There is an error in regard to Mr. [George A.F.] Ruxton,[19] an Englishman who came up to our camp at Val Verde on his way east, leaving Dr. Connelly in Chihuahua and consequently could not have furnished any information to him as stated in your letter. An incident concerning him was said to have occurred in camp at Val Verde, when one of the wagoners who was plying him with questions to which he got very curt and unsatisfactory answers finally asked him if he was an American, and on being told that he was an Englishman remarked, "Well, you must have lived in the States a good while for you talk 'Merican' damn nigh as well as I do."

In reply to your other question, it was understood that Captain [John W.] Reid who had distinguished himself at the fight on the Xmas previous above El Paso should lead the charge [at Sacramento] with one hundred picked men. They were well advanced when Adjutant [James A.] De Courcy ordered a halt. Captain Reid and some others, not hearing the order, kept on alone and finding his men had halted rode back and asked the reason. Upon hearing that De Courcy had ordered them to stop, he exclaimed "Well, I order you to charge", which was gallantly done.

This circumstance is of course from hearsay as I was bringing up the four columns of wagons, Major Owens having left me in charge and gone on with Reid. In this charge Major Owens was killed within twenty feet of the breastworks.

I think [James L.] Collins and [James] Kirker were along [in the charge] but I am not positive.

Yours truly,
Edward J. Glasgow

73 East 92[20]nd Street
New York Jan 22 1907

Mr W[m] Connelley
Topeka Kas.
My dear Sir

In reply to your favor of three weeks ago I can only say that, although it is strange, I have no recollection of Major Campbell, nor do I know anything about Skillman's early history, or nativity but am of the opinion he was an American.

When I first knew him he had the reputation of being a noted Indian fighter. As to my photograph, while not personally ambitious of notoriety myself, my family and several others of my relatives seem to desire you should carry out your intention. Having none on hand myself, my grand niece Miss Eleanor Glasgow Voorhis has sent you one by mail, which please return to her when you have used it.

Wishing you success with your forth coming book I remain

Your's very truly
E. J. Glasgow[21]

73 East 92nd Street
New York Feb 26. 1907

Mr W[m] E. Connelley
My dear Sir

Your letter came duly to hand and copies of the prospectus to your book.[22] It was a real treat to see the pictures of my old friends and brought back remembrances of auld lang syne which had almost passed out of memory. It will give me much pleasure to distribute the prospectus where they will bring subscribers for the book. I have already disposed of two, possibly three, which I think will have that result, and on my return to St. Louis will continue my efforts in that way, for which purpose, you might when convenient, send a few more.

It was gratifying to see my face reproduced in the company of old friends, to know whom was a pleasure and an honor, although, personally, I have not cared for notoriety and have rather avoided being conspicuous.

One of the copies I have sent to my friend Judge Joseph Magoffin[23] at El Paso, Texas who is among the most prominent men in that city, and who is the son of James Magoffin. The latter named gentleman was a prominent trader in Chihuahua many years before I went there and probably antedated D^r. Connelly as a merchant, being associated in business with his brother Samuel of a prominent Kentucky family.

When I was in El Paso I saw at the Judge's house,[24] a portrait of his father, and if you would write the Judge he might give you items about his father, and, if you desired a photograph of his father's portrait.[25]

There is an item about our Battalion which I would reiterate which is the way it has been treated by the Government. As you know, when Doniphan reached El Paso expecting to report to Gen. Wool at Chihuahua, he learned [that] Wool was not there, but instead there was a Mexican Army, far outnumbering his, awaiting him in a fortified position. In this emergency he called for artillery from Santa Fe and ordered the Traders and their men over 200 in number to be organized into a Battalion and mustered into the U.S. Service.

They responded willingly and cheerfully, and stood by him until he reached Chihuahua after participating in The Battle of Sacramento where the Mex^n. force was defeated and dispersed.

One of the men of my company Richard C. Cabeen afterwards applied for a pension, but was refused on the ground that the Battalion was not "duly enlisted" and mustered in" the U.S. Army.[26] The reason they were not "duly" enlisted was a legal technicality that Doniphan had no power or authority to create new companies of troops

As a very large number of the volunteer army in New Mexico never heard a hostile gun fired, but have regularly drawn pensions, it looks like simple justice that the Trader's Battalion ought to have received equal consideration and treatment, having rallied to Doniphan's aid at a time, his action showed he considered the emergency called for it

Very Truly your's
E J Glasgow

HEADQUARTERS THE ATLANTIC DIVISION
OFFICE OF THE AIDES-DE-CAMP
GOVERNOR'S ISLAND, NEW YORK

Mch 22/07

Mr Wm E. Connelley
Topeka
Dear Sir:

I have disposed of the copies of your prospectus where I think they will bring you some subscribers. Among others I sent one to Henry S Kearny, son of General Kearny His address is 100 Broadway New York[27]

Mr Western Bascom of St Louis who married a daughter of General Kearny would probably like to have a copy.[28] and I suggest that you mail him one and write a few lines at the same time His address is Century Building St Louis Mo.

Yours truly
E J Glasgow
I expect to return to St Louis by middle of April. My address there is 213 N. 2nd Street

TELEPHONE 6800 BROAD

GOVERNORS ISLAND
NEW YORK

March 30th 1907

Mr Wm E. Connelley
My dear Sir

I have just rec^d a note from Mr Henry S. Kearny 100 Broadway thanking me for the prospectus and saying he would order several copies of the book

He is, as I wrote, the son of Gen Stephen W Kearny who took possession of New Mexico and conquered California, where his battle at San Pascual was the bloodiest of the whole war, taking into consideration the numbers engaged.[29] Many of his officers were killed. I had no prospectus left to send Mr. Bascom — son-in law of Genl Kearny. whose address as I wrote, is Century Building St Louis

your's truly E J Glasgow

["HEADQUARTERS. . . " scratched out on stationery]
GOVERNOR'S ISLAND, NEW YORK

April 17th 1907

Mr Wm E. Connelley
My dear Sir

Your last favor was received some days [back] asking for a more detailed history of my experiences in early life, but that was so uneventful that I do not think it would interest the readers of your book. The natural affection of my niece Miss Voorhis magnifies little occurrences into greater importance than they would otherwise be considered.

The last picture she sent was from a miniature painted when I was about to leave on my first trip to Mexico.[30]

I was then only 20 years old.

When I started, my expectation was to locate our business at Guaymas in the State of Sonora, but on arriving there I decided to change location to

Mazatlan State of Sinaloa, where I remained two years and a half and disposed of the cargos of three vessels.

Before leaving home I was appointed U.S. consul for Guaymas by President Van Buren but as I did not remain at that Sea Port, I resigned my commission.

Being much younger than Dr. Connelley [Connelly], I was kept on the plains with our trains, pretty constantly, while in business with him. Always fond of hunting, the buffalos and antelopes furnished full occasion for this pastime, while the moderate danger from Indians, kept up an excitement, not particularly unpleasant except for the trouble and constant watchfulness at night, to guard against stampedes. I was surprised at the information in your last letter, that Col [Thomas Hart] Benton had stated that the occupation of New Mexico was secured by negotiations of Mr Magoffin with Armijo, something I had never heard before.[31] Gen. Kearny incurred the hatred of Benton by sending Col. John C Fremont home from California under arrest for insubordination, of which I think, he was convicted by a court martial, and suspended for a while.[32]

I had hoped to be back at St Louis before now, but serious illness in my family in New York has detained me

Very truly your's

E. J. Glasgow

TELEPHONE 6800 BROAD

GOVERNORS ISLAND

NEW YORK

May. 15"/07

Mr. Wm E. Connelley,
My dear Sir;

Miss Voorhis by telephone has told me of the particulars you desire of Mr. [Ceran] St. Vrain,[33] my acquaintance was slight with him compared with that of his partners Chas. W^m & George Bent at Bents Fort, sometimes called "Bents & St. Vrains Fort" on the Arkansas. He was a French gentleman of polished manners & intrepid character which made him feared by the Indians more than his partners who were of milder tempers. I've heard an incident related of him which illustrates his character as a man of nerve. When camped at Pawnee Fork for the noon day meal two Pawnees came into camp on foot & while being entertained a body of Pawnees came from under the bank & drove off all their oxen over which contrary to the custom of the traders they kept no guard. The two Indians broke and ran but were captured & brought back to camp. Mr. St. Vrains horse was tied to a wagon & he told one of the Indians to mount him & bring back his oxen & if they were not returned before sun down he would cut the other Indians throat, the oxen were returned in time. In my trips across the plains I generally took the "Cimmaron" route & passed the [Bent's] Fort on only two occassions. Wishing I could give you more information

I am,

Very truly yours,

E J Glasgow.

["HEADQUARTERS . . . " scratched out on stationery]
GOVERNOR'S ISLAND, NEW YORK
May 23rd 1907

Mr Wm E. Connelley
My dear Sir

Your letter of 21st is received. I had no acquaintance with the Sublettes, being very young when they figured in St. Louis, in business connection with Robt. Campbell.[34]

Neither did I know Beckwith or Beckwourth, who I believe was a prominent trapper.[35] My only recollection of Gen Wm Ashley is having been at his house when I was a boy, at which time, I think it was, he was Representative in Congress. I think his wife was a Missouri lady, Miss Wilcox — his widow afterwards married John J. Crittenden of Ky.[36]

The Bent family comprised four or five brothers of whom I knew four, Charles, William, George and Silas.[37] The latter was an officer in the Navy and resigned before or about the time of the Civil War

I think his wife was Miss Tyler of Kentucky — his widow and daughter live in St. Louis.[38]

When Gen. Kearny was at Santa Fe he set up a temporary Government
and, as you probably know, appointed Charles Bent as Governor of New
Mexico, and, as you also know, Governor Bent was killed at Taos in an
uprising of Mexicans and Pueblo Indians, against the new Government. I
will be on the lookout for information as you request, and will be pleased
if I can collect any that will interest you.

Very truly your's

E. J. Glasgow

NOTES

1. The following letters were written to historian William E. Connelley in reponse to his
   inquiries concerning Edward Glasgow's life and experiences along the Santa Fe Trail and
   during the Mexican War. Connelley quotes many of them in the notes to his *War with
   Mexico, 1846–1847: Doniphan's Expedition and the Conquest of New Mexico and California* (Kansas City:
   Bryant & Douglas Book and Stationery Co., 1907). The originals are now housed at the
   Kansas State Historical Society in Topeka. They are here published in their entirety for
   the first time.
       Governors Island (often spelled with an apostrophe in the official stationery of the
   day) was an administrative center for the U.S. Army. Edward's son, Captain William
   Jefferson Glasgow, arrived here from the Philippines as an aide-de-camp to Major
   General James F. Wade about 1905. He served in that capacity until April 14, 1907,
   when Wade retired. William remained at Governors Island on "special duty" at the
   headquarters, Department of the East, until late August 1907. George W. Cullum,
   Biographical Register of the Officers and Graduates of the U.S. Military Academy at West Point, New York,
   Since Its Establishment in 1802, Supplement, vol. 5, 1900–1910, ed. Charles Braden (Saginaw,
   Mich.: Seemann & Peters, 1910), 5:468; and Lewis S. Sorly and Octavia Magoffin
   Glasgow, "Official Biography of Gen. Glasgow," *Southwesterner* 5 (May 1966):2 and 6.
   Edward stayed with his son at Governors Island off and on during this period. As will
   be seen from the following letters, he occasionally used stationery from his son's office
   to respond to Connelley's inquiries.
2. Connelly married Dolores Perea, the widow of Mariano Jose Chavez, in 1849 (Connelly
   was also a widower at this time). Their residence was on a large rancho near Peralta
   known as Los Pinos. In 1846 Wislizenus wrote that the widow Chavez's "hacienda is
   the largest we have yet seen. It embraces a large tract of land, with cornfields and an
   extensive pasture, shaded by cotton trees, and fenced in by a wall made from adobes,
   and by a ditch with running water. The comfortable dwelling-house of the owner, with
   the opposite huts of the Indian serfs, bore a striking resemblance to a southern
   plantation in the United States." From 1862 to 1867 Los Pinos served as a military post,
   Connelly and his stepsons leasing the property to the U.S. government. Marc Simmons,
   Murder on the Santa Fe Trail: An International Incident, 1843 (El Paso: Texas Western Press, 1987),
   2–3 and 74; Ralph Emerson Twitchell, *The Leading Facts of New Mexican History*, 2 vols. (Cedar
   Rapids, Iowa: Torch Press, 1911 and 1912), 391, n. 316; Frederick Wislizenus, *Memoir
   of a Tour to Northern Mexico, Connected with Colonel Doniphan's Expedition in 1846 and 1847* (1848;
   facsimile reprint, Albuquerque: Calvin Horn Publisher, 1969), 35; and Darlis A. Miller,

"Los Pinos, New Mexico: Civil War Post on the Rio Grande," *New Mexico Historical Review* 62 (January 1987):4–5 and 1.

3.   Connelly was appointed territorial governor of New Mexico by President Abraham Lincoln in 1861 and reappointed in 1864, serving until July 16, 1866. He died the following month, on August 12, 1866. Connelley, *Doniphan's Expedition*, 282, n. 65; and Calvin Horn, *New Mexico's Troubled Years: The Story of the Early Territorial Governors* (Albuquerque: Horn & Wallace, 1963), 110.

4.   José Francisco Chavez (1833–1904) commanded New Mexico troops during the Civil War and was elected New Mexico's delegate in Congress in 1865. A "staunch republi-can," he served in the territorial legislature for several years. He was "assassinated" on November 26, 1904. Twitchell, *Leading Facts of New Mexican History*, 400–401, n. 326. See also William A. Keleher, *Turmoil in New Mexico, 1846–1868* (Santa Fe: Rydal Press, 1952), 480–481, n. 1.

5.   Henry Skillman was the wagonmaster for Francisco Elguea's train of wagons in 1846–1847. Edward remembered him as having a "reputation of being a noted Indian fighter." He was among those Americans who left for Santa Fe when Doniphan evacuated Chihuahua in late April 1847. According to historian Ralph Bieber, Skillman served as an interpreter and guide for troops sent to El Paso in October. He later returned to Santa Fe, where, in February 1848, General Price "engaged" him and about fifteen men as "spies" for the Chihuahua campaign. In 1851 Skillman was living in El Paso, Texas. According to his claim for bounty land submitted that year, he was thirty-seven years old. In the early 1850s he operated a mail and stage service between San Antonio, El Paso, and Santa Fe. Bieber reports that Skillman served with the Confederacy during the Civil War and was "killed near Presidio del Norte on the night of April 13, 1864." George R. Gibson, *Journal of a Soldier Under Kearny and Doniphan, 1846–1847*, ed. Ralph P. Bieber, Southwest Historical Series, vol. 3 (Glendale, Calif.: Arthur H. Clark, 1935), 328; Connelley, *Doniphan's Expedition*, 109; Philip St. George Cooke et al., *Exploring Southwestern Trails, 1846–1854*, ed. Ralph P. Bieber in collaboration with Averam B. Bender, Southwest Historical Series, vol. 7 (Glendale, Calif.: Arthur H. Clark, 1938), 311–312, n. 258; Skillman Bounty Land File (BLF) 3525-Rejected-55, Record Group (RG) 15, National Archives (NA); *Santa Fe Republican*, February 12, 1848; W. H. Timmons, *El Paso: A Borderlands History* (El Paso: Texas Western Press, 1990), 138–139; and Santa Fe *Weekly Gazette*, January 14, 1854.

6.   Several members of the Traders Battalion applied for bounty land based on their service with Doniphan. Some received their service with Donipan. Some received their land warrants and some did not. Although Edward Glasgow had filed the muster rolls for the two companies with the secretary of war in June 1849, they were apparently misplaced or lost at different times (some records indicate that only the roll for Glasgow's company was filed). Many bounty land claims from members of the Traders Battalion were rejected because no evidence of their service (i.e., the muster rolls) could be found. Edward and William Glasgow, however, both received their land warrants. When Edward was seeking a pension based on his service in the Traders Battalion, the military secretary at the War Department reported in 1906 that "it does not appear that such an organization . . . was ever mustered into the military service of the United States, and there are no rolls of the organization on file in this office." Yet it was hoped by those assisting Edward that evidence of his having received a land warrant would be sufficient proof of his military service. The acting commissioner of the Pension Bureau, however, informed them that this tactic had been used with another individual in Edward's company, Richard C. Cabeen, and his case had been rejected. And if a claim was filed for Edward Glasgow, he was "reasonably certain . . . it would have to be rejected

on the ground that he was not duly enlisted or mustered into the service of the United States." As mentioned in the Editor's Introduction, a bill was introduced in the House of Representataives by H. M. Coudrey to grant Edward a pension, but Edward's death in 1908 apparently ended the effort. Hamilton G. Fant to George C. Whiting, Washington, D.C., May 19, 1857; F. C. Ainsworth to H. M. Coudrey, Washington, D.C., January 28, 1907; Julian K. Glasgow to W. C. Taylor, St. Louis, January 2, 1907; J. L. Davenport to W. C. Taylor, Washington, D.C., February 5, 1907; and J. L. Davenport to H. M. Coudrey, Washington, D.C., February 5, 1907; all in E. J. Glasgow BLF 76336-160-55, RG 15, NA; U.S. Congress, House, *Suppression of Hostilities in New Mexico*, H.R. Rep. 52, 37th Cong., 3rd sess., March 3, 1863 (Serial 1173), 1–3. While in Washington, D.C., in September 1990, I made a special effort to locate the lost rolls of the Traders Battalion at the National Archives. Today the rolls would prove extremely valuable in identifying the many traders and teamsters on the Santa Fe and Chihuahua trails in 1846–1847. Although ably assisted by the staff of the Military Reference Branch and others, I was unsuccessful. However, many of the bounty land claims for members of the Traders Battalion survive and can be traced as long as one knows the names of the particular individuals.

7.   Missouri had adopted a state constitution in 1820, but it was not admitted to the Union until 1821.

8.   Albert Speyer (or Speyers), a Prussian Jew, was by 1846 known in the Santa Fe trade "for his energy, perseverance and fearlessness" (Wislizenus, *Memoir of a Tour to Northern Mexico*, 5). Most sources agree that he left the trade after the Mexican War. In the 1860s he was residing in New York City. The Mercantile Agency reported in 1861 that he had formerly been in the lager beer-brewing business. At the time, however, he was purchasing goods for the sutlers of a German regiment near Washington. In 1863 he was a member of the firm of Speyers & Dupre (later Speyers, Dupre & Co.), dealers in bullion and specie and manufacturers of silver nitrate. Speyer was the sole member of the business in late 1864 and two years later the Mercantile Agency was told that he was worth $100,000. In 1867 the credit agency reported that Speyer was "a large and bold speculator estimated worth from 30 @ 40^m\$, at present not doing much supp[osed] to have lost largely." Speyer's bold speculating came to an end with the "Black Friday" crash of 1869, Speyer having purchased millions of dollars worth of gold for Jay Gould and others when the crash occurred. The Mercantile Agency report for September 29, 1869, contained one word: "Failed." What appears to be the last report for Speyer, dated October 17, 1870, states that he "is very largely in debt in consequence of his gold transactions, during the panic last year — cannot do bus[iness]. on the street & has no cred[it] (New York City, vol. 378, 279, R. G. Dun & Co. Coll., BLHBS). Speyer is said to have committed suicide sometime thereafter. There is, however, a Mercantile Agency report for an Albert G.P. Speyers, stockbroker, dated October 9, 1888 (New York City, vol. 378, 409, R. G. Dun & Co. Coll., BLHBS). Whether this is the same Speyer or a relation I have been unable to determine. See also James Josiah Webb, *Adventures in the Santa Fe Trade, 1844–1847*, ed. Ralph P. Bieber, Southwest Historical Series, vol. 1 (Glendale, Calif.: Arthur H. Clark, 1931), 54, N. 67; and Susan Shelby Magoffin, *Down the Santa Fe Trail and into Mexico, 1846–1847*, ed. Stella M. Drumm (New Haven: Yale University Press, 1926), 246–247, n. 105.

9.   Edward is in error here. Manuel Armijo's train was one of the early caravans to leave Independence, and for that reason Edward may not have been aware of it. The Armijo train may have been traveling with Speyer's wagons. See Louise Barry, *Beginning of the West: Annals of the Kansas Gateway to the American West, 1540–1854* (Topeka: Kansas State Historical Society, 1972), 580; Webb, *Adventures in the Santa Fe Trade*, 179; and Bieber, introduction in Gibson, *Journal of a Soldier*, 41, n. 81.

10. According to James Josiah Webb, who traveled with Speyer from Santa Fe to the fair at San Juan de los Lagos, Speyer's train did indeed have two wagonloads of Mississippi rifles and ammunition the Chihuahua governor had ordered the previous year. Speyer was afterwards arrested by Lieutenant Colonel Mitchell at Chihuahua and put on trial. James Josiah Webb tells us, however, that before the trial Speyer "kept 'open house' and entertained liberally. Whist parties with wine were held every night in his rooms, and many articles of bric-a-brac which he had bought at the fair, such as silver bridle reins, silver fans, and other Mexican curiosities, disappeared from his shelves. And after a couple of weeks he was tried before a court-martial and honorably acquitted." The St. Louis *Missouri Republican* of May 18, 1847, received correspondence from Chihuahua that reported that Speyer was "innocent of any crime. He had six kegs of powder when he left Independence, and sixty muskets, which the Mexicans took from him." The two wagons had been taken from Speyer's train at Chihuahua and, according to historian Stella Drumm, Speyer later submitted a claim for payment to Governor Trias. It is quite possible that the two wagons contained more than the sixty muskets and six kegs of powder reported in St. Louis. Webb, *Adventures in the Santa Fe Trade*, 181, 206–207, 210, and 275–276; and Magoffin, *Down the Santa Fe Trail*, 247, n. 105.

11. Edward may have been trying to protect the memory of his old friend. He himself had written to his sister shortly after the battle that Owens "no doubt sought his own death." See E. J. Glasgow to Mary Susan Glasgow, Chihuahua, March 12, 1847, in Part I.

12. This is an important comment made by Edward, which is supported by other primary sources. Captain Philip St. George Cooke reported in 1843, after spending a summer escorting trains along the Santa Fe Trail, that "the trade is falling into the hands of the Mexicans: of about 200 wagon loads which I have escorted this year, I do not believe ten have belonged to Americans who were resident citizens" (Cooke, "A Journal of the Santa Fe Trail," ed. William E. Connelley, *Mississippi Valley Historical Review* 12 [September 1925]:254). Josiah Gregg wrote that "in 1843, the greater portion of the traders were New Mexicans, several of whom, during the three years previous, had embarked in this trade, of which they bid fair to secure a monopoly" (Gregg, *Commerce of the Prairies*, ed. Max L. Moorhead [Norman: University of Oklahoma Press, 1954], 332). In1846 a soldier of the Army of the West at Santa Fe noted that "many of the [overland] traders are native Mexicans from the south" (St. Louis *Weekly Reveille*, January 4, 1847). By the early 1840s, much of the goods transported over the Santa Fe Trail were intended for the richer markets of Chihuahua and points below. Although there were several Mexican merchants involved in this trade as well, William H. Glasgow wrote of Chihuahua in 1843 that "the Commerce of this place is generally in the hands of the Americans and a few German & French merchants" (W. H. Glasgow, "Memorandums of a Trip Through Mexico in 1842 & 1843," in W. M. Glasgow Coll.).

13. Manuel X. Harmony's goods were not confiscated. See Part I, note 9.

14. Peter Connelly was a son of Henry Connelly. Peter served for a time as clerk to the New Mexico Territory Supreme Court. In 1868 he married Cornelia Davy, daughter of Chihuahua trader Cornelius Davy. At the time of Edward's letter he was living in Kansas City, Missouri. Connelley, *Doniphan's Expedition*, 280, n. 1.

15. Kirker died in California about 1853. The only full-length biography is William Cochran McGaw's *Savage Scene: The Life and Times of James Kirker, Frontier King* (New York: Hastings House, 1972).

16. Ebenezer W. Pomeroy (1806–1861) was involved in the Santa Fe trade at least as early as 1844. He was a sutler for Doniphan's regiment and traveled in that capacity to Chihuahua, temporarily joining the ranks for the Battle of Sacramento. Pomeroy left

Chihuahua for Santa Fe with a group of traders and others in early April 1847. Traveling with this party was George R. Gibson, who described Pomeroy as "an agreeable and pleasant companion." Pomeroy returned to Chihuahua a few months later to take charge of the estate of James Aull, his brother-in-law. When General Price arrived there in March 1848, Pomeroy accompanied his forces to Santa Cruz de Rosales, where he served Price as an aide-de-camp during the battle. Pomeroy traveled with Edward James Glasgow back to Missouri over the Santa Fe Trail. James and Robert Aull, "Letters of James and Robert Aull," ed. Ralph P. Bieber, *Missouri Historical Society Collections* 5 (1928), 295, n. 59; Barry, *Beginning of the West*, 514; Edwards, *Campaign in New Mexico*, 114; George R. Gibson, *Over the Chihuahua and Santa Fe Trails, 1847–1848*, ed. Robert W. Frazer (Albuquerque: University of New Mexico Press, 1981), 13–14; and Price to Jones, Chihuahua, March 31, 1848, in U.S. Congress, House, *Message from the President* . . . , Ex. Doc. 1, 30th Cong., 2nd sess., 1848 (Serial 537), 119.

17. According to the diary of Philip Gooch Ferguson, a soldier under Price, James L. Collins "made his escape from prison by cutting through the wall with a picket pin." Abraham Robinson Johnston, Marcellus Ball Edwards, and Philip Gooch Ferguson, *Marching with the Army of the West, 1846–1848*, ed. Ralph P. Bieber, Southwest Historical Series, vol. 4 (Glendale, Calif.: Arthur H. Clark, 1936), 353.

18. John P. Campbell (1804–1851), founder of Springfield, Missouri, was a beef contractor to the Army of the West. According to a biographical sketch prepared by his daughter, Campbell "engaged in the trade with northern Mexico and with Texas." Campbell accompanied Doniphan to Chihuahua and took part in the Battle of Sacramento. Although he is given the title of major in most accounts, he was not an enlisted volunteer in Doniphan's regiment (see also Part I, note 101). Connelley, *Doniphan's Expedition*, 77, 260, 451–453, n. 111; and Edwards in *Marching with the Army of the West*, 264.

19. George Augustus Frederick Ruxton (1821–1848), an English adventurer and sometime British agent, had arrived at Valverde about November 28, 1846, from Chihuahua. According to Lieutenant Abert, Ruxton had come there to "attend to the interest of those traders who acknowledge allegiance to Her Majesty." Ruxton had brought with him the circular from General Trias promising the traders safe entry for their goods if they employed Mexican teamsters and paid "proper duties." Abert, *Western America in 1846–1847* . . . , ed. John Galvin (San Francisco: John Howell, 1966), 66–69. Ruxton remained at Valverde until December 14, when he traveled north to Santa Fe with Lieutenant Abert's party. His own account of his experiences at the traders' camp is found in his *Adventures in Mexico and the Rocky Mountains*, (1847; reprint ed. Glorieta, N.Mex.: Rio Grande Press, 1973), 174–183. See also *Ruxton of the Rockies*, collected by Clyde and Mae Reed Porter, ed. LeRoy Hafen (Norman: University of Oklahoma Press, 1950).

20. This was the address of Julia Clark Voorhis (1842–1922), daughter of Edward's sister Eleanor. Also living at that address was Julia's daughter, Eleanor Glasgow Voorhis (1863–1919), and Mrs. Jefferson Kearny Clark. Mrs. Clark was Edward's younger sister, Mary Susan. Eleanor Glasgow Voorhis states in a letter to Connelley of January 1907 that Edward was spending the winter in their home. Eleanor Glasgow Voorhis to W. E. Connelley, New York, January 22, 1907, Connelley Coll., Manuscripts Department, Kansas State Historical Soceity (KSHS), Topeka, Kansas; and Clark Genealogy and "Cousin Wills $25,000 to Julian K. Glasgow," newspaper clipping, both in folder 14, box 10, Clark Family Papers, Missouri Historical Society, St. Louis, Missouri.

21. Eleanor Glasgow Voorhis wrote the following description of Edward for William Connelley:

As to Edward James Glasgow's personality, he is in full mental vigor at nearly eighty seven years of age. He speaks several languages, reads without glasses, & still takes

long journeys of over a thousand miles, spending much time in New York. Mr
Glasgow is a quiet man, devoting many hours to reading, but on any subject which
interests him, his conversation becomes brilliant, possessing the two-fold quality of
the rich and varied experience of so many years that are told, together with a wide
knowledge of the progressive thought of modern times.

He is a modest man, caring little for general society. At a dinner, however, he is the
life of the company, with his amusing stories & glowing anecdotes, told with a serious
face while his keen, dark brown eyes gleam with merriment. He can quote at great
length from the various poets of different periods.

His knowledge of the Bible is unusual and he has a deep reverence for religion
and the things of Eternal Truth. (Eleanor Glasgow Voorhis Manuscript, Connelley
Coll. KSHS)

22. William E. Connelley had printed a small pamphlet advertising his forthcoming book,
     which contained several photographs of individuals who figured in his text, including
     Edward Glasgow. Connelley's book, Doniphan's Expedition, was apparently available only by
     subscription.

23. Joseph Magoffin, born in Chihuahua in 1837, served with the Confederacy during the
     Civil War, taking part in General Henry H. Sibley's disastrous New Mexico campaign in
     1862. After the war he resided at El Paso, filling various elected positions, including
     that of mayor. Joseph Magoffin's daughter, Josephine, married William Jefferson Glas-
     gow, son of Edward James Glasgow, on October 29, 1896. Frank W. Johnson, History of
     Texas and Texans, 5 vols. (Chicago: American Historical Society, 1916), 5:2071–2072; and
     Sorly and Glasgow, "Official Biography of Gen. Glasgow," 2 and 6.

24. William J. Glasgow and his wife, Josephine, lived for many years in this adobe house,
     built by Joseph Magoffin in 1875. It is now a state historic site.

25. This portrait is reproduced in Connelley, Doniphan's Expedition, 196.

26. See Richard C. Cabeen BLF 75497-160-55, RG 15, NA.

27. Henry Stephen Kearny was born May 30, 1846, at Fort Leavenworth. Dwight L. Clarke,
     Stephen Watts Kearny: Soldier of the West (Norman: University of Oklahoma Press, 1961), 106.

28. Western Bascom (or Bascome) married Ellen Kearny, born at Jefferson Barracks on
     January 10, 1843. Clarke, Stephen Watts Kearny, 85 and 121.

29. The Battle (or rather skirmish) of San Pasqual was fought on December 6 and 7, 1846.
     Historian Dwight Clarke states that "few engagements can exceed San Pasqual's record
     for the deadliness of the combat." See Clarke, Stephen Watts Kearny, 195–232.

30. This miniature is reproduced in the Editor's Introduction.

31. In his Thirty Years' View, Benton credits Magoffin's negotiations with Armijo and
     Archuletta as the sole cause of the "bloodless conquest" of New Mexico. Magoffin, in
     his claim for remuneration for "secret and personal services" stated that "bloodless
     possession of New Mexico was what President Polk wished. It was obtained through
     my means." Despite the statements of Benton, Magoffin, and others, this episode of the
     Mexican War has remained clouded. The degree to which Magoffin contributed to the
     U.S. success is still questioned. If Magoffin's efforts were indeed as important as he and
     Benton claimed they were, it is interesting that the Mexican War letters of Edward and
     William Glasgow make no mention of them, and that as late as 1907 Edward was still
     unaware of them. Edward knew James Magoffin, as did his partner, Henry Connelly.
     Connelly also knew Armijo and Archuletta and provided intormation to Magoffin on
     whether the Mexicans intended to resist the U.S. army. Connelly later gave a deposition
     for Magoffin in which he states that it had been reported in Chihuahua that Magoffin

had "been the cause of non resistance and that he had bought over Genl. Armijo and Col. Archuletta." But Connelly does not personally substantiate the claim. Edward was in Chihuahua when James Magoffin arrived there after his release from imprisonment and certainly had many opportunities to learn of Magoffin's negotiations with Armijo and their impact, even if he did not report this information back to his family. It is also somewhat curious that Edward had not learned of this episode from Joseph Magoffin, James Magoffin's son, whom Edward calls a friend. Joseph Magoffin was aware of Benton's account, as he pointed it out to historian William E. Connelley. At any rate, Magoffin's services were considered important enough that a secret session of the Senate voted him an appropriation of $50,000. This was later reduced to $30,000 by the secretary of war. Magoffin's own statement of expenses and losses he incurred amounted to $37,780.96. Thomas Hart Benton, *Thirty Years' View; or, A History of the Working of the American Government for Thirty Years, from 1820 to 1850 ... by a Senator of Thirty Years*, 2 vols. (New York: D. Appleton & Co., 1854 and 1856), 2:682–684; "The Magoffin Papers," in Ralph Emerson Twitchell, *The Story of the Conquest of Santa Fe, New Mexico, and the Building of Old Fort Marcy, A.D. 1846*, Historical Society of New Mexico Publication No. 24 (Santa Fe: Historical Society of New Mexico, 1923); and Connelley, *Doniphan's Expedition*, 197, n. 39½. See also Max L. Moorhead, *New Mexico's Royal Road: Trade and Travel on the Chihuahua Trail* (Norman: University of Oklahoma Press, 1958), 158–161; and Daniel Tyler, "Governor Armijo's Moment of Truth," in Odie B. Faulk and Joseph A. Stout, Jr., eds., *The Mexican War: Changing Interpretations* (Chicago: Swallow Press, 1973).

32. The court-martial sentenced Fremont to be dismissed from the U.S. service. On February 17, 1848, President Polk remitted the sentence, however, and ordered that Fremont "report for duty." Fremont immediately resigned rather than "admit the justice of the decision." Benton, *Thirty Years' View*, 2:719. See also Clarke, *Stephen Watts Kearny*.

33. Ceran St. Vrain (1802–1870) was born in St. Louis. He first started across the plains for New Mexico in 1824 and formed his now-famous partnership with Charles Bent seven years later. See Harold H. Dunham, "Ceran St. Vrain," in LeRoy R. Hafen, ed., *The Mountain Men and the Fur Trade of the Far West*, 10 vols. (Glendale, Calif.: Arthur H. Clark, 1965–1972), 5:297–316; and David Lavender, *Bent's Fort* (Garden City, N.Y.: Doubleday, 1954).

34. Fur trappers and traders William Sublette and Robert Campbell formed the partnership of Sublette & Campbell in 1833. The firm was still in business as late as 1849. See Harvey L. Carter, "Robert Campbell," in Hafen, *Mountain Men and the Fur Trade*, 8: 49–60; and James Neal Primm, *Lion of the Valley: St. Louis, Missouri* (Boulder, Colo.: Pruett, 1981), 175.

35. James P. Beckwourth (1798–1866) is one of the more famous trappers and fur traders of the ninteenth-century West, primarily because of T. D. Bonner's *The Life and Adventures of James P. Beckwourth, Mountaineer, Scout, and Pioneer, and Chief of the Crow Nation of Indians*, first published in 1856 (reprint ed., Lincoln: University of Nebraska Press, 1972). During the Mexican War Beckwourth carried dispatches between Santa Fe and Fort Leavenworth. See Bonner, *James P. Beckwourth*, 476; *Santa Fe Republican*, February 12, 1848; and Barry, *Beginning of the West*, 730, and 764–765.

36. William H. Ashley (c. 1782–1838), the famous fur trader who along with Andrew Henry founded what eventually became the Rocky Mountain Fur Company, was a representative to Congress from 1831 until his death. Ashley's third and last wife was Elizabeth Moss Wilcox. She was also the third and last wife of John J. Crittenden (1787–1863), at various times U.S. senator and governor of Kentucky. Elizabeth outlived him as well. See Harvey L. Carter, "William H. Ashley," in Hafen, *Mountain Men and the Fur Trade*, 7:23–34; and Allen Johnson and Dumas Malone, eds., *Dictionary of American Biography*, vol. 4 (New York: Charles Scribner's Sons, 1930), 546–549.

204 et Lavender, Bent's Fort.

37. There were seven sons in the family of Judge Silas Bent, Sr.: Charles (1799–1847), John (1803–1845), William (1809–1869), George (1811–1847), Robert (1816–1841), Edward (1819–1824) and Silas (1820–1887). Frederic L. Billon, *Annals of St. Louis in Its Territorial Days from 1804 to 1821* (1888; reprint ed., New York: Arno Press, 1971), 200–201; and Lavender, *Bent's Fort.*

38. According to David Lavender, Bent resigned from the navy in 1861. Lavender also identifies Bent's wife as "wealthy Ann Eliza Tyler of Louisville, Kentucky," whom Bent married in 1857. Lavender, *Bent's Fort*, 418, n. 5.

APPENDIX
INTERVIEW WITH EDWARD J. GLASGOW

[The following interview of Edward James Glasgow appeared in the editorial section of the March 11, 1906, issue of the St. Louis *Daily Globe-Democrat*.]

EARLY DAYS OF SOUTHWEST TRADE PERIL-FRAUGHT

HUMAN LIFE SACRIFICED

Edward J. Glasgow Recalls
Enterprise of Van Buren's Time

"Northern Mexico is St. Louis territory, and St. Louis can control it by pushing its own specialties," said Mr. Edward J. Glasgow to a caller who asked his opinion as an expert. "Of course, we have to meet European competition from the gulf ports," he added, "but the territory is ours for our shoes, our machinery and other goods of our own make we send there."

Mr. Glasgow's knowledge of southwestern trade from the St. Louis standpoint probably covers a longer period than that of any one else now living. His opinion as expert belongs as much to the romance of history as it does to the present possibilities of business. He founded a St. Louis dry goods store in Chihuahua more than sixty years ago, and in carrying it on rode five times over the trail from Chihuahua to Independence, when the only white settlement between Las Vegas and Independence was Bent's fort on the Arkansas. He has probably ridden more miles on horseback in extending the "trade territory" of St. Louis than any one now living, and in the opinion of his friend, Gen. Bernard G. Farrar, he holds the nineteenth century record for the longest continuous ride on horseback made in North America. This stretch of 2000 miles was from Mazatlan, on the Pacific coast of Mexico, at the mouth of the gulf of California, to Independence, via

Chihuahua and Santa Fe. Now well past 80, Mr. Glasgow watches the enterprise with which St. Louisans of the present push into the "trade territory" he helped to open with "headquarters in the saddle," and no one is likely to doubt his right to speak with expert knowledge of what St. Louis enterprise means.

"Yes," he said, "I made the connection between Mazatlan and Missouri on horseback before I began business at Chihuahua. In fact, I had made two trips to Mazatlan before opening at Chihuahua. I had been appointed consul by President Van Buren at another Mexican port, and at Mazatlan I served as vice consul. I came back to the United States round the Horn, and returned to Mazatlan, riding then across country to Independence. I rode alone through Mexico except that I had my camp servants with me, but from Santa Fe to Independence I traveled with a trading party. I opened a dry goods store in Chihuahua in 1842 [1843], and did business there until the trade was broken up by the Mexican war."

PLANS FOR TRADE DEVELOPMENT

At the time he rode thus alone through Mexico unmolested from the Pacific coast across the Cordilleras to the Rio Grande and on to Santa Fe with no other escort than his own camp servants, Mr. Glasgow now remembers that plans were being devised in Washington for "developing" this trade territory in a way neither he nor the friendly Mexicans were then aware of. After Van Buren, under whose administration he went to Mexico, had been succeeded by James K. Polk, he began to hear more and more of the "destiny of the conquering Saxon in the halls of the Montezumas."

"The plans of getting Mexican territory as a means of controlling the United States, which developed out of the Polk administration," he says, "took me out of my store at Chihuahua, and after Doniphan had marched from Missouri to Chihuahua by way of Santa Fe, I was one of the two companies of Americans belonging to the southwestern trade who joined him. We formed these companies of teamsters and helpers, and going with Doniphan as volunteers, we were in the fight at Sacramento. But we got no pay, no glory nor anything else. When Doniphan marched through Mexico to the coast and came back to Missouri by way of the gulf and the Mississippi river, he said nothing about us who were left there in Mexico behind him.

So after my experience in the war, all that was left for me was to wind up business in Chihuahua and come back to St. Louis. In the five trips I had made between Missouri and Mexico I had seen the life of the southwestern plains at a time [when] buffalo and other game were so plentiful that the merchants crossing the country with their wagon trains relied on the rifles of their hunters for provisions. Indians were plentiful, of course, but even when they were hostile, they were held in contempt by the force of armed men which always went with a wagon train. It was a common saying of the teamsters that one white man was worth ten Indians. The Indians were seldom armed with rifles, and on the southwestern plains they could be seen approaching for miles. Sometimes there was trouble with them unexpectedly when they seemed friendly. They were confirmed horse thieves, and their usual plan was to stampede the animals of a wagon train after it had gone into camp. Once, after I had passed through a camp of Arapahoes near Bent's Fort, and traded them tobacco and some surplus corn I had for buffalo robes, we went on afterward and camped for dinner. Suddenly the whole band of Indians came whooping down on the camp and stampeded our entire outfit. Our horses and mules broke from the camp, and the Indians woul have got all of them but for the presence of mind of one of our Mexicans. We had a bell mare the rest of the animals were trained to follow.

Jumping on her back, the Mexican rode after the stampeded animals, and they all followed her bell back to camp, except one the Indians had lariated. Between Santa Fe and Chihuahua we had the Apaches to deal with, but I had no serious trouble with them in traveling through their territory. The staples of our trade with Chihuahua were calicoes and bleached cottons, with silks and fancy goods.

ONLY WOOL AND SILVER

We had trouble I told projectors of the first southwestern railroads they would always have. The Mexicans had nothing except wool and silver to give up for return freight, so that our profits were all on business one way. We brought back silver in $5000 packages we made by skinning an ox and sewing the silver up in the green hide. Then we left it in the sun to dry. When the sun had shrunk it down on the metal, the only way to get at the money was with an ax. I was mistaken about the railroads, however, for they made return trade for themselves by developing it where it did not exist. Out of twelve American merchants doing business in Chihuahua I was the only one from St. Louis. The rest were mostly Kentuckians. Chihuahua was then a town of about 1200 people. It has developed since, but now, as then, it still depends largely on its silver mines. Northern Mexico develops slowly, because it has the alkali soil which belongs to New Mexico. The railroads of the present which are opening up the whole country southwest of us follow our old wagon roads so closely that between Topeka and Bent's Fort the Atchison and Topeka scarcely gets 400 yards away at any time from the old route we traveled when we turned to pass Bent's Fort and go through the passes of the Ratton mountains. With a team of ten mules to the wagon, it generally took about three months and a half to make the trip between Independence and Chihuahua, with about thirty days of the time spent on the road between Santa Fe and Chihuahua.

After I had returned to St. Louis and opened up in the grocery business, the record time on the southwestern trade route was broken by a customer of mine, a tough wiry Canadian named Francis [François] Xavier Aubrey [Aubry], who made the most remarkable ride between Santa Fe and Independence ever made at all. New Mexico was then occupied by the United States army, and Aubrey had a candle contract with the quartermaster's department. After he had reached Santa Fe with his train he found himself far short of the supplies the contract called for. To fill it, he was obliged to return to St. Louis. He provided himself with two horses, one to be ridden and the other led, alternately.

When the time he had set himself to make the trip was known, he had bets offered on all sides that he could not make it from point to point, as he had planned, and other bets that he would fail on the whole schedule. He took all these bets, and then another of $250 that he would win every bet he had made. He did it, riding the 800 miles in six days and a half. He killed one of his horses, but he got another from a wagon train he met and went on without stopping, except to change from the saddle of one horse to that of the other. He told me in St. Louis that he slept in the saddle and had no other sleep during the whole ride than that he got in this way. He bought his candles from me, and, as I did not have enough to fill his order, I exhausted, or came near exhausting, the entire stock in the St. Louis market before collecting the quantity necessary. Aubrey, poor fellow, got back to Santa Fe in time to fill his contract, but he did not live many years afterward.

Capt. [Richard H.] Weightman, who went to New Mexico with the army of occupation, remained there and started a small newspaper. When he and Aubrey were drinking together, he explained that this paper had died a natural death for lack of subscribers. He had published an article giving some one else credit for some topographical work Aubrey thought he ought to have had credit for himself. He spoke of the possible connection between the death of the paper and the "lot of lies" it had published. He was armed with pistols, but in the fight which followed Weightman stabbed him repeatedly and killed him before he had time to draw a weapon.

From the time the first wagon train from St. Louis reached Chihuahua, the southwestern trade was profitable, though the expense of carrying it on was enormous. Mr. Glasgow might recall, perhaps, not a few cases besides that of Aubrey, illustrating the fact that the expense was not of money alone. Almost every station on the trade routes St. Louis opened, both to the southwest and the northwest, has some such romance as that of poor Aubrey. If his ride had not given him a claim to be considered as perhaps the most enterprising of all the enterprising men who carried St. Louis business to the Rio Grande and beyond, the tragedy of his death might have been lost sight of among many others of the same kind.

A.W.

BIBLIOGRAPHY

ARCHIVAL MATERIALS

Adams County Probate Records, Natchez, Mississippi.

Baker Library, Harvard University Graduate School of Business Administration.
R. G. Dun & Co. Collection.

Colorado Historical Society, Denver.
Dawson Scrapbooks.
O. C. Pratt Diary, "Trip over Santa Fe Trail, 1848," Coll. #1034 (microfilm).

Jackson County Historical Society Archives, Independence, Missouri.
Copy of John C. McCoy Manuscript, "Early History of Col Saml C Owens & James Aull."

Jefferson National Expansion Memorial, National Park Service, St. Louis.
Photograph Collections.

Joint Collection: University of Missouri, Western Historical Manuscript Collection/State
Historical Society of Missouri Manuscripts.
James Aull Business Records, 1825–1851, Coll. #3001 (microfilm).
Abiel Leonard Collection.

Kansas State Historical Society, Topeka.
William E. Connelley Collection.

Lafayette County Probate Records, Lexington, Missouri.

Missouri Botanical Garden, St. Louis.
Inventory of Henry Shaw Papers.

Missouri Historical Society, St. Louis.
William G.B. Carson Collection.
Clark Family Papers.
Fur Trade Ledgers Collection (microfilm).
Typescript of William H. Glasgow Manuscript, "Memorandums of a Trip Through
Mexico in 1842 & 1843."
William Carr Lane Collection.
Mullanphy Papers.
Necrology Scrapbooks.
St. Louis Court House Papers.
James Josiah Webb Papers.

National Archives, Washington, D.C.
*Applications and Recommendations for Public Office During the Administrations of
James Polk, Zachary Taylor, and Millard Fillmore, 1845–1853*, Microfilm M873, roll
33.

Bureau of Pensions Correspondence and Pension and Bounty Land Case Files, Records of the Veterans Administration, RG 15.

Correspondence 1845 to 1848, U.S. Consulate General, Mexico City, Mexico, RG 84.

Correspondence Received, 1829 to 1841/1842 to 1844, U.S. Consulate General, Mexico City, Mexico, RG 84.

Despatches from United States Consuls in Mazatlan, 1826–1906, Microfilm M159, roll 1.

Records of the United States Senate, RG 46.

Registers and Indexes for Passport Applications, 1810–1906, Microfilm M1371, roll 1.

U.S. Census Population Schedules (Seventh, Eighth, Ninth, Tenth, Twelfth).

New Mexico State Records Center and Archives, Santa Fe.

Manuel Alvarez Papers (microfilm).

E. Boyd Collection.

Felipe Chavez Papers.

Mexican Archives of New Mexico (microfilm).

Private Collections.

Wade Shipley, Lovington, New Mexico.

W. Merrill Glasgow, Houston, Texas.

Isabel Glasgow, El Paso, Texas.

Edward J. Glasgow, Nashville, Tennessee.

City of St. Louis Deed Records.

City of St. Louis Probate Court Records.

University of New Mexico Library, Special Collections, Albuquerque.

José Felipe Chaves Papers.

NEWSPAPERS AND PERIODICALS

Colorado Springs Gazette

Congressional Globe

Daily Globe-Democrat (St. Louis)

Glasgow Missourian

Manitou Springs Journal

The Merchants' Magazine, and Commercial Review

Missouri Republican (St. Louis)

Missouri Intelligencer (Fayette)

Missouri Statesman (Columbia)

Niles' National Register

Reveille (St. Louis)

St. Louis Republic

Santa Fe Republican

Weekly Gazette (Santa Fe)

Weekly Reveille (St. Louis)

Weekly Tribune (Liberty, Mo.)

Western Journal, and Civilian (St. Louis)

GOVERNMENT DOCUMENTS AND PUBLICATIONS

Carter, Clarence E., ed. *The Territorial Papers of the United States*, vol. 15, Louisiana-Missouri, 1815–1821. (Washington: U.S. Government Printing Office, 1951).

Condition of the Indian Tribes: Report of the Joint Special Committee, Appointed Under Joint Resolution of March 3, 1865 (Washington: Government Printing Office, 1867).

Heitman, Francis B. *Historical Register and Dictionary of the United States Army*, 2 vols. (Washington: Government Printing Office, 1903).

Index to the Congressional Record: Sixtieth Congress, First Session, from December 2, 1907, to May 30, 1908, vol. 42 (Washington: Government Printing Office, 1908).

Regulations Prescribed for the Use of the Consular Service of the United States (Washington: Government Printing Office, 1888).

Switzler, William F. *Report on the Internal Commerce of the United States for the Fiscal Year 1889.* Treasury Department Doc. #1243b (Washington: Government Printing Office, 1889).

U.S. Congress. House. *Changes in Commercial Systems of Foreign Nations.* House Doc. 29, 27th Cong., 3rd sess., 1842 (Serial 419).

———. *Message from the President of the United States . . . Relative to the Occupation of the Mexican Territory.* House Ex. Doc. 19, 29th Cong., 2nd sess., 1846 (Serial 499).

———. *Message from the President . . . .* Ex. Doc. 1, 30th Cong., 2nd sess., 1848 (Serial 537).

———. *. . . Report of Lieutenant Colonel Hitchcock, Respecting the Affairs of the Cherokee Indians, &c.* House Ex. Doc. 219, 27th Cong., 3rd sess., 1843 (Serial 425).

———. *Report of Missouri River Commission*, Appendix D. House Ex. Doc. 2, 55th Cong., 2nd sess., 1897 (Serial 3636).

———. *Report on H.R. Bill 441: To Establish Ports of Entry in Arkansas and Missouri, and to Allow Debenture, &c.* H.R. Rep. 540, 26th Cong., 1st sess., 1840 (Serial 372).

———. *Report on the Petition of Manuel X. Harmony.* H.R. Rep. 458, 30th Cong., 1st sess., 1848 (Serial 525).

———. *Suppression of Hostilities in New Mexico.* H.R. Rep. 52, 37th Cong., 3rd sess., 1863 (Serial 1173).

U.S. Congress. Senate. *Documents Relating to the Bill (S. 347) "to Establish Ports of Entry in the States of Arkansas and Missouri. . . ."* S. Doc. 472, 26th Cong., 1st sess., 1840 (Serial 360).

———. *Message from the President . . . .* S. Ex. Doc. 1, 30th Cong., 1st sess., 1847 (Serial 503).

———. *Report: The Committee on Finance, to Which Was Referred the Petition of Glasgow, Harrison, Boyd & Co.* S. Rep. 271, 27th Congress, 2nd sess., 1842 (Serial 398).

UNPUBLISHED STUDIES

Boyle, Susan Calafate. "Comerciantes, Fiadores, Arrieros, y Peones: The Hispano in the Santa Fe Trail."

Dreesen, Donald. "Founders of Albuquerque, 17th and 18th Century," vol. 3. University of New Mexico Library, Special Collections.

Fowler, Pauline S. "History of Home and Lands of James W(iley) Magoffin and Wife, Dolores, in Jackson County, Missouri." October 1989.

BOOKS AND ARTICLES

Abert, James W. *Abert's New Mexico Report, 1846–'47* (1848; facsimile reprint, Albuquerque: Horn & Wallace, 1962).

————. *Through the Country of the Comanche Indians in the Year 1845 ...* , ed. John Galvin (San Francisco: John Howell, 1970).

————. *Western America in 1846–1847 ...*, ed. John Galvin (San Francisco: John Howell, 1966).

Allison, W. H.H. "Colonel Francisco Perea," *Old Santa Fe* 1 (October 1913): 210–222.

Atherton, Lewis E. *The Frontier Merchant in Mid-America* (Columbia: University of Missouri Press, 1971).

————. "James and Robert Aull: A Frontier Missouri Mercantile Firm," *Missouri Historical Review* 30 (October 1935): 3– 27.

————. "The Santa Fe Trader as Mercantile Capitalist," *Missouri Historical Review* 77 (October 1982): 1–12.

Aull, James, and Aull, Robert. "Letters of James and Robert Aull," ed. Ralph P. Bieber, *Missouri Historical Society Collections* 5 (1928): 267–310.

The Baltimore Directory for 1845 (Baltimore: John Murphy, 1845).

Barry, Louise. *Beginning of the West: Annals of the Kansas Gateway to the American West, 1540–1854* (Topeka: Kansas State Historical Society, 1972).

Bartlett, John Russell. *Personal Narrative of Explorations and Incidents in Texas, New Mexico, California, Sonora, and Chihuahua ...* , 2 vols. (New York: D. Appleton & Co., 1854).

Benton, Thomas Hart. *Thirty Years' View; or, A History of the Working of the American Government for Thirty Years, from 1820 to 1850 ... by a Senator of Thirty Years,* 2 vols. (New York: D. Appleton & Co., 1854 and 1856).

Billon, Frederic L. *Annals of St. Louis in Its Territorial Days from 1804 to 1821* (1888; reprint ed., New York: Arno Press, 1971).

Bonner, T. D. *The Life and Adventures of James P. Beckwourth, Mountaineer, Scout, and Pioneer, and Chief of the Crow Nation of Indians* (1856; reprint ed., Lincoln: University of Nebraska Press, 1972).

Boyd, E. *Popular Arts of Spanish New Mexico* (Santa Fe: Museum of New Mexico Press, 1974).

Bryant, Edwin. *What I Saw in California* (1848; reprint ed., Minneapolis: Ross & Haines, 1967).

Catlin, George. *Letters and Notes on the Manners, Customs, and Conditions of the North American Indians ...* , 2 vols. (1844; reprint ed., New York: Dover Publications, 1973).

Carson, William G. B. "Secesh," *Bulletin of the Missouri Historical Society* 23 (January 1967): 119–145.

Chamberlain, Samuel E. *My Confession* (New York: Harper & Brothers, 1956).

Chaput, Donald. *François X. Aubry: Trader, Trailmaker and Voyageur in the Southwest, 1846–1854* (Glendale, Calif.: Arthur H. Clark, 1975).

Christopher, Mrs. Max A. "Red Bridge," in *Vital Historical Records of Jackson County, Missouri* (Kansas City: Daughters of the American Revolution, Kansas City Chapter, 1934).

Clarke, Dwight L. *Stephen Watts Kearny: Soldier of the West* (Norman: University of Oklahoma Press, 1961).

Cobos, Ruben. *A Dictionary of New Mexico and Southern Colorado Spanish* (Santa Fe: Museum of New Mexico Press, 1983).

Connelley, William E. *War with Mexico, 1846–1847: Doniphan's Expedition and the Conquest of New Mexico and California* (Kansas City: Bryant & Douglas Book and Stationery Co., 1907).

Cooke, Philip St. George. *The Conquest of New Mexico and California* (1878; reprint ed., Albuquerque: Horn & Wallace, 1964).

———. "A Journal of the Santa Fe Trail," ed. William E. Connelley, *Mississippi Valley Historical Review* 12 (September 1925): 227–255.

———, et al. *Exploring Southwestern Trails, 1846–1854,* ed. Ralph P. Bieber, with Averam B. Bender. Southwest Historical Series, vol. 7 (Glendale, Calif.: Arthur H. Clark, 1938).

Cullum, George W. *Biographical Register of the Officers and Graduates of the U.S. Military Academy at West Point, N.Y., from Its Establishment, in 1802, to 1890,* vol. 1 (Boston: Houghton, Mifflin & Co., 1891).

———. *Biographical Register of the Officers and Graduates of the U.S. Military Academy at West Point, New York, Since Its Establishment in 1802, Supplement,* vol. 5, 1900–1910, ed. Charles Braden (Saginaw, Mich.: Seemann & Peters, 1910).

Cutts, James Madison. *The Conquest of California and New Mexico* (1847; reprint ed., Albuquerque: Horn & Wallace, 1965).

Davis, W. W. H. *El Gringo; or, New Mexico and Her People* (1857; reprint ed., Chicago: Rio Grande Press, 1962).

Drumm, Stella M. "The Kennerlys of Virginia," *Missouri Historical Society Collections* 6 (October 1928): 98–123.

Dry, Camille N., and Compton, Richard J. *Pictorial St. Louis: The Great Metropolis of the Mississippi Valley* (1875; reprint ed., St. Louis: Knight Publishing Company, 1979).

Eddlemon, Sherida K. *Missouri Genealogical Records & Abstracts,* vol. 1 (Bowie, Md.: Heritage Books, 1990).

Edwards, Frank S. *A Campaign in New Mexico with Colonel Doniphan* (Philadelphia: Carey and Hart, 1847).

Edwards, Richard, and Hopewell, M. *Edwards's Great West and Her Commercial Metropolis, Embracing a General View of the West, and a Complete History of St. Louis* ... (St. Louis: Edwards's Monthly, 1860).

Edwards' St. Louis Directory, editions for 1864 through 1872.

Elliott, Richard Smith. *Notes Taken in Sixty Years* (St. Louis: R. P. Studley & Co., 1883).

Emory, William H. *Lieutenant Emory Reports: A Reprint of Lieutenant W. H. Emory's Notes of a Military Reconnoissance,* ed. Ross Calvin (Albuquerque: University of New Mexico Press, 1951).

Evans, Mrs. E. E., and Thompson, Mrs. J. Frank. *Tombstone Records of Boone County, Missouri* (Columbia: Mrs. E. E. Evans and Mrs. J. Frank Thompson, 1934).

Franzwa, Gregory F. *Maps of the Santa Fe Trail* (St. Louis: Patrice Press, 1989).

Gardner, Mark L., ed. *The Mexican Road: Trade, Travel, and Confrontation on the Santa Fe Trail* (Manhattan, Kans.: Sunflower University Press, 1989).

Garrard, Lewis. *Wah-to-yah and the Taos Trail* (1850; reprint ed., Norman: University of Oklahoma Press, 1955).

Gibson, George R. *Journal of a Soldier Under Kearny and Doniphan, 1846–1847,* ed. Ralph P. Bieber, Southwest Historical Series, vol. 3 (Glendale, Calif.: Arthur H. Clark, 1935).

———. *Over the Chihuahua and Santa Fe Trails, 1847–1848,* ed. Robert W. Frazer (Albuquerque: University of New Mexico Press, 1981).

Gould's St. Louis Directory, editions for 1872 through 1896.

Green's St. Louis Directory (No. 1) for 1845 (Saint Louis: James Green, 1844).

Green's St. Louis Directory for 1847 (Saint Louis: James Green and Cathcart & Prescott, 1847).

Gregg, Josiah. Commerce of the Prairies, ed. Max L. Moorhead (Norman: University of Oklahoma Press, 1954).

————. Diary and Letters of Josiah Gregg, ed. Maurice Fulton, 2 vols. (Norman: University of Oklahoma Press, 1941 and 1944).

Hafen, LeRoy R., ed. The Mountain Men and the Fur Trade of the Far West, 10 vols. (Glendale, Calif.: Arthur H. Clark, 1965–1972).

Hammond, George P. The Adventures of Alexander Barclay, Mountain Man (Denver: Old West Publishing Company, 1976).

History of Howard and Chariton Counties, Missouri (St. Louis: National Historical Company, 1883).

Hobbs, James. Wild Life in the Far West: Personal Adventures of a Border Mountain Man (1872; reprint ed., Glorieta, N. Mex.: Rio Grande Press, 1969).

Hodges, Nadine, and Mrs. Howard W. Woodruff, comps., "Jackson County, Missouri, Abstracts of Wills & Administrations 1849–1854," in Missouri Pioneers: County and Genealogical Records, vol. 4, (1969).

Horn, Calvin. New Mexico's Troubled Years: The Story of the Early Territorial Governors (Albuquerque: Horn & Wallace, 1963).

Hyde, William, and Conard, Howard L., eds. Encyclopedia of the History of St. Louis, 4 vols. (St. Louis: Southern History Company, 1899).

Jackson County, Missouri: Census of 1850, ed. Hattie E. Poppino (Kansas City: Hattie E. Poppino, 1959).

Johnston, Abraham Robinson; Edwards, Marcellus Ball; and Ferguson, Philip Gooch. Marching with the Army of the West, 1846–1848, ed. Ralph P. Bieber, Southwest Historical Series, vol. 4 (Glendale, Calif.: Arthur H. Clark, 1936).

Johnson, Frank W. History of Texas and Texans, 5 vols. (Chicago: American Historical Society, 1916).

Jostes, Barbara Donohoe. John Parrott, Consul, 1811–1884: Selected Papers of a Western Pioneer (San Francisco: Lawton and Alfred Kennedy, 1972).

Keleher, William A. Turmoil in New Mexico, 1846–1868 (Santa Fe: Rydal Press, 1952).

Kennerly, William Clark. Persimmon Hill: A Narrative of Old St. Louis and the Far West, as told to Elizabeth Russell (Norman: University of Oklahoma Press, 1948).

Lavender, David. Bent's Fort (Garden City, N.Y.: Doubleday & Co., 1954).

Loyola, Sister Mary. The American Occupation of New Mexico, 1821–1852 (1939; reprint ed., New York: Arno Press, 1976).

Lytle, William M., and Holdcamper, Forrest R., comps. Merchant Steam Vessels of the United States, 1790–1868, ed. C. Bradford Mitchell (Staten Island, N.Y.: Steamship Historical Society of America, 1975).

McElroy's Philadelphia Directory for 1846 (Philadelphia: Edward C. & John Biddle, 1846).

McGaw, William Cochran. Savage Scene: The Life and Times of James Kirker, Frontier King (New York: Hastings House, 1972).

McNierney, Michael, ed. Taos 1847: The Revolt in Contemporary Accounts (Boulder, Colo.: Johnson Publishing, 1980).

Magoffin, Susan Shelby. Down the Santa Fe Trail and into Mexico, 1846–1847, ed. Stella M. Drumm (New Haven: Yale University Press, 1926).

Miller, Darlis A. "Los Pinos, New Mexico: Civil War Post on the Rio Grande," New Mexico Historical Review 62 (January 1987): 1–31.

Miller, Nyle H.; Langsdorf, Edgar; and Richmond, Robert W. *Kansas in Newspapers* (Topeka: Kansas State Historical Society, 1963).

Mooney, Sylvia D. "Cave Spring: Historic Landmark on the Santa Fe Trail," *Wagon Tracks* 3 (November 1988): 6–7.

Moorhead, Max L. *New Mexico's Royal Road: Trade and Travel on the Chihuahua Trail* (Norman: University of Oklahoma Press, 1958).

———, ed. "Notes and Documents," *New Mexico Historical Review* 26 (January 1951): 68–82.

Morgan, Dale. *Overland in 1846: Diaries and Letters of the California-Oregon Trail*, 2 vols. (Georgetown, Calif.: Talisman Press, 1963).

Myer, Mrs. Max W. "Sarah Beaumont: Her Life and Loves," *Bulletin of the Missouri Historical Society* 17 (October 1960): 16–44.

The New York City Co-Partnership Directory, for 1844 and 1845 (New York: John Dogett, Jr., 1844).

Oliva, Leo E. *Soldiers on the Santa Fe Trail* (Norman: University of Oklahoma Press, 1967).

———, ed. *Adventure on the Santa Fe Trail* (Topeka: Kansas State Historical Society, 1988).

Pearce, T. M. *New Mexico Place Names: A Geographical Dictionary* (Albuquerque: University of New Mexico Press, 1965).

Peck, John Mason. *Forty Years of Pioneer Life: Memoir of John Mason Peck D.D.*, ed. Rufus Babcock (Philadelphia: American Baptist Publication Society, 1864).

Porter, V. M. "A History of Battery 'A' of St. Louis," *Missouri Historical Society Collections* 2 (March 1905): 1–48.

"Preliminary Report of Survey of Inscriptions Along Santa Fe Trail in Oklahoma," *Chronicles of Oklahoma* 38 (Autumn 1960): 310–322.

Primm, James Neal. "Henry Shaw: Merchant-Capitalist," *Gateway Heritage* 5 (Summer 1984): 2–9.

———. *Lion of the Valley: St. Louis, Missouri* (Boulder, Colo.: Pruett, 1981).

———. "Seal of the Territory of Louisiana: A Discovery Amid a Clark Family Collection," *Gateway Heritage* 4 (Spring 1984): 17–21.

Reps, John W. *Saint Louis Illustrated: Nineteenth-Century Engravings and Lithographs of a Mississippi River Metropolis* (Columbia: University of Missouri Press, 1989).

Richardson, William H. *Journal of William H. Richardson, a Private Soldier in Col. Doniphan's Command* (1847), reprinted in *Missouri Historical Review* 22 (January, April, July, 1928): 193–236, 331–360, 511–542.

Rittenhouse, Jack D. *The Santa Fe Trail: A Historical Bibliography* (Albuquerque: University of New Mexico Press, 1971).

Robinson, Jacob S. *A Journal of the Santa Fe Expedition Under Colonel Doniphan* (1848; reprint ed., New York: De Capo Press, 1972).

Rodgers, Thomas L. "Recollections of St. Louis — 1857–1860," *Glimpses of the Past* 9 (October-December 1942): 111–121.

Russell, Elizabeth Kennerly. "The Narrow-Gauge and Its Patrons," *Bulletin of the Missouri Historical Society* 6 (April 1950): 273–287.

Ruxton, George A. F. *Adventures in Mexico and the Rocky Mountains* (1847; reprint ed., Glorieta, N. Mex.: The Rio Grande Press, 1973).

———. *Ruxton of the Rockies*, comp. Clyde Porter and Mae Reed Porter, ed. LeRoy R. Hafen (Norman: University of Oklahoma Press, 1950).

St. Louis Directory 1859 (St. Louis: R[obert] V. Kennedy & Co.).

St. Louis Directory 1860 (St. Louis: R[obert] V. Kennedy & Co.).

St. Louis Genealogical Society, StLGS Index of St. Louis Marriages, 1804–1876, vol. 1 (St. Louis: St. Louis Genealogical Society, 1973).

Sandweiss, Martha A.; Stewart, Rick; and Huseman, Ben W. Eyewitness to War:Prints and Daguerreotypes of the Mexican War, 1846–1848 (Washington: Smithsonian Institution Press, 1989).

Scharf, J. Thomas. History of Saint Louis City and County, 2 vols. (Philadelphia: Louis H. Everts & Co., 1883).

Seematter, Mary E. "Merchants in the Middle: The Glasgow Brothers and the Mexican War," Gateway Heritage 9 (Fall 1988): 34–43.

Sheldon & Co's Business or Advertising Directory ... of the Cities of New-York, Boston, Philadelphia, Baltimore, &c., &c. (New York: John F. Trow & Co., 1845).

Shriver, Thomas D., comp. Missouri General Assembly , 1812– 1976 (Jefferson City: Office of Secretary of State, 1976).

Simmons, Marc. "A Humorous Incident of the Santa Fe Trade," Westport Historical Quarterly 7 (March 1972): 3–4.

———. Murder on the Santa Fe Trail:An International Incident, 1843 (El Paso: Texas Western Press, 1987).

———, ed. On the Santa Fe Trail (Lawrence: University of Kansas Press, 1986).

Smith, Justin H. The War with Mexico, 2 vols. (New York: Macmillan, 1919).

Sobel, Robert. Conquest and Conscience: The 1840s (New York: Thomas Y. Crowell, 1971).

———. Machines and Morality: The 1850s (New York: Thomas Y. Crowell, 1973).

Sorley, Lewis S., and Glasgow, Octavia Magoffin. "Official Biography of Gen. Glasgow," Southwesterner 5 (May 1966): 2 and 6.

Stadler, Frances Hurd. "Letters from Minoma," Bulletin of the Missouri Historical Society 16 (April 1960): 237–259.

Stanley, Lois; Wilson, George F.; and Wilson, Maryhelen, comps. More Death Records from Missouri Newspapers, 1810–1857 (1985).

Stevens, Walter B. St. Louis: The Fourth City, 1764–1909, 2 vols. (St. Louis and Chicago: S. J. Clarke,1909).

Stimpson's Boston Directory, editions for 1840 through 1844.

Strickland, Rex W. "Six Who Came to El Paso: Pioneers of the 1840s," Southwestern Studies 1 (Fall 1963): 3–48.

Swift, Roy L., and Corning, Leavitt, Jr. Three Roads to Chihuahua: The Great Wagon Roads That Opened the Southwest, 1823–1883 (Austin: Eakin Press, 1988).

Thomas, James. From Tennessee Slave to St. Louis Entrepreneur: The Autobiography of James Thomas, ed. Loren Schweninger (Columbia: University of Missouri Press, 1984).

Timmons, W. H. El Paso: A Borderlands History (El Paso: Texas Western Press, 1990).

Turner, Henry Smith. The Original Journals of Henry Smith Turner, with Stephen Watts Kearny to New Mexico and California, 1846–1847, ed. Dwight L. Clarke (Norman: University of Oklahoma Press, 1966).

Twitchell, Ralph Emerson. The History of the Military Occupation of the Territory of New Mexico from 1846 to 1851 (1909; reprint ed., Chicago: Rio Grande Press, 1963).

———. The Leading Facts of New Mexican History, 2 vols. (Cedar Rapids, Iowa: Torch Press, 1911 and 1912).

————. The Story of the Conquest of Santa Fe, New Mexico, and the Building of Old Fort Marcy, A.D. 1846, Historical Society of New Mexico Publication No. 24 (Santa Fe: Historical Society of New Mexico, 1923).

Tyler, Daniel. A Concise History of the Mormon Battalion in the Mexican War, 1846–1847 (1881; reprint ed., Chicago: Rio Grande Press, 1964).

Tyler, Daniel. "Governor Armijo's Moment of Truth," in Odie B. Faulk and Joseph A. Stout, Jr., eds., The Mexican War: Changing Interpretations (Chicago: Swallow Press, 1973).

The United States Biographical Dictionary and Portrait Gallery of Eminent and Self-Made Men, Missouri vol. (New York: United States Biographical Publishing Company, 1878).

Utley, Robert M. Fort Union and the Santa Fe Trail, Southwestern Studies Series No. 89 (El Paso: Texas Western Press, 1989).

Vineyard, Mrs. John. Original Land Entries of Jackson County, Missouri (Mrs. John Vineyard, 1971).

Waugh, Alfred S. "Desultory Wanderings in the Years 1845–46," ed. John F. McDermott, Bulletin of the Missouri Historical Society 7 (January 1951): 216–264.

Webb, James Josiah. Adventures in the Santa Fe Trade, 1844–1847, ed. Ralph P. Bieber, Southwest Historical Series, vol. 1 (Glendale, Calif.: Arthur H. Clark, 1931).

Weber, David J., ed. The Extranjeros: Selected Documents from the Mexican Side of the Santa Fe Trail (Santa Fe: Stagecoach Press, 1967).

Weichselbaum, Theodore. "Statement of Theodore Weichselbaum, of Odgen, Riley County, July 17, 1908," Collections of the Kansas State Historical Society, 1909–1910 11 (1910): 561–571.

Wells, Eugene T. "The Growth of Independence, Missouri, 1827–1850," Bulletin of the Missouri Historical Society 16 (October 1959): 33–46.

Wetzel, David, ed. The Santa Fe Trail: New Perspectives (Denver: Colorado Historical Society, 1987).

Wilhelm, Paul, Duke of Wuerttemberg. First Journey to North America in the Years 1822 to 1824, Trans. William G. Bek, South Dakota Historical Collections, vol. 19 (1938), 7–474.

Windham, Margaret Leonard, ed. New Mexico 1850 Territorial Census, vol. 4 (Albuquerque: New Mexico Genealogical Society, 1976).

Wislizenus, (Frederick) A. Memoir of a Tour to Northern Mexico, Connected with Colonel Doniphan's Expedition in 1846 and 1847 (1848; facsimile reprint, Albuquerque: Calvin Horn Publisher, 1969).

INDEX

Fe (Fay), Mr., 81, 85, 142(n24),
147(n55), 148(n60)
Ferguson, Alexander C., 77, 97(fig.), 138–
39(n5), 141–42(n22), 157(n115)
Ferguson, Mary Susan, 82, 88, 143(n31),
147(n57)
Ferguson (Fergusson), Charles (Charley),
81, 141–42(n22)
First Regiment Missouri Mounted Volun-
teers, 31, 32(fig.), 102, 145(n43)
Flemming & Marshall, 146(n49)
Fort Leavenworth, 95
France, 13
Francisco, A. F., 176(n5)
Fray Cristóbal (N. Mex.), 31–32
Fremont, John C., 195, 203(n32)
Fristoe, John, 157–58(n115)

Gaoucillo. See Guajoquilla
Garcia, John, 139(n9)
Gay, Caroline M. Page, 154(n95)
Gay, Edward J., 61(n66)
Gay, Glasgow & Co., 14, 61(n66)
Gay, John H., 61(n66), 143(n31),
154(n95)
Gay, John H., Jr., 108, 154(n95)
Gay, Sophia Mitchell, 61(n66)
Gentry, Reuben, 25, 63(nn84, 85),
67(n138), 155(n99)
Gibson, George R., 201(n16)
Glasgow, Anita Damon, 47(fig.), 52
Glasgow, Brother & Co., 48–50, 52, 55,
72(nn217, 220)
Glasgow, Carlota Nestora Fales, 46,
47(fig.), 52
Glasgow, Charles, 57(n21)
Glasgow, Edward James, 1, 3, 6–7, 7(fig.),
24–25, 28(fig.), 48, 52, 54(fig.), 55,
62(n75), 69(n181), 71(nn201, 204),
72(n217), 76(fig.), 141(n21),
149(n65), 162(n139), 185, 201–
2(nn21, 22); and Chihuahua trade,
30, 37, 38, 39–40, 64(n105), 89,
119, 122, 125, 154(n92),
157(n115), 158(n118), 160(n131),
205–6; in Doniphan's expedition, 33,
36, 176(n5); and Glasgow & Brother,
40, 43; marriage of, 46–47; in Mazatlan, 59–60(n51); in Mexican War, 31,
39, 198–99(n6), 202–3(n31); in Mexico, 9–10, 11–12; in Santa Fe, 100,

149(n69); and Santa Fe trade, 26, 27,
28–29, 66(n127), 145(n44),
147(n53); in Valparaiso, 13– 14
Glasgow, Edward James, Jr. (William H.'s
son), 46(fig.), 46, 48, 50, 52
Glasgow, Edwardo, 69(n181)
Glasgow, Eleanor (grandmother), 2
Glasgow, Eleanor Ann. See Clark, Eleanor
Ann Glasgow
Glasgow, Harriet Clark Kennerly ("Tea"),
47, 48, 55, 71(n201), 73(n233),
159(n125)
Glasgow, Harrison, & Co., 58(n32)
Glasgow, Harrison, Boyd & Co., 11, 12,
14, 24, 62(n78)
Glasgow, Harrison, Valois & Co., 6, 7–8, 9,
11, 12
Glasgow, James (grandfather), 2
Glasgow, James (uncle), 4, 7, 8(fig.),
58(n32), 61(n66), 159(n121)
Glasgow, Jefferson Clark, 52
Glasgow, John P., 57(n21)
Glasgow, Josephine Magoffin, 202(nn23,
24)
Glasgow, Joseph Magoffin, 54(fig.)
Glasgow, Julian Kennerly, 52, 55
Glasgow, Mary (William H.'s daughter),
71(n198)
Glasgow, Mary Frances Wright, 46, 70–
71(nn196–98)
Glasgow, Mary Susan (sister). See Clark,
Mary Susan Glasgow (Sue)
Glasgow, Mary Susan (William H.'s daugh-
ter), 52
Glasgow, Octavia Magoffin, 54(fig.)
Glasgow, Sarah Lane, 13, 147(n58)
Glasgow, Sarah Mitchell (mother), 3,
4(fig.), 71(n201)
Glasgow, William, Jr. (cousin), 13, 48,
61(n66), 127–28, 133, 147(n58),
151(n77)
Glasgow, William, Sr. (father), 3(fig.), 8–
9, 47(fig.), 64(n102), 71(nn201,
204), 159(n122); as merchant, 2–4,
7, 10, 11, 12, 56–57(nn11, 16, 19,
30), 58–59(nn32, 38), 61(n66)
Glasgow, William Henry, 1, 3, 6, 14,
15(fig.), 27, 46(fig.), 47(fig.), 48,
51(fig.), 53(fig.), 55, 70–71(nn196–
98, 201), 73(n227), 75(fig.), 90,
176(n1); business interests of, 43, 46,

50, 52–53, 72(nn216, 217, 222, 223;
and Chihuahua trade, 16–19, 31–32,
37, 38, 39–40, 66(n129, 89, 132,
155(n98, 157(n115), 158(n118); diary of, 14, 16–23, 61(n67); "Memorandums of a Trip Through Mexico in
1842 & 1843," 16–23; in Mexican
War, 31–32, 33, 35, 36, 39, 176(n5),
198(n6); and Santa Fe trade, 19–23,
87, 145(n44)
Glasgow, William Jefferson, 43, 52, 55,
62(n75), 72(n219), 197(n1),
202(nn23, 24)
Glasgow, William Wright, 71(n198)
Glasgow & Brother, 40, 41(fig.), 42(fig.),
43(fig.), 43–44; success of, 45–47;
New Mexico customers of, 43–44
Glasgow & Connelly, 25, 40
Glasgow & Nevins, 56(n11)
Gnesire, Ilsey, 79
Gold, 12, 60(n57)
Gonzales, José, 30, 66(n118), 151(n76)
Gonzales, Juana, 69(n181)
Governors Island, 197(n1)
Grahm, Bernard, 139(n9)
Grant, Julia Dent, 150(n72)
Grant, Ulysses S., 150(n72)
Gregg, Harmon, 138(n1)
Gregg, Josiah, 28, 58(n34), 77, 138(n1),
139(n6)
Grier (Greer), William N., 170
Grim, Mr., 132
Guajoquilla (Mex.), 122–23, 171
Guaymas, Sonora (Mex.), 7, 194
Guerrilleros, 174–75, 178(n19)

Hamelin, Joseph P., Jr., 161(n136),
162(n139)
Harmony, Manuel X. 78, 81, 139–
40(nn9, 10), 145(n44), 147(n53),
187, 200(n13)
Harmony, Peter, 139(n9)
Harmony Report, 145–46(n49)
Harmony's Nephews & Co., P., 139(n9),
146(n49)
Harper, Fanny Owens, 143(n30)
Harper, John H., 82, 143(n30)
Harrison, H. C., 176(n5)
Harrison, James, 7–8, 10(fig.), 10, 24,
57–58(n32), 59(n43), 61(n66),
62(n78), 139(n7)

Harrison & Co., James, 57–58(nn20, 32)
Hawks, Cicero Stephens (Bishop),
154(n94)
Hawks, Mrs. Cicero Stephens, 107,
154(n94)
Hayward (Haywood), George, 101, 111,
153(n87)
Henry, Andrew, 203(n36)
Herculaneum (Mo.), 3–4, 187
Heredia, José, 33, 177(n9)
Hicks, Bethel, 156–57(n112)
Hicks, Young E., 157(n112)
Hobbs, James, 155–56(n103)
Hoffman, J. Tilghman, 160(n132)
Hoffman & Barney, 160(n132), 186
Home Bitters Co., 72(n223)
Houck, Solomon, 157(nn114, 115),
158(n119)
Houghton, Joab, 113, 152(n86),
156(n104)
Howard, George T., 142(n25)
Howard, John, 161(n136), 176(n5)
Hughes, John T., 1, 154–55(nn97, 99),
156(nn106, 112)
Huston, John Calvin, 176(n5)
Hynes, Andrew, 140(n15)
Hynes, Mary Jane. See McCreery, Mary Jane
Hynes

Ibarra (Ivarra, de la Vara), Manuel de la,
178(nn17, 18)
Independence (Mo.), 141(nn19, 20)
Indians, 142(n25); in Chihuahua, 122–
23, 155(n99), 189; in Mexico, 170–
71, 172, 173, 178(n18); in New
Mexico, 90, 91, 92, 93, 98, 110; on
Santa Fe Trail, 148(n60), 152(n86),
186, 207
Ingleside, 47
Inscription Rock (Okla.), 28(fig.)
Irwin, Douglass Simms, 154(n96)
Irwin, Sarah Beaumont, 108, 154(n96)
Isletas (Isleta) (N. Mex.), 92

Jackson, Congreve, 98, 151(n79)
Jarvis Creek (Kan.), 22, 62(n74),
Jesús Maria, Chihuahua (Mex.), 17
Jones, Martha (Patsy), 71(n201), 78,
141(n17)
Jornada del Muerto, 32(fig.)
Juarez. See El Paso del Norte